ASPECTS OF GREEK AND ROMAN LIFE

General Editor: Professor H. H. Scullard

CHARITIES AND SOCIAL AID IN GREECE AND ROME

A. R. Hands

CORNELL UNIVERSITY PRESS
ITHACA, NEW YORK

First published 1968

Library of Congress Catalog Card Number: 69–11154

PRINTED IN ENGLAND

CONTENTS

PREFACE

THE TITLE OF THIS BOOK (or at least its first word) may seem to beg a large question as probably no two readers will agree as to what should be included under it. This may be one reason why much of the material assembled here is generally distributed over a wide range of books dealing with Greek and Roman social life in general, or with specific aspects of it, rather than organized in the present way. It may also explain why, in one recent attempt to treat of much the same subject, H. Bolkestein followed a comparative method by which Ancient Egyptian and Jewish 'charity' provided the contrast with classical 'well-doing'. To some extent I, too, shall follow such a method, but, having had the advantage of referring to recent works of great interest concerning English philanthropy in modern times, shall place greater emphasis on the comparisons and contrasts to be made with the latter.

Philanthropic activity can never be understood (or defined) except against the background of the social *ethos* of the age to which it belongs. Hence the early chapters discuss the philosophy of life or theory of the city-state rather than its actual practice or institutions. The advanced scholar will find parts of these chapters rather elementary, but without them the subsequent chapters would, for the more general reader, seem almost irrelevant. On the other hand, few people, other than lawyers themselves, find a chapter on law easily digestible. Since, however, benefactors of almost every age, whether they regard the law as an enigma or merely as an ass, have had to contend with it when they have wanted to establish a permanent fund or foundation, such a chapter was unavoidable. I have tried to simplify its technicalities (for myself, as much as for the reader) by concentrating on a few specific instances in which such benefactors either conformed to or circumvented the current demands of the law.

The argument of these early chapters—like that of a Platonic dialogue—does not run consistently in one direction. This simply reflects my doubt whether a simple formula is to be found to explain human behaviour in this field. The answer to a whole series of questions implicit here can be neither a complete positive nor a complete negative. So, if the reader finds himself left with a question rather than an answer as regards, for instance, the apparent similarity between classical ethical theory at its highest and the ethics of Christianity, this is largely intended. And should he wish to take further one essential difference relevant to our subject, he might find it in the contrasting idea of 'immortality'— and the qualifications for it.

The following chapters, dealing with the application of theory, are self-explanatory. The documents bring us a step nearer to actuality in the life of the classical city-state. Just because the topics discussed in this book are more commonly dealt with in more general studies, the reader often has to be content merely with a reference to epigraphical publications for a statement's illustration or substantiation. But between reference to such publications and a sight by the reader of the inscriptions themselves there is normally a great gulf; nor is a translation always available to the more general reader. Indeed, even a document in translation is still only partly satisfactory, and in a book of this kind it is scarcely practicable to indicate by complicated typographical means the exact character of each inscription, its gaps and uncertainties. None the less, in dealing with a subject of this kind, where much depends on personal interpretation of the word 'charity', I consider the inclusion of these documents to be particularly valuable.

The square brackets used in the documents indicate either an abbreviation of the text, where line numbers are given, e.g. [*ll.* 11–13], the restoration of the text where the inscription is defective, or, occasionally, the anglicized form of the technical term appearing in the original document. I gratefully acknowledge permission to use translations in certain instances from the books and journals cited in the introduction to the documents.

For the reader without a knowledge of Greek a word about the pronunciation of the Greek words here transliterated may be useful; in particular that all Greek vowels are sounded, so that *tīmē* is a dissyllable—the anglicized name Irene, from the Greek word for 'peace', should strictly be pronounced as a trisyllable. The length of certain vowels is indicated when a term first appears.

Perhaps nobody but the author should be too closely implicated in an attempt to cover in a narrow compass a subject which touches upon so many fields—philosophy, religion, law, economics, and others. The number of authors named in the Notes, will indicate the extent of my debt to many scholars. Among recent work, the articles of R. Duncan-Jones merit a special mention for the wealth of detail and skilful analysis which they provide regarding gifts and foundations in Italy and Roman Africa. On several topics, especially those relating to the earlier chapters of this book, I have benefited from discussion with colleagues at Queen Mary College. As to the presentation of the material, the reader will benefit not least from one of Professor Scullard's helpful suggestions, namely that some of my more 'periodic' (or insufferably long) sentences should be broken up. Such assistance has made this a better book than it might have been; but the author alone is wholly responsible wherever it could have been better than it is.

My wife provided the final *philanthropia* as far as the book's composition was concerned, by her invaluable help with the Index.

Queen Mary College,   A. R. H.
  London, 1968

CHAPTER I

INTRODUCTION

IN HIS ACCOUNT of social and economic conditions in the Greek cities of the Hellenistic Age—an age which, together with the first two centuries of our own era, provides most of the evidence for our study—W. W. Tarn wrote: 'Amid all the philanthropic feeling and public spirit of the time, philanthropy in our sense— the organized aid of the poor by the rich—was almost unknown.' By 'philanthropy in our sense' Tarn had in mind that oriental concept which was stressed as a religious duty in Ancient Egypt and Israel and in large measure inherited by Christian ethics. This concept H. Bolkestein, in his *Wohltätigkeit und Armenpflege im vorchristlichen Altertum*, compared with the classical term 'beneficence', which he showed to have a broader intention and therefore not to be synonymous with *Armenpflege* (poor-relief), as the oriental concept tended to be. Yet it is plain that the term 'philanthropy', while it may indeed be used today in this narrower sense, is more commonly used in a wider sense. The same is true of the term 'charity'; and not only of charity in the abstract, but also of charities—or 'charitable uses', as they are spoken of in English law. Consider the Elizabethan Act of Charitable Uses of 1597, which relates to wealth left by sovereigns and

> by sondrie other well disposed persons, some for releife of aged, impotent, and poore people, some for maintenance of sicke and maymed souldiers and marriners, schooles of learninge, free schooles and schollers in universities, some for repaire of bridges portes havens causewaies churches seabankes and highwaies, some for education and preferments of orphans . . . some for supportacion ayde and helpe of younge tradesmen, handie-craftesmen and persons decayed, and others for releife or redemption of prisoners or captives, and for aide or ease of

any poore inhabitants concerning paymente of fifteenes,
settinge out of souldiers and other taxes.

This most un-Socratic of definitions, so 'starkly and coldly secular'
in its wording, Lord Macnaghten tried in 1891 to render more
concisely. But since to his three basic categories, 'the relief of
poverty, the advancement of education and the advancement of
religion', he found it necessary to add an omnibus category—
'trusts for other purposes beneficial to the community, not falling
under any one of the preceding heads'—the attempt was abandoned. Today the definition of the term, or rather its enumeration, in English Law remains as wide as ever. It is consistent with
this legal position that entered under 'charity' in the *Encyclopaedia
Britannica* we find reference to a 'disciplined and habitual mood
in which the mind is considerate of the welfare of others individually and generally', followed by the comment that 'it thus has no
necessary relation to relief or alms'. This again is merely to say that
the terms 'charity' and 'philanthropy' have come to admit of
classical as well as oriental conceptions, and it is therefore somewhat misleading to say that 'philanthropy in our sense' was
'almost unknown' to the Greeks (or to the Romans).[1]

Connected with Tarn's statement is a further difficulty,
namely that in discussing philanthropy in his limited sense one
can hardly avoid the question of motive and the temptation to
emphasize a single motive at the expense of all others. And so we
are led on to the generalization that 'broadly speaking, pity for
the poor had little place in the normal Greek character'. Indeed
there is considerable evidence to support this statement, but if
we wish to go beyond theory to practice it is impossible to confine
the term 'charitable' to acts or institutions the performance or
creation of which are motivated only by pity. Apart from the
fact that the motives must always be a matter of speculation,
even when they are reported by the subject himself, they will
generally appear to be complex rather than simple in character.
For example, Jordan ascribes the upsurge of English philanthropy
in the century following the Elizabethan Act of 1597, not only to
'an increasing sensitivity to pain and suffering', but to the 'Tudor

concern for the whole basis of public order in the face of social upheavals and the doctrine of trusteeship put abroad by Calvinism'. Again, Owen attributes to seven Victorian philanthropists a variety of motives, ranging from 'religious commitment through humanitarianism, social idealism, civic patriotism and personal satisfaction to an undeniable, though not necessarily ignoble, desire for self-perpetuation'. A similar variety is evident in the history of classical beneficence. And if the role of pity in classical beneficence often appears minimal, we may note the comparatively recent instance of an English testator, quoted by Owen, who left £300 to be applied for ever to the payment of a man 'who has been unsuccessful', as the testator expressed it, 'in the diffusion of my opinions in my published works'.[2]

This latter bequest, though a striking illustration of Mr Justice Vaisey's view that 'the legal conception of charity has its origin in the eccentricities of the benevolent', would scarcely answer to the common notion of a charity. The latter requires at least that a charity should (1) not be *blatantly* self-regarding, (2) be motivated to some degree by a sense of compassion, and (3) be biased in favour of, though not necessarily devoted exclusively to, those most in need. It is certainly not intended in this study to deny these emphases nor their mainly oriental derivation. Rather, by putting classical beneficence in its full and proper context, we shall seek to explain why it is that these emphases are so much less evident than in oriental charity. We shall go on to notice the ways in which this beneficence did nevertheless ameliorate the conditions of the poor—even where it appears to have done so in the absence of any explicit expression of pity. We shall also notice how the motives which are emphasized in the classical context reappear in the context of post-classical charities and schemes of social aid. In this way we may come to a fairer estimate of classical philanthropy—perhaps even to a conclusion near to that of Tenney Frank in his account of social behaviour at Rome: 'Just because Christianity discovered how well the altruistic instinct served as a foundation for religion we must not assume that it did not exist before. It did, but it expressed itself in other forms.'[3]

Bolkestein cites the evidence of language as well as the social thought and practice of the classical world in his attempt to show how its beneficence was transformed into something approaching the concept of oriental *Armenpflege*, not simply as a result of the spread of an oriental religion, but also through the growing social and economic assimilation of the West to the East in the early centuries of the present era. He also tried to show that these social and economic changes were having their effect on Roman thought and practice as early as the first century AD. As to this date, the evidence he provided was not entirely convincing, since those inscriptions on which he largely relied seem to belong to a period later than that to which he assigned them, or to relate to persons who, although domiciled in the west, were almost certainly (to judge by their names) of oriental origin. But it is not our concern to date the beginning of such a transformation, which in any case must have affected different parts of the classical world at different times. Rather shall we aim to define the spirit of classical beneficence and illustrate the main features by considering a wide range of sources unlikely to be much contaminated by non-classical ideas. We shall take as our extreme chronological limit a date *c.* AD 250, and direct our attention particularly to three fields in which both modern charity and classical philanthropy or social aid have operated: the provision of foodstuffs, of education and of medical attention. In so doing, however, we shall not neglect the third of Macnaghten's three main categories, since the advancement of religion, or at least the maintenance of its outward forms, will be found involved in these fields, to various degrees. Finally, we shall present a series of documents (indicated in the text by the letter D) which may enable the reader to judge for himself how far the actions or institutions to which they relate conform to his own or any other definition of the charitable.[4]

Inevitably we shall hazard broad generalizations. The evidence itself, which is never full, always uneven, and narrowed by selection, relates to city-states in an area stretching from Spain to the Black Sea, and from the Rhine and Danube regions to North Africa. Such cities would have different characteristics at different periods, while even within a given period Athenians and

Spartans, Thebans and Corinthians—to look no further than the
Greek mainland—differed widely. This being so, there is little
point in our making a fundamental division between Greeks and
Romans, especially since the latter when first they appeared at the
centre of the historical stage were already taking over much of
the tradition of the Greek world. It will be more appropriate for
present purposes to treat Rome as just one among many instances
of the classical city-state, though we shall not ignore evidence
suggesting that the Romans had a peculiar contribution to make.

A further limitation of our study is the fact that we shall be
almost exclusively concerned with the ideas and practice of a
comparatively narrow and wealthy upper class—of people who,
in today's terms, could afford to give in hundreds rather than in
fractions of pounds. For there exists little or no evidence relating
to the lower classes; it is often merely assumed that their attitude
to the less fortunate of their members was less generous than that
of their betters—an assumption based largely on the grounds that
charitable attitudes develop in step with education and culture.
However, as we shall see, there were in the ancient world no
organized charities comparable with those to which the small man
contributes with confidence today. Nor would it be appropriate
for us to make a rigid distinction between the private actions and
the public policy of the upper class. There are various reasons for
this: for example, in the Greek city-state many of the apparently
public funds devoted in whole or part to benevolent purposes,
derived in some measure at least from private gifts which, in the
absence of independent charities, had to be publicly administered.
Moreover, these gifts themselves were not infrequently called
forth by the state in circumstances which make it largely a matter
of speculation whether they were the outcome of private initiative
or public insistence. The latter doubt applies also to a large number
of 'gifts' given in association with the tenure of magistracies,
especially where the election to a magistracy depended on a prior
undertaking to provide such a gift. It is often no less difficult to
decide whether the funds created by donors are more properly
to be regarded as private or public, an obvious case being the
booty of war falling to the Roman military commanders, which

they were expected to use for the benefit of the state, though technically it 'belonged' to them.[5]

Finally, we shall not, except in passing, concern ourselves here with public measures directed to what we might regard as immediate and permanent solutions to social ills. For example, there is clearly a legitimate sense in which it may be said that the tribune Tiberius Gracchus was introducing a measure of public philanthropy when in 133 BC he proposed a redistribution of public land, in order to resettle small farmers whom the changing social and economic conditions in Italy and the constant demand of the state for military personnel had forced to give up their allotments. It is true that Plutarch uses of an alleged first draft of this law the very Greek epithet from which derives the English word 'philanthropic', though significantly he means by it that Tiberius' law did not *unduly* serve the interests of the poor at the expense of the rich. In another sense, however, such measures were designed to eliminate the need for private charity or public aid, and since they were in any case seldom carried into effect or adequate for long, there normally remained to a lesser or greater degree in every city-state scope for private benevolence and the founding of public charitable institutions. It is to the latter that we shall in the main confine our attention, although we shall have occasion to observe that just because contemporary political thinking—especially that of the Greeks—was more optimistic than modern thought, it tended to concentrate on the former type of solution rather than the latter.[6]

CHAPTER II

CHARITIES AND LEGAL PERSONALITY

MODERN CHARITIES are generally institutions 'existing in their own right' with a view to achieving certain specific purposes, the continuance of which may depend upon an indefinite series of gifts used directly to meet recurrent expenditure, or upon a steady income deriving from the investment of a capital sum, usually a permanent endowment. It is particularly with charities where the income is of the latter kind, involving the maintenance of a clear distinction between capital and income, that English law is concerned; but in either case the funds will be in the hands of trustees who receive title of ownership only for the performance of duties in accordance with the stated object of the charity, and are otherwise in the eyes of the law simply a group of private individuals. By contrast, in dealing with charities (or their nearest approximations) in the classical city-state, we shall make frequent reference to gifts, whether for immediate expenditure or (more relevant to permanent charitable purposes) for investment, to the cities themselves, that is to the body politic as a whole or to one or more of its constituent groups—gifts which, once handed over, become the legal property of the recipient. It is essential, therefore, as a first step in our study, to make clear our reasons for dealing with gifts which *prima facie* are so different in character.[7]

The explanation turns largely on a point of law—the concept of 'legal personality'—according to which a modern charitable fund is conceived of as 'existing in its own right', independently of the continued existence of the particular body which may be administering it at any given time. The establishment of permanent endowments, administered by trusts of this nature was notably encouraged by the Elizabethan Act of Charitable Uses in the post-Reformation period, when there was considerable uncertainty as to what could be regarded in law as a good charitable object. Briefly, the Act's effect was to extend to charities serving mainly social or welfare purposes (as enumerated in the previous chapter) privileges similar to those which in the Middle Ages had been granted by the Ecclesiastical Courts to charities more narrowly concerned with the advancement of religion (though these might also involve the advancement of education and the relief of poverty). For example, it waived an existing rule which limited the duration of a trust, and provided that, according to the doctrine of cy pres, a new objective might be specified, as near as possible to the original, should the latter become incapable of execution. Again, it provided machinery for checking abuses in the administration of trusts, namely *ad hoc* commissions which were the ancestors of the permanent Charity Commission of today. In this way individuals of great wealth were encouraged to believe that the wider purposes of their gifts could be achieved in perpetuity. Later, particularly after the late seventeenth century, men of more modest resources, inspired perhaps by the progress of joint-stock companies, were also encouraged to pool their individual gifts in order to effect a common purpose by 'associated philanthropy'.[8]

In the classical city-state, however, there existed no such concept of 'legal personality'. If a wealthy Greek or Roman wished to establish or to contribute to a fund with a view to a permanent objective, the only way in which he could hope to achieve this was by making over money or real property to a person or group of persons, either during his life-time or upon his death. He would have to call upon the recipients, firstly, to use the derived annual income to effect the desired purpose and, secondly, to pass on the 'gift' to others who would after their own death take over the property, with the same obligation attaching, and so on *ad infinitum*. As Laum declared, the Greek foundation—and the Roman was no different—was from the legal viewpoint no more than a gift with an obligation attached. As such, the classical 'foundation' was likely to be at risk in two ways. Firstly, however careful the arrangements, there

was always the chance of a break in the chain of recipients resulting from unforseen contingencies, especially in a world where
chance often seemed to rule and the average expectation of life
was low. What was wanted was some artificial person or body
not subject to such contingencies. Secondly, even if chance did
not intervene, how could one guarantee that the immediate
recipient, let alone the series of persons who succeeded to the
property, would in fact use it for the purpose for which it had
been given? In the case of the immediate recipient, indeed, it was
possible to think of a variety of devices, such as the appointment
of joint recipients (the one to watch the other), a provision for
revoking the fund, or for its reversion to a third party, in case of
departure from the stated purpose of the gift; or the threat of a
fine or the invocation of the gods to curse the offender and bless
the faithful. These (and other) devices were in fact resorted to by
classical donors, but their very number tends to suggest that it
was not only the last which was difficult to implement. The
Greeks, in particular, were notorious, not least in the eyes of
fellow Greeks, for their unreliability in handling money. It has
been noted how, even in the case of a family-foundation, that of
Epikteta of Thera at the turn of the second century BC, the
donor provides against the possibility of her own daughter
Epitelcia's failing to carry out her obligations. Moreover, as
long as the gift was to a private individual or any group of people
unrecognized by the state, any undertaking of the immediate
recipient was not backed by the state, and any legal action
would normally depend entirely upon the initiative of an
interested party, which, even if successful, could not cause the
fund to be redirected to its original purpose. As for future
recipients yet unborn, there was no way in which the donor
could bind their wills.[9]

In Roman law the fulfilment of the donor's intention was
originally even more uncertain, since his right to bind the will—
even of the immediate recipient—was not admitted. After the
time of Augustus, however, the *fideicommissum* could be enforced
in the case of the immediate recipient, but the law still remained
hostile to the idea that a donor could bind the will of persons yet

unborn. Not that this deterred either Greeks under Roman rule or Romans themselves from having drawn up wills and other documents which tacitly assumed the contrary. This may be seen, for instance, in the case of a certain Titus Flavius Praxias, a Phrygian who had gained Roman citizenship. About AD 85 he tried, through the agency of six freedmen and their successors, to establish an annual banquet in his memory and provide for the purchase of roses to be strewn on his statue: the annual income from certain property was to be put to this purpose and no other 'during the unending rule of Rome'. Again, in Italy itself a century or so later we find a Flavius Syntrophus assigning to a freedman, Aithales, certain gardens 'with buildings and vineyard enclosed by a wall', the usufruct of which he was to enjoy in association with fellow freedmen so long as they continued to perform services with a similar purpose, passing on their obligation together with the property to their successors. Aithales was really in the position of a trustee, and the continued acceptance of the obligation attaching to the gift would depend thereafter on the good will of those who inherited the property.[10]

There are certain aspects of the arrangements made by Flavius Praxias, however, as distinct from those of Flavius Syntrophus, which exemplify the method which had come to be adopted by many persons who wished to circumvent the double hazard attaching to gifts of this kind to private persons. Flavius Praxias had caused the provisions attaching to his gift to be embodied in a bill presented to the council of his native town, Akmonia, and, remarkably enough, had apparently had the bill submitted to the Roman authorities in advance, obtaining their approval. This method of handing over property to the city, or one of its official organs (the magistrates or the council, etc.) so that they became entitled to the usufruct (or part of it), but undertook to use it as specified by the donor, had clearly come to be employed in Greece some time before the advent of Roman domination in 146 BC. We have a number of documents dating earlier than this which record both the offer of the donor and the formal acceptance of the city or some official group within it. Such a method obviously seemed to many donors to offer a better chance of affecting a long-term purpose, because (1) although individual citizens died, the city itself went on living, and (2) the Greek city could bind by its laws the actions of citizens yet unborn, making them as well as the initial recipients subject to penalties in case of default or misappropriation: a share of the money-fine imposed was frequently offered to anyone who brought a successful prosecution (D. 47, 71). Under Roman law, indeed, it was comparatively late—not until the time of Nerva—that all Roman municipalities were accorded the right to receive gifts, and not until the time of Hadrian were the obligations attaching to them enforceable. Even then the life of the city was not conceived of as indefinite but was limited to a hundred years. But by the latter part of the second century AD such gifts were not uncommon, no doubt seeming to be investments at least as sound as their Greek counterparts.[11]

Yet the perpetuation of the donor's intention could still not be completely assured. Even at the time of accepting a gift the receiving body, besides itself deciding the more detailed regulations (the nature of any fines, for instance) for the administration of the fund, might secure from the donor some modification of his original intention and, once the gift had officially been handed over and technically become the property of the recipient, it could be treated henceforth as was deemed best by the assembly or council, in the light of changing circumstances. But what of the sanctions which were now supposed to have state backing? The answer is that by the time this type of gift, with obligation attached, became common, the courts which would normally try anyone accused of departing or of proposing departure from the obligation in question, were in most cities no longer popular courts. They were courts empanelled from a small group of families which exercised all real political power and, more important, supported almost all the financial burdens of the state. If, then, such a court felt that these burdens might be eased by applying property assigned for a charitable or social purpose to some other purpose, they were unlikely to convict those responsible, even supposing the magistrate, who came from the same class, were ready to admit a charge under this head. By this time, too, the audit to which, in democratic cities at any rate, all magistrates who handled public money had once been subject at the end of their term of office, was simplified or abolished, so that no redirection of funds by a magistrate was likely to arouse complaint, unless it infringed the interests of the wealthy minority. Laum cites an example from early in the second century AD, namely the lavish endowment of C. Vibius Salutaris of Ephesus, part of which was intended to provide an annual payment to the six tribes of the city. Of this sum fully half had disappeared or been diverted to other purposes within a few years of its acceptance.[12]

Before the time of this endowment the Greeks had hit upon another device aimed at assuring the original purposes of such gifts, a device already seen in part in the case of Titus Praxias— that of securing the additional backing of Rome for its continuance, despite the Roman law's abhorrence of entail. It was again at Ephesus, about a century earlier, that Vedius Pollio had established a benevolent fund which included among its purposes the provision of an annual sum to defray a special tax levied on certain local priesthoods. With respect to this a decree of Paullus Fabius Persicus, the imperial legate of the province of Asia in Claudius' reign, is of interest; for while reproving the Ephesian authorities for resorting to various devices through which individual magistrates might prey upon temple revenues and treasure, it allows the priests to maintain their exemption under this endowment as being 'under the guardianship of Augustus'. It is evident that Vedius Pollio, a favourite of Augustus, had obtained something like the personal intercession of the Emperor to supplement the protection already theoretically given by the council and people of Ephesus to his fund at its inception. Tracing the further development of this practice we see that in the case of Vibius Salutaris' endowment the interest of the Emperor is expressed by the fact that the fine payable, in case of any misdirection of funds, is to be divided between the imperial treasury and the temple of Artemis (since the Emperor now had divine status, this was in one sense a way of placing a fund under divine protection). At the same time a specific legal formula provided

for action against any real or would-be evader. A generation
or so later this formula was standardized, and by the end of
the second century, at the request of the people of Antioch, the
Emperor Commodus himself, rather than his representatives in
the province, had issued a declaration protecting an endowment
from embezzlement by the city magistrates. Yet even if the sanctions now imposed were more impressive, their imposition upon
the guilty could do nothing to divert misdirected funds back to
their original purpose; nor could yet another device, probably
invented in the Greek east during the Roman period, namely
provision for the transfer of the fund to another municipality
or association, the means of enforcing which it is equally difficult
to discover (see D. 40, 71, 74).[13]

When eventually the way was open at Rome for the benevolent
legally to confer legacies upon towns or associations for philanthropic purposes, they were faced with much the same problems.
'Suppose you pay over the money to the state,' writes Pliny
(D. 17) to a correspondent who was considering this possibility,
'there is the fear that it will be misdirected; suppose you hand over
land, then once it has become public it will be neglected.' We
have no way of checking the proposals of benefactors in the
Roman world against acceptance decrees of cities receiving their
gifts, since our Latin documents are mainly simple honorary or
commemorative inscriptions. Laum concluded that the absence in
the west of evidence for the backing of sanctions protecting
foundations by provincial governors or the Emperor might
indicate a higher degree of security for these foundations than for
their counterparts in the east. More recently, however, it has been
suggested that it was the very considerable gifts which came into
the coffers of some Italian municipalities that caused the Emperors
to establish *curatores*, with a general commission to guard against
financial inefficiency, if not dishonesty, in the west as well as in
the east. We may note, too, how the name of the Emperor is
invoked unofficially to protect a fund in Italy (D. 31).[14]

Emperors of the second century AD themselves were ready on
occasion to take the initiative in diverting funds from the purposes
for which they had been intended, though notably in a context

which modern feeling would approve: in seeking to restrict expenditure on gladiatorial games and similar entertainments. Here we should bear in mind that even under English law a hard-fought compromise has had to be worked out 'between regard for the spirit of the intention of the founder and the claims of the present'. 'There is no inherent right belonging to those who have played their part in this world to dictate in what manner their former worldly goods shall be used,' wrote Sir Arthur Hobhouse in 1880 in protest against the control of the 'Dead Hand'. But everything, once this is admitted, depends on the disinterested and independent character of the body which is empowered to effect such redirections. Thus, in England the present-day Charity Commission, two of whose three paid members must be legally qualified, deals primarily with proposals initiated by trustees where the object of a trust has become, for example, obsolete, useless, or prejudicial to public welfare. It was (on one recent view) because of his doubts as to such impartiality that Flavius Syntrophus resorted to his foundation '*par des substitutions à l' infini*', rather than rely on the town-council or the magistrates to secure his mainly funerary purpose.[15]

For men of wealth who were concerned simply to confer upon their fellow townsmen a really lasting benefit the best solution in the circumstances might appear to be the provision, not of money or property, the income from which was still capable of misdirection, but of amenities such as baths, libraries, theatres—and many benefactors did, indeed, provide these. Yet, even then, such amenities would need a permanent fund to ensure their maintenance, and though the donor might provide this, it too would be susceptible to misdirection. If then, as was normally the case even in periods when the foundation came to cover a wide variety of social objectives, the classical donor—like his modern counterpart—was still concerned to secure his own memory by his gifts, he might be considered merely prudent if he concluded that this would probably be best effected through an endowment for the annual distribution of food or cash within the particular social group to which he belonged (the whole citizen-body, if he was wealthy enough, but otherwise a smaller group).

He would thus be relying on the individual self-interest of the beneficiaries to secure the continuance of the fund, and consequently tended to make this type of gift his main, if not his only, benefaction. Moreover, such a conclusion appears to have been most acceptable to the beneficiaries themselves, if we may judge from a rebuke delivered by the Emperor Antoninus Pius to the people of Ephesus for their failure to show due gratitude for the generous programme of building carried out by a certain Vedius Antoninus and a greater readiness to honour those who lavished their wealth on 'shows and distributions and prizes for the games' (D. 25).

Such may have been some of the considerations of which wealthy men took account in attempting to set up permanent funds in the context of the city-state. This does not mean that any failure of the wealthy to meet social ills through such funds was due simply to lack of appropriate machinery; here we may accept Le Bras' judgment that 'institutions do not depend in a servile manner upon the progress of technique'. In other words, if these men had been more concerned about such problems they would have found a way. None the less, this chapter may properly serve, not only to account for the frequent mention of gifts to municipalities (or their constituent parts) in subsequent chapters, but also to emphasize the very imperfect character of this device, as soon as such a concern, in however limited a form, did come to be felt by the classical donor.[16]

CHAPTER III

GIVING FOR A RETURN

IN THE VAST MAJORITY of texts and documents relating to gifts in the classical world, it is quite clear that the giver's action is self-regarding, in the sense that he anticipates from the recipient of his gift some sort of return. To the modern mind such 'giving' may seem more like an economic transaction than an altruistic gesture. Yet as anthropologists, such as Marcel Mauss, have pointed out, simple societies can be found even today in which such giving, far from being amoral, let alone immoral, is the whole basis of friendly intercourse and exchange of *any* kind. The first aspect of the matter is that in such societies the money market, the use of money and idea of sale are unknown, and so the 'giving' of one article and the explicit expectation or demand of the 'giver' that he be 'given' another in return must inevitably do duty for sale and purchase. But in addition to this, particularly as between the chiefs within such communities or of neighbouring communities (and it will normally be only the leading men who are in a position to exchange 'gifts' of any consequence), the offer of a gift represents an offer of friendship, an offer not lightly to be rejected, since the number of friends which a man has may well be as important to his security and prestige as the value of his material possessions. If the offer is to be accepted, there is only one way in which this can be done, by the offer of a counter-gift, while the failure to offer a counter-gift is *ipso facto* a declaration of enmity.[17]

Further consequences ensue, once it is decided to accept the offered 'gift'. Since prestige as well as security is involved, the recipient will wish not merely to make an equal return, but to outdo the gift which he has received, thereby asserting his superior worth or status—which the original giver can question only by offering in turn an even larger 'gift'. Thus, to use a Greek term, an 'agonistic' attitude to giving is established as the two parties engage in what sometimes proves a ruinous competition. Indeed, any undue delay on the part of either in making an adequate return will involve his becoming in some sense the dependent of the other; for ultimately, not being able to offer any material return, he might even offer himself.[18]

Such communities are still to be found today, not only in continents such as Africa, where among the Bantu of Kavirondo, for instance, it has been observed that 'the larger gifts which are exchanged at definite occasions between different categories of person are rather mutual obligations than gifts, as they are not voluntary but strictly reciprocal. In the case of refusal, the gift is either fetched by force, or the relationship ceases to exist.' Even in present-day Greece, in the remote, mountainous areas, J. K. Campbell has described certain communities in which 'where a man does a personal service for an affine, some return of favour is always awaited. In these relations the element of contract is always present, and a certain competitive attitude as to which set of affines fulfils its obligations with greater punctilio.' Nor, of course, in more advanced society is the feeling unknown, as between 'friends' in the more diluted sense of the term, that one must always seek to return a gift or favour; while internationally the symbolic nature of reciprocal gifts between heads of 'friendly' states is evident. In all these cases it is not the isolated 'gift' which is significant, but the whole sequence of giving and receiving of which it is a part, and the kind of relationship which it establishes or confirms.[19]

In the case of early Greece and Rome, language itself points to the original significance of giving and countergiving as doing duty for purchase and sale. Thus, to cite merely a few of the more obvious illustrations, the common classical Greek verb which we translate 'to sell' is merely a middle compound form of *didonai*, indicating 'to give of one's own accord'. In Latin the parallel verb is again a compound form of the verb 'to give', *venum dare*, while *emere*, commonly translated 'to buy' means basically no more than 'to take'. Significant, too, are reciprocal terms such as *xenos* in Greek, *hospes* in Latin, which may mean either the person who offers *or* the person who receives entertainment. The Greek verb *nemein* may be used of a person either giving or receiving a share in a distribution, the Latin term *mutuum* of the loan either given or received, *munus* of the burden readily accepted or almost compulsorily undertaken in return for a favour previously received. Finally, such terms as *nexus*, *obligatus*, *damnatus*, which came to be used in the context of penalties for debt, originally clearly reflected the condition of one who is 'bound' to return a 'gift' and who must, if no other way is possible for him, make that return by placing himself at the disposal of his 'creditor', becoming his dependant, at least until in that way he has returned something of equal value. Although by that time—even if he regains his freedom—he will have lost much of his prestige.[20]

The earliest Greek literature we possess shows us the practice of giving in expectation of a return, with the same dual object of establishing friendship and asserting one's worth. Thus, in the *Iliad*, Glaukos and Diomedes break off fighting when they discover that their grandfathers had once entertained each other, 'after which they gave each other the splendid gifts that host and guest exchange', thus honouring and confirming the friendship previously established between their families. In the *Odyssey* Menelaus asserts his prestige by giving Telemachus a mixing-bowl of wrought metal, 'the loveliest and most precious of the treasures that my palace holds'; nor does he omit to let the recipient know that he himself had previously received it from the king of Sidon. Where the giving and receiving of presents is a matter of prestige there is felt to be nothing remarkable in passing them on, especially when the donor could boast such a source. Again in the *Odyssey*, Athene, appearing to Telemachus as the Taphian chieftain Mentes, asks him to keep an offered gift till later, with the unblushing suggestion that he should make it the best he could find, since he would not lose by the exchange. This attitude towards gifts has been discussed more fully in *The World of Odysseus*, by M. I. Finley, who has argued that 'marriage gifts' are also to be seen in much the same light, rather than as merely representing a 'bride-price': that is to say, when offered by the suitor they are to be regarded as the assertion of his worth against other suitors; and as such he will not expect to reclaim his 'stake', should he fail in the contest. It is in keeping with such an interpretation that gifts should sometimes accompany the bride rather than be 'exchanged' for her, indicating that the conclusion of the marriage alliance will bring more prestige to the bride's family than that of her suitor. So *hedna*, the technical term for such gifts, if not *dōra*, may be precisely parallel to *xenia*, the gifts so commonly exchanged between guest and host, being simply 'gifts accompanying marriage . . . regardless of the direction in which the gifts travelled'.[21]

At this stage in social development, as Evans Pritchard has observed, the moral criteria by which we normally judge the practice of giving are simply irrelevant; 'such gifts are at once and the same time moral, economic, juridical, aesthetic, mythological and social phenomena.' However, within two centuries of the time that the Homeric epics were first written down, the Greeks were already familiar with the use of coinage and a money market (although we shall notice that among them, as later among the Romans, services done between members of the upper class were for a long time not paid for in cash). Faced with this new social and economic development, they were not slow to criticize a system according to which a 'giver' could openly indicate in advance the return which he expected for his 'gift' and consider himself wronged if he did not receive it. Clearly they no longer fully understood the background against which such behaviour was to be viewed. Thus Finley has noted how Thucydides (writing *c.* 430–400 BC) regards as a curiosity in the kingdom of Sitalkes 'the custom of taking rather than giving, more disgrace being attached to not giving *when asked* than to asking and being refused'. In the same period the philosopher Democritus was declaring, if the fragment is genuine, that 'the generous man is not the man who looks for a return, but he who is predisposed to confer a benefit.' A little later the orator Lysias is found declaring that 'it is a good man's part to benefit his friends even though no one should come to know of it'; and Demosthenes insists that 'the benefactor should not remind a man of what he has received, for this almost amounts to rebuking him.' For Aristotle it is the conferring of a benefit where a return is not sought that is morally acceptable (*kalon*); and comedy re-states the theme: 'If you receive a favour, keep it in mind, if you confer a favour, forget it.'[22]

This same point was to be taken up in Latin, as for instance in a line of Terence, '*istaec commemoratio quasi exprobatio est immemori benefici*' ('this reminder to the forgetful of a service rendered is almost a reproach'), or in Cicero's description of such unkind remembrancers as a 'hateful class of men'. In moral philosophy Cicero re-states the Aristotelian doctrine in asserting that 'if we are truly liberal and beneficent we do not make a profitable business of doing good' (*beneficium faenerari*). A century later Seneca makes similar points repeatedly in his *de beneficiis*: 'Doing good means simply paying out; if you receive anything in return, then you do good business; but if there is no return, you make no loss'; or, more directly, 'He who has given in order to receive back has not given'; or again, more paradoxically, 'Often he who has returned a favour is ungrateful; it is the man who has not returned it who is grateful.' He also repeats the dictum of Aristotle that the value of a gift is not to be judged by its intrinsic worth, but by the spirit of the giver and the resources from which he gives. Aristotelian, too, is the frequent insistence on the idea of the 'cheerful giver' (which found its way into the Septuagint at Alexandria and so into the letters of St Paul). But Seneca carries the point still further and urges that certain *beneficia* are to be conferred anonymously: 'On occasion the very person who is being helped is to be kept in the dark.'[23]

Yet, though the very terminology of this critique of the Homeric picture—including the term 'gratitude' itself—is quite out of place with reference to the original significance of giving and countergiving, and offers indication enough of the different social and economic conditions in which these writers lived, further attention to the context reveals to what a large extent the attitude to giving remained the same. The essential point is that there remains basic to the discussion the assumption that the gifts, benefits or favours in question are to be conferred upon somebody who *can* make a return, so that a return, even though it may no longer decently be asked for, is confidently expected. The discussion, then, never reaches the obvious conclusion, namely that the surest way to avoid any suggestion of giving with a view to a return is to confer one's gift on someone who is incapable of giving in return. This is the doctrine of the Christian apologist, John Chrysostom: 'Do not give to the rich who can give back.' Taken out of context certain remarks of classical writers may indeed seem to be suggesting as much. We find Cicero declaring that in the placing of a good turn, other things being equal, one should follow above all the principle that the help should go where the need is greatest. But the tone of the whole work, *de officiis*, makes it quite clear that the proviso is a very considerable one; even if the verb which Cicero uses for the 'placing' of a good turn, *collocare*, commonly used of financial investment, represents (like its Greek parallel) a dead metaphor, it is significant that Cicero is applying his principle not merely to the conferment but to the repayment of favours. Similarly in Seneca, to counterbalance the paradox already quoted, there may be found the advice that 'although we assert that he who has gladly accepted a good turn has returned it, yet we urge him to return something similar to what he has received.' Indeed, the recipient is expected to engage in what the third-century BC Greek philosopher Chrysippus had described as 'a most honour-able competition', the outdoing of one good turn by another an expression of the continuing 'agonistic' attitude to giving, which was our starting point. So, again, Cicero asserts that, while each of us has the right to decide in the first place whether or not he is going to make a gift, when the question of returning a gift arises we have not the same right, at any rate if we are 'good men.'[24]

All this in turn merely recapitulates what had been said long before by the Greeks. Precisely because of the strong sense of obligation to return favours or gifts, we find in Thucydides such aphorisms as: 'He who has done a favour is in a stronger position, while he who is in the position of owing one finds that friendship has lost its edge, since he is aware that by making a return he will not obtain a response of gratitude but will merely be paying back the generosity.' The same point lies behind the well-known remark of Aristotle that 'people who have done a good turn seem to regard as their friends those for whom they have done it, rather than *vice versa*'. A line of Menander goes still further: 'There are some who even hate those who do them a good turn.' Demosthenes, after declaring that people should not be reminded of benefits received, immediately adds that it is up to the recipients to make a return without *needing* to be reminded; and a letter, ascribed to Aristotle, declares that 'giving and returning is that which binds men together in their living , as some give, others receive, while others again make a return gift for what they have received.'[25]

The limitations of this critique of the earlier concept of reciprocity in giving are largely explained by the fact that it is set in the context of the proper relations of persons of equal or near-equal status within the upper strata of society in the city-state, where the assertion of personal worth (*aretē/dignitas*) through the maintenance of friendships remained of fundamental importance. This assertion still depended not least on a claim to generosity (*eleutheriotēs/liberalitas*) which, by definition, any member of this narrow class would have some power of exercising. It is in this context, indeed, that we find Aristotle emphasizing that the 'just' man will need to be a man of means, with a view to the repayment of gifts received, and that liberality can be defined not merely as giving the proper amount to the proper ends but also as *receiving* the proper amount from the proper sources. As to the latter, the question *whether* he is to receive in return does not arise, his problem being simply to ensure that the balance between his giving and receiving is maintained to the best advantage of his own prestige.[26]

For this class of men the need to maintain 'friendships' turned in part on the fact, already briefly noticed, that even in a money economy there were still a considerable number of services essential to comfort and security which could not be bought for money. Aristotle does not speak sentimentally when he asserts that 'nobody would choose to live without friends, even though possessed of all other blessings'; for, even though his highest form of friendship is that between men of like mind and heart, he also recognizes the type of friendship based essentially on the consideration of mutual advantage (*to chrēsimon*). Such a relationship he recognizes as being easily dissolved, yet it *is* for him a type of 'friendship'—and he uses the term in no philosophic or esoteric sense. Not all philosophers followed Aristotle's usage. It may have been the Stoic Panaetius, some two centuries later, who inspired Cicero's protest that 'friendship does not follow upon advantage, but advantage upon friendship'; but the latter found the protest the easier because in Roman society there was freer use of two correlative terms, *patronus* and *cliens*, expressing the same kind of relationship, but making it clearer where the advantage in status lay; and so in practice there was little difference between Greek and Roman. Little or no mutual affection was essential to the relationship of either *philia* or *amicitia*: originally, we recall, the adjective *philos* was used of something which was one's own.[27]

In the aristocratic state it was almost exclusively among men of like status that men of quality needed such friendships; their 'friends' supplied services analogous to those provided by bankers, lawyers, hotel owners, insurers and others today. Thus, if any member of this class wished to raise a loan, it would be to a friend that he would normally look for assistance. If he needed representation in the lawcourts he would seek a man of culture, who virtually by definition would be a man of wealth, among his friends; if he needed accommodation outside his own town, the only respectable place he could look for was a villa owned by some wealthy friend. In the matter of personal 'insurance' against contingencies of any kind, he must rely upon the moral obligation felt by those whose 'friendship' he had secured by prior services. No payment in cash for such services would be acceptable to the person who rendered them. In the upper class of both Greece and Rome the acceptance of payment in money remained shocking, for it implied that the recipient was the *employee* of the other party, that he needed to accept such for his living, and was not a man of quality at all. As has been emphasized, both for Rome and (perhaps more truly) for Athens, it was not so much work in

c

itself, but the implications of accepting payment for work, of being at another's beck and call, which was felt to be demeaning. By the late first century AD we find in Quintilian the grudging admission that a 'poor' orator will need to make charges sufficient to meet his needs, but even then there follows the immediate qualification that 'he will not take it as a fee, but will enjoy it as a reciprocal kindness [*mutua benevolentia*], since he knows [having taken *no more* than was sufficient] that his own contribution has been so much the greater.' These services had, then, in theory at least to be disinterested (*beneficii loco*); the return expected (but not to be demanded) was an equivalent service by the recipient in the not too distant future. There was no legal way of ensuring this; the sanction ensuring that the 'debt' would be honoured was simply the social disgrace (*adoxia/ infamia*) resulting from default—and the loss not merely of one 'friend' but possibly of many, who would take warning and repudiate their 'friendship'.[28]

Such a loss was not readily to be admitted. Agreeing with Aristotle, Cicero asks: 'Whose wealth can be or ever has been of such proportions that it can stand without the services of friends?' The question had point since, even if money was acquired in vast quantity, there was little which could be done with it, for luxury goods which could be bought were comparatively few, and there was usually little scope for investment except in land, and that too was limited. It becomes less surprising, then, that the old rural aristocracy of Attica, for instance, 'never considered their wealth as primarily a means of amassing further wealth'. Rather than accumulate money for its own sake it was better to invest it in friendship, that '*optimam et pulcherrimam vitae, ut ita dicam, supellectilem*' as Cicero, following Xenophon, described it (though perhaps not many a 'friend' today would consider it flattering to be spoken of as a piece of furniture). There was good sense in Aristotle's generous man's prizing his wealth 'not for its own sake, but as a source of his giving' and in the dictum that wealth consists 'in its use as a means of securing friendships, rather than in its being possessed'. Martial puts the same point in a couplet:

What's given to friends is outside fortune's grasp:
Your gifts will prove the only wealth to last.

And Seneca says of the miser, as so often with an almost New
Testament nuance, that he is not in possession of riches but 'his
riches are in possession of him' ('*divitiae illum tenent*').²⁹

But in addition to friendship between status-equals 'with a
view to advantage' there was also for Aristotle, within the same
category, friendship of unequals and even of opposites. We should
scarcely grace the latter relationship with the name of 'friendship'
at all; but, according to Aristotle's definition, as long as there
exists an association which is of mutual advantage, to which each
contributes something (however wide the difference in kind
between that which is given and received), a kind of friendship
exists. In the case of friendship between the poor and the wealthy,
it is obviously material assistance which the wealthy can provide.
What can the poor man offer? The answer given is 'honour', in
the form of social and political allegiance, increasingly important
as the social and political life of the city-state became more
democratic. In the social club as well as in the body politic the
friendship of the poor, collectively, if not individually, came to
be worth having.³⁰

It is at this point that we can best understand how the Greek
root-word of our term 'philanthropy', which is applied in one
direction only, that is of benefits conferred by the rich upon the
poor (or not so rich), came in Greece to be characterized by that
zweiseitigkeit which is common to the terms *xenos/hospes, philos/
amicus, charis/gratia*, etc. In contrast with the latter the noun
philanthropia and its associated adjective had originally a one-way
direction, being used, as its basic form might suggest (love of
man—by someone other than a man) of the gods' relationship
with men, especially of the beneficence of such a god—or demi-
god—as Prometheus in giving fire to mortals. By the fourth
century, however, by a natural extension of usage, it came to be
applied to all-powerful rulers who were generous to their
subjects—so it is applied to Philip by Isocrates and to the Persian
Cyrus by Xenophon—or to great men generally who were kind

to their dependants, particularly as religious belief declined and it seemed increasingly that it was the attitude of such men, not that of the gods, which really mattered. And yet, just because of the widespread acceptance of the idea that the common man should have at least a nominal part to play in the life of the Greek state and of other associations which it embraced and, again, because of the innate tendency to assume that any gift, once received, naturally gave rise to a counter-gift, the reaction of the poor and weak to the generosity of the great and powerful came also to be designated as *philanthropon*. So it is that in many resolutions in which such generous acts are formally accepted by the benefici-aries, whether in social or religious clubs, in professional associa-tions or in political assemblies, the honours voted in return to the benefactors are also not infrequently styled as *philanthropa*. In modern terms, the generosity of the donor of £50,000 to an impoverished college would be styled as *philanthropon*, but so would any plaque recording the gift and any annual college dinner held in the donor's honour. Indeed, the very title of *benefactor/euergetes* was itself *philanthropon*, since it did not simply state a fact but conferred a status, indicating that the person on whom it was conferred was in credit, as it were, in respect of the balance of friendly acts. In this sense it was true that the classical benefactor, by virtue of his very title, had his reward.[31]

Now this reciprocity of *philanthropa* (or, in Latin, *beneficia*) was vital to the whole life of both club and state, the latter being, as Aristotle argued, merely an association or club writ large, of a more permanent kind and with more long-term aims than most private associations. In particular, each was made up of members, some of whom were rich but the majority comparatively poor, and each depended on the willingness of the rich to meet the bulk of the running expenses of the association, including the financial burden attached to its chief offices, which were normally unpaid. This probably remained true of the most burdensome offices, even in the radical Athenian democracy. These offices were acceptable to the wealthy precisely because, although costly, they did bring honour with them. Indeed, *timē* in Greek and *honos* in Latin indi-cate primarily the honour associated with a position rather than the position itself. As long as each party, the wealthy and the poor, could be seen to be making its own distinctive contribution to the association, there remained that common interest which was the basis of its existence. As long as this was true, the state did not degenerate into a tyranny in which, according to Aristotle's theory, the ruler sought to monopolize both honour and material advantage himself. 'There is little or no *philia* in a tyranny,' he declares, 'for where there is nothing in common for the ruler and the ruled, neither is there any friendship. . . .' It is friendship which in fact seems to act as a bond within cities. Three centuries later Lucretius was to say that human societies were linked by *amicitia* before the emergence of the city-state.[32]

For a considerable period, as long as the city-state retained its health, the distinction of holding office was regarded by the upper class as an adequate return for the burdens which it involved —though these were by no means always unassociated with the opportunity for material gain. At Rome, especially with the expansion of the Empire, both the prestige and the material advantage of the *honos* remained for long very obvious. Sooner or later, however, a situation arose in most cities, in which members of the upper class were called upon to provide more than what they considered to be their fair share in contributing to the well-being of the city-state, whether by accepting offices where the financial burden was increasingly disproportionate to the honour or by assuming financial burdens which entailed little or no honour. This latter imbalance is represented by Aristotle as the upper-class definition of a 'liturgy'. It is a 'liturgy' (a compulsory obligation), and not *philia*, if the rewards do not match the value of the services rendered—though even these, as the Greek orators knew, could be exploited to make a claim of 'friendship' upon the recipients. Eventually the stage was reached at which the traditional *honores* themselves were seen in no other light than liturgies. At Athens, for instance, from the late fourth century no distinction was made between them. At certain periods (the evidence is particularly good for Roman Africa in the first two centuries AD) it became customary for the citizen-body, the 'club-members' as it were, to specify in advance what sum of money (in Latin, *summa honoraria*) it expected from those upon whom office was conferred, a practice which might appear to us tantamount to offering the magistracies for sale to the highest bidder, but which in fact was only making explicit a principle of give-and-take which had always applied. When the office itself became unwelcome, the expenditure accompanying it became still more clearly something entirely other than a purchase price. Hence Rostovtzeff's question: 'Where shall we find in our own time thousands of rich men who would not only spend their time (without remuneration) in managing the affairs of their city, but also pay for it in the shape of *summa honoraria* and voluntary gifts?'[33]

Where a degree of resistance to the acceptance of office arose, however, something could be achieved by way of multiplying and carefully grading honours and titles. Aristotle supplies a whole series for the life of the Greek *polis*, and a still larger collection may be drawn from the extant inscriptions relating to the life of both city and club. One particularly distinctive title was the epithet *aionios* attached to the office or liturgy undertaken, indicating that its holder had endowed the office permanently, so providing for the expenses of future occupants. To encourage the generosity of wealthy outsiders, citizenship itself might be treated as an honour available as one *philanthropia* in return for another (in more material form), comparable to the entrance fee required by many a social club. In terms of prestige it might be worth becoming an Athenian, or even a citizen of Tarsus or Thasos, if one came from some remote or less civilized city, with no distinction of its own.[34]

If it appears remarkable, even so, that funds could be raised in such quantity and for so long in these ways, we should recall the small size of the typical state, which allowed something very like a club-spirit to assert itself. Hence the constant reference to the ideal of *homonoia* in the Greek-, and of *concordia* in the Latin-speaking city, both of which are suggestive of Aristotle's conception of friendship, since they indicate that happy condition in which every person and group within the state is conscious of working towards a common end. The Greek term appears on the coinage of the south Italian city of Metapontum as early as 400 BC, and both *homonoia* and *concordia* become the object of cult in many cities. The actual consciousness of this common end was regarded by Aristotle as more important than the rules which governed a city. He declares that it was at *homonoia* above all that constitution-makers aimed; for 'where there is friendship there is no need of justice, but those who are just still need friendship'— a secular antecedent of St Paul's 'love is the fulfilment of the law.' On the same principle the maxim that 'friends have everything in common' provides the basis of Aristotle's doctrine of private ownership but common use of property within the city.[35]

Aristotle refers to Tarentum (D. 1) in particular as actually applying this latter doctrine; but it was applied too in all the others in the sense that the financial burdens essential to the well-being of the city as a whole were undertaken largely by the wealthy, whether or not in association with office, on a voluntary basis. 'Everywhere there was an early stage of civic life when the revenue consisted largely in gifts from the wealthier citizens,' it has been observed of the Greeks in general; but not only at an early stage, for a similar picture has been presented of the Greek cities of Asia Minor under Roman rule: 'In all probability income accrued from sums paid by magistrates and others on entering office; liturgies and gifts were the most important items of revenue.' For this reason a carefully worked out 'budget' was held scarcely necessary or possible. No surplus was normally kept in hand to meet contingencies—witness fourth-century Athens, which 'like all other ancient states . . . lived from hand to mouth'. And just because there *were* for every state a series of contingencies (not least a failure of the corn supply), each tended to live with a succession of financial crises. It was to meet the latter that in Greek cities and clubs there developed a practice particularly relevant to our present study, namely the appeal for subscriptions (*epidoseis*) to special funds, directed to the wealthy class in general (D. 2). A proposal would be made in the assembly or council that a subscription fund be set up to meet a particular need and, once it was accepted, immediate contributions were expected.[36]

The wealthy in England today pay surtax according to the

demands of an impersonal Department of Inland Revenue and remain in inglorious anonymity (if not furtive obloquy) as far as society is concerned. The wealthy of the Greek city-state, by contrast, gave 'gifts', which, however near-obligatory in character, had their reward in the publicity of the subscription-list, quite apart from any other public honours. It is of some interest to compare how for two generations after the promulgation of the Elizabethan Act of Charitable Uses the two 'rich and aggressive classes'—merchants and gentry—then coming into prominence responded to its challenge, accepting 'burdens which were now fully understood'. 'At no time before 1660,' writes W. K. Jordan, 'was more than a slight burden of responsibility ever assumed by taxation, by public intervention, so immediate, so sustained and so generous was the private response.' Hence, 'the failure of a London merchant to settle some substantial and conspicuous trust or gift was generally regarded as little short of shocking.' The Act itself has been seen as something of a propaganda document, in so far as it was intended to suggest to other donors that they should follow the example set by sovereigns and 'sondrie other well-disposed persons'. In the Greek world, of course, the motive for publishing the subscription-lists was, as much as anything, to indicate those who had *not* contributed and remind them of their shocking omission, according to the standard of *homonoia*. It was also fair game to make public the name of any person who, having promised his subscription, then failed to give it. This is made clear by a passage in Isaeus, referring to a certain man whose name had appeared on a list, posted up before the statues of the twelve heroes at Athens, under the rubric: 'these men, having promised of their free will to give money to the people for its security, then failed to do so.' Sometimes, again, the state might indicate the size of contribution acceptable, as on one occasion in third-century Athens when a minimum of fifty *drachmae* and a maximum of two-hundred was authorized.[37]

Particularly in a democracy, where the fortunes of the wealthy tended to be at the mercy of a popular jury, the pressure upon the man of means to contribute was considerable. Common in the law-courts was the argument that a defendant who had subscribed to this and that subscription-fund was clearly not a person who would descend to the sort of crime with which he was being charged. On the same principle a defendant would not blush to declare before a jury that he had accepted a much heavier financial burden than he need have done, 'so that you might have a better opinion of me and so that, if I should meet with misfortune [face a charge in the law-courts] I might be able to put up a better case.' The nearest equivalent in an English court of law might be a declaration by one accused of misappropriation of public funds that he had always been most scrupulous in declaring his full liability for income tax.[38]

The danger which the wealthy had to face in many city-states was that, even though they did continue to make contributions in accordance with the demands of 'friendship' (*homonoia*), the popular jury might listen to vexatious prosecutions and deprive them not only of their wealth by confiscation but also of honour. And in the more aristocratic type of state, such as Rome, it seems often to have been, not so much the financial penalty itself, but the *infamia* attaching to it, which seemed to matter. That the wealthy were by no means always successful in urging the people to keep their side of the bargain may be illustrated by the self-congratulation of a speaker in one of Xenophon's dialogues on having disposed of his wealth and with it his fear of vexatious prosecutions, or by Isocrates' allegation that 'to seem to be wealthy is more dangerous than to be an open wrongdoer'. Aristotle saw the extent of the danger and offered his remedy, a law preventing fines imposed in the law-courts from becoming public property and so an incentive to such prosecutions. But no remedy was totally successful, and at the turn of the first century AD we find Plutarch making the same complaint: 'The masses hate a rich man who does not share his prosperity more than a poor man who steals public property.' Shortly afterwards Dio of Prusa declares that it was enough merely to seem rich to earn that hatred, having himself to convince his fellow-citizens that his personal fortune is much less than their demands imply.[39]

Despite the near-contradiction of theory and reality, the city-state in its classical form continued to be financed largely on this

'voluntary' basis. One of its attractions for the wealthy man was
that it enabled him, even in a radical democracy, to publicize his
worth (and perhaps overshadow a rival) by his generosity. It
allowed him to play the part of a truly free and liberal man
instead of subjecting him to laws which called for a merely
passive acquiescence in meeting the financial needs of the state.
For this reason most well-to-do Greeks would have seen good
sense in Aristotle's criticism that the abolition of the ownership
of private property among members of the upper class, as Plato
had suggested, would 'destroy liberality'. They saw liberality as a
political no less than a moral virtue and as a positive expression
of their real interest in the state. Another important factor was
that the average city-state did not possess and could not afford the
machinery for an elaborate system of taxation. The voluntary
system was also admirably adaptable to the needs of those
Hellenistic monarchies where, as long as the king could represent
himself as the supreme benefactor, the essentially passive loyalty
of his subjects might be made to appear as an active and spontaneous response of gratitude. In Egypt, in particular, almost
any decision of the Ptolemies referred to in official documents,
whether relating to fiscal immunities, rights to land or property
or even to guarantees against arbitrary action by the king's own
officers, is almost invariably styled as *philanthropon*; though their
non-Greek subjects might see in the term no more than the
Greek equivalent of that oriental 'grace' and 'mercy' familiar
to them for generations under the Pharaohs.[40]

But while it is possible to see the advantages of the voluntary
system, it becomes the more difficult to estimate the degree to
which there operated in the classical city-state that genuine regard
for others characteristic of a charity or scheme of social aid. Consider also the objectives for which the wealthy gave, whether in
response to the announcement of a public subscription or in connection with a magistracy received: on one occasion it might be
towards a fund to secure the distribution of cheap corn or oil in
the city or within the narrower group to which the donor
belonged, on another towards the repair of a temple—objectives
of a kind clearly associated with charitable endeavour today. But

the same people would also contribute on exactly the same basis
to a fund for rebuilding the city walls (D. 4) or the financing of a
war—objectives which for us (though not so much for the wealthy
Englishman of some three centuries ago) scarcely fall into the
same category—and clearly they received and expected to receive
the same public commendation for both types of contribution.
Similarly the wealthy magistrate of a Roman township would
pride himself equally on his distribution of cheap food and the
provision of a gladiatorial show, and not infrequently would
cover both objectives with a single donation (D. 32). It is quite
misleading to quote the former as a 'charitable benefaction' out
of context (hence the collection of inscriptions, quoted at some
length, at the end of this book).

Still more important, in the records of the acceptance of such
gifts, the motive which is constantly ascribed to the donor by the
recipient—and, indeed, asserted by the donor himself—is *philotimia* or *philodoxia* (love of honour or glory); and although the
language is less flexible, the same motive is clearly implicit in the
Latin inscriptions recording acts of beneficence. Yet it would be
as naïve to deduce from this that every public gift was simply
an expression of self-regard as it would be to assume that every
act designated 'charitable' was motivated by nothing except
selfless pity (this is the reason for the varied translation of the
Greek terms in the documents). Both terms when relating to
benefactions are blanket terms which obscure lesser, and sometimes even major, motives. The Greeks, in particular, believed
that the good man would pursue honour, admiring as they did a
strong competitive element in a man's psychology—so much so
that Plato defined one of the three 'parts' of the soul as *to
thumoeides*, which is virtually untranslatable but which comes very
near to 'self-regard'. This 'self-regard', however, to quote a recent
commentator, 'ranges from self-assurance, through self-respect,
to *our relations with others* and our concern for our reputation and
good name' (my italics), so reminding us of Butler's coupling of
'self-love' and 'benevolence'. In other words, this 'part' of the
soul tends to overlap with others and seldom, if ever, acts alone.
Accordingly Aristotle clearly indicates that even his 'friendship

with a view to advantage', if it is really to come under the category of friendship at all, must at least be tinged with regard for others, however convenient it may be to disregard this for purposes of classification. Conversely we have already noted some of the complementary motives which the study of English philanthropy must consider. Perhaps we may appositely add at this point Owen's reference to philanthropy as 'a ladder for social climbing' and Jordan's emphasis on its attraction as a means of securing 'fame among fellows and . . . promise of spiritual reward in the world to come'. The Greeks would have understood.[41]

We are now, of course, verging upon the philosophical question of whether in any sense a man is capable of a wholly altruistic act. Here, however, we must be content to note that some Greek thinkers recognized that the advantage which a benefactor obtained from his benevolence might be of a distinctly immaterial and subtle kind, and even claimed—though they could hardly prove it—that this type of advantage was 'best' and most satisfying. Thus, Aristotle could not accept the cynical interpretation that the benefactor 'loves' the man he has benefited in a way no different from that in which a creditor clings to a debtor. On the contrary, he insists that 'the benefactor . . . has a sincere kindness and affection for the man he has assisted, even if he gets no immediate, nor expects any future, good out of him.' Aristotle prefers to draw an analogy with the artist's joy in something which he has *created*', an aesthetic rather than a material gain on the part of a man who 'loves his handiwork because he loves existence; it is part of the nature of things'. Consistently it is one of his arguments for the retention of private property within the state that 'a very great pleasure is to be found in doing a kindness and giving some help to friends, or guests or comrades' —with all allowance made for the latter qualification. Clearly deriving from such an outlook is Seneca's definition of *beneficium* as a 'benevolent action *which gives pleasure* and *finds pleasure in so doing*, the outcome of a *natural and spontaneous inclination*' (my italics). For Seneca 'friendship' was not a matter of having 'someone to sit by one's sickbed . . . but of having somebody at whose bedside one can sit oneself or whom one can help in financial need'—a more particular version of Aristotle's statement that 'friendship consists in befriending rather than in being befriended'. Although Seneca emphasizes that 'everybody in serving another has thereby served his own advantage', he insists that this advantage does not arise from the fact that, 'once the example of beneficence has been set, it returns, as in a circle, to its initiator, but from the fact that the reward of all the virtues is inherent in themselves'. The dictum that 'you must live for another if you wish to live for self' (in this case recalling a line of Menander) is intended to state a fact of life, not simply suggest a motive for beneficence. Against this standard Seneca might well have met any criticism of the latter with the reply that 'there is no beneficent act so perfect as to defy the carping of the cynic'; and it becomes understandable how at least one Christian apologist, Origen, was led to accept the complaint of the pagan Celsus that in their ethical *teaching* Christians had nothing new to offer.[42]

It would be misleading to emphasize these passages in isolation or to forget that practice often fell short of precept, not least for Seneca. Yet, in considering the former, any over-isolation of the expressed motive of 'love of honour' would tend to blur the distinction between 'beneficent' acts which were almost blatantly self-regarding and those where the self-regarding element is at least much less evident. Thus we shall refer to examples of benefactions which their authors knew would not secure the widest popular applause, precisely because they were directed (in the younger Pliny's words) *'communibus magis commodis quam privatae iactantiae'*—towards the common good rather than towards self-display. The reward for such benefactions had to be found in their authors' awareness of the value of what they were doing. Perhaps Vedius Antoninus at Ephesus (D. 25) believed himself to be acting on such principles in refusing to submit to a popular demand that he should expend his wealth on public games and distributions; so perhaps did the orator Dio Chrysostom of Prusa in incurring unpopularity for similar reasons. It is true that, even in such cases, the cynical spirit (that *malignitas* of which Seneca speaks) might observe that the approval of *somebody* more influential than the crowd, perhaps that of the Emperor himself,

was being sought, and quote the case of a famous Greek benefactor, T. Claudius Atticus, a near-contemporary of Pliny, who
had offered to surrender his immense fortune to Nerva, but had
been instructed by that Emperor to 'keep it and use it well'.
Indeed, our knowledge of some of these benefactors arises in part
from the fact that they succeeded in gaining such approval. Yet
such claims as Pliny's can hardly be altogether discounted.[43]

However, there remains another group of acts which we might
call beneficent, namely that involving minimal gifts or services.
Some modern writers have held that it was through these gifts
and services that the classical world came nearest to altruism.
To this group of acts are related the so-called *arai Bouzygeiai*—
curses which were called down upon any man who failed to
provide water for the thirsty, fire for anyone in need of it, burial
for an unburied corpse, or directions for a lost traveller. The
range of these curses was eventually extended to cover a coin for
a beggar and a crust for a starving man. Within their original
limits these requirements are clearly of considerable antiquity,
as is indicated by the nature of the sanction which protected them.
In one sense at least it is proper to distinguish them from gifts
and services which we have so far been considering, in that they
came to be expressly excluded from the status of *beneficia* precisely
because they were conceived of as non-reciprocal. They were
the kind of gifts, in Seneca's words, 'whose very worthlessness
deprives them of real [moral] value', even though at a particular
moment they are of the greatest consequence to their recipients.
It is therefore held that the person capable of providing them is
not entitled, before he renders them, to consider the recipient's
'worth', in the sense of his ability and readiness to offer a return;
nor should he expect a return after he has rendered them. It
follows, or might seem to follow, that they were the kind of gifts
which might be given to any man in need, and ought to be so
given. Yet in moral philosophy they seem to be associated with
the concept of a very extended 'friendship' which is natural to the
largest 'society' of all, that of the human race itself. Thus Cicero
(as usual, following Greek thought) mentions these basic human
obligations in the context of the doctrine of an *omnibus inter omnes*

societas (a universal association). Against this background, then, we may be inclined to see the principle *do ut des* (I give that you may give) being applied here as well, especially when we notice that, in the case of some of these obligations—most obviously that due to the dead man in need of burial—it followed from their very nature that a return *could not* be expected from the person benefited. Yet behind the act of one who performed the needed service, apart from any religious scruple, there might lie the half-conscious calculation that he too might one day stand in need of a like service from someone to whom *he* would be unable to make any return. None the less, it is worth noticing Seneca's dismissal of such casual gifts and services as mere trivialities, if only to compare it with our occasional readiness to grace even acts of this type (for example, those associated with 'flag days') with the name of charity.[44]

As already noted, Bolkestein suggested that, quite apart from the *arai Bouzygeiai*, there developed among wealthy Romans, as early as the first century AD, a tendency to give to the poor, irrespective of the likelihood of an equivalent return. This suggestion is based on the recognition, on the one hand, that the Roman aristocrat had always tended to give *ob honorem* (in the concrete sense of an office expected or received) and, on the other, that from the reign of Tiberius onwards the common people had no further significant part to play in elections to these offices. Since the upper-class Romans continued to be lavish in their gifts, we must posit, according to Bolkestein's argument, an attitude to giving on their part more 'oriental' in character. Few would dispute the first half of the argument, that the Roman aristocrat under the Republic gave largely, if not exclusively, *ob honorem*. Even in Cicero there is little to suggest any consciousness of the social obligations of the man of property: when he and others talk of *concordia*, they tend to use the term of co-operation between the two upper sections of society, the knights and the senators, rather than of the mutual obligations of rich and poor. Nor does it appear at Rome that the people were able, through a device comparable to that of the Greek *epidosis*, to 'do themselves a good turn' (the language of the fifth-century Athenian pamphleteer) by virtually extorting financial sacrifices from the upper class, action in the law-courts being threatened if the latter did not respond. If the gifts of the Roman upper class tended to increase in lavishness, this seems mainly to reflect the increasing prestige and material advantages attaching to high office at Rome as the Empire expanded and competition became more intense. In the Latin west as a whole the municipal magistracies tended to decline in attractiveness more rapidly than at the heart of the Empire; but the evidence of recently-collected inscriptions suggests that, while these magistracies were still flourishing, generosity directed to social needs as ends in themselves was quite rare. Another review of inscriptions, concerned specifically with Roman Africa, suggests that precisely because the conferment of office was the most common occasion for munificence, the phrase *ob liberalitatem*, which appears in a relatively small number of cases, may reflect the rare occasions when there had *not* been an explicit *quid-pro-quo* basis for giving.[45]

If this apparently Roman characteristic—at least of the upper class—whereby, in Polybius' caustic words, 'nobody ever gives anything of his own willingly to anybody', is admitted, however, it would be all the more paradoxical, if it were true, that there occurred under the Principate that swift or early change of attitude posited by Bolkestein. In fact political patronage had not so much disappeared at Rome as come to be monopolized by one man, the *Princeps*; and the emperor's supremacy still depended to some extent on the loyalty, if not on the votes, of the populace—a loyalty arising out of gratitude for benefits received or anticipated. Moreover, throughout the remainder of the upper class the client-patron relationship remained as important as ever in terms of social prestige. There is clear evidence of this in the letters of Pliny and in the satires of Juvenal and Martial. 'Sometimes it seems', wrote Gilbert Highet, 'as though nine out of ten Romans were living on charity at this time, five of them on public-welfare schemes run by the government, and the other four as dependents of the tenth.' In general, therefore, it appears that the emphasis on reciprocity in giving continued at Rome well into the Empire period, that the lure of honour remained a powerful and essential motive.[46]

CHAPTER IV

THE NATURE OF THE
RETURN

HONOUR IS ASSERTED by Aristotle to be the greatest of external goods: it is that 'which we assign to the gods as their due and which is desired by the eminent and awarded as the prize of victory in the most glorious contests'. Another dictum, reminiscent of that of Aristotle on friendship, is attributed to Theophrastus: 'Generous actions and honour and the giving of assistance provide the bond between men in their life.' Demosthenes asserted of the Athenians collectively what Aristotle asserted of the individual, when he told them: 'You are more concerned about a good reputation than about material goods, and this is not only true of you but was true of your forefathers also.' One of the chief ways of acquiring honour within the social or political group was by giving; and neither Greek nor Roman shrank from the admission that this was an essential motive of their beneficence. 'It is quite clear', says Cicero, 'that most people are generous in their gifts not so much by natural inclination as by reason of the lure of honour—they simply want to be seen as beneficent.' Pliny makes the same point more epigrammatically in speaking of those who embellish their own acts of beneficence in fair words: 'Their boasting as to their good deeds is considered to be, not the consequence of the latter, but their motive.'[47]

It is, of course, to this very fact, and the open admission of it, that we owe much of our detailed evidence of the giving of members of the upper class in the classical world, their concern for honour causing them to seek public recognition of their generosity, not only by word of mouth, but through lasting memorials in stone or bronze, many of which survive to the present day. The donor not infrequently gave the most precise instructions as to the nature and placing of the memorials which he expected, as did a donor of Gytheion (D. 71): 'I wish to confer my gracious gift . . . on the stated conditions, which are to be published upon three marble stones; of these, one should be set up in the market before my house, one should be erected in the temple of the Caesars, close by the gates, and one in the gymnasium, so that to citizens and non-citizens alike at Gytheion my philanthropic and kindly act may be evident and well known.' Similarly a donor of Petelia in Italy (D. 31) made conditional a clause in his will bequeathing a sum of money for annual distribution to his fellow townsmen: 'If a pedestrian statue has been set up in the upper forum, with a stone foundation . . . I wish to be given, etc.' Where such a request was not made by the donor himself, the recipients would recognize the response expected and frequently include among the honours assigned to him a sum of money to pay for a statue beneath which an appropriate inscription would appear. Thereupon the benefactor would demonstrate his generosity still further by returning this sum—an act which would be mentioned in the inscription—and by providing a public feast or distribution at the dedication of the statue. Thus, a certain Q. Flavius Lappianus (D. 46) was following a widespread and long established custom when, c. AD 250, in accepting the honour of a statue in recognition of his munificence to the town of Thabarbus in Libya, he returned all the money (the amount of which is stated to the last sesterce) 'being content with the honour alone' (compare D. 10, 55).

The acceptance resolutions of social clubs and political assemblies alike follow almost a set formula in stating the various honours which the donor is to receive in return for his gift, a fact which makes possible the almost certain restoration of quite fragmentary inscriptions. The formula runs to the effect that in recognizing the generosity of the donor the recipients have conferred upon him honours which are not less, but rather more, than the equivalent of his gift. The implication of this was threefold: firstly, that the obliged party had repaid his obligation, as honour demanded, with interest; secondly, that it was now for the donor, both as a matter of material interest and moral obligation, to display his generosity still further; and, thirdly, that others should be inspired to emulate it. Occasionally the expectation of further gifts in return for honours conferred would be even more explicitly spelt out, as for instance in a third-century AD resolution giving the status of 'patron' to a certain Rutilius Viator at Beneventum in the following terms: 'We are hopeful of receiving still more lavish gifts hereafter from a man of whose high worth we have been conscious in the past and *therefore* we co-opt Rutilius Viator as patron' (my italics).[48]

The careful grading of honours and distinctions could be illustrated from a whole variety of inscriptions, relating to gifts for purposes as diverse as the adorning of the temple of Hera by the citizens of Samos, or the building of a temple to Dionysus by the members of a religious society (*thiasos*) at a Black Sea colony, on the one hand, and the strengthening of city-walls at Kolophon, on the other. Thus, an inscription, *c.* 310 BC, relating to the latter records how 'in order that the citizens may contribute as generously as possible towards the walls, it is resolved by the people that any citizen who wishes shall promise whatever amount he desires'. But the sting is in the tail, for the inscription continues: 'with regard to the promises made, in the month of Lenaion the people in plenary session are to take council, so that each of those who have promised a gift shall be honoured worthily in proportion to his generosity, in the measure that seems good to the people'. Still more explicit is a decree from Oropus, about a century later, relating to a similar fund where those who contributed more than a talent would receive the title of *proxenos* and *euergetēs*, while, concerning those who might give less than this 'the people is to make an investigation as to what degree of honour each deserves to receive'. It was perhaps a fair response to such pressure that in this case apparently only a single contributor came forward; nor was it an unparalleled response, as we may judge from a third-century inscription from Olbia (D. 4). On the other hand, social or political pressure might lead a donor, even if grudgingly, to increase the size of his gifts, as apparently did a certain Diotimos at Cibyra, who declares in an inscription that he has now decided to give more than he had originally intended 'since he has come to recognize what is expected of him'. The principle here involved is not essentially different, of course, from that commonly followed today in the case of subscriptions to a hospital fund, whereby the donor of £25 may perhaps have a bed named after him, while a whole ward will be named after a subscriber of £5,000. In the city-state, however, the pressure on the wealthy was considerably greater in that, should they fail to display the expected degree of generosity, they might find themselves not only deprived of the honours which they coveted but also burdened with unwanted liturgies; they might even be subjected to vexatious prosecutions in the lawcourts, involving positive dishonour (*adoxia/infamia*), as well as confiscation of their property.[49]

The inscriptions also make it abundantly clear that the mere acceptance of an office, whether in club or state, was often seen as tantamount to making a gift to the body concerned, and welcomed in exactly the same terms as the latter (the verb *epididonai*, with which the noun *epidosis* is connected, could be used of giving a sum of money or of giving *oneself* for public service, e.g. D.9). Ziebarth observed that the honouring of deserving members was the central point about which the life of Greek clubs revolved, so that the passing of an honorary resolution was not the exception but the rule at the conclusion of a member's year of office—a year which would certainly have involved him in some expenditure of the club's behalf. Much the same is true of the Roman club, as may be seen from one of the clauses of the charter of a society of humble folk at Lanuvium (D. 28) which was mainly concerned with securing the proper burial of its members. It lays down that the chief officer (*quinquennalis*) is to receive certain honours and immunities, some to be enjoyed during his term of office and others afterwards, assigned with the intention 'that other *quinquennales* also may hope for the same by properly performing their duties'. The last phrase in this case referred to the provision of oil for members of the society in the public baths before the annual banquet in honour of Diana and Antinous. Such expenditure at club level might be comparatively modest, but in the city-state most public offices called for parallel, but more costly, services to all citizens. High-priesthoods were especially notable (though not uniquely so) for involving their incumbents in sacrificial feasts, the expense of which might often be covered only in part by regular funds. Other offices, especially those connected with the purchase or distribution of corn or other commodities within the city, those of the *agoranomoi*, *sitonai* or *elaionoi* in Greek cities, for example, or that of the *aediles* in Republican Rome (though the corn distributed there often seems to have come from the provinces or outside sources) were expected to subsidize the market price, often at enormous expense.[50]

The Greeks invented a number of special terms which were used of the activities of officers who, in pursuit of controlling the market or securing the supply of corn or oil, had subsidized their fellow citizens by selling at below purchase price (e.g. D. 9) or had persuaded merchants to co-operate towards that end. Where they had gone so far as to supply free rations, the inscriptions often state the current market price in order to make quite clear the extent of the magistrate's financial sacrifice; where some charge was made, both the current market price and the price at which the commodity was distributed may be stated. It is not surprising, therefore, that many honorary inscriptions mention both the holding of office and the conferment of gifts as calling forth the gratitude of those who had benefited. So an inscription from Aphrodisias groups together the honorand's 'magistracies and public services and embassies and lavish *agoranomiai* and contributions to public subscriptions and generous undertaking of public burdens and most lavish high-priesthood' (D. 79 offers a further example). In some areas of the Greek east in the period of the Roman Empire the exercise of priesthoods in particular tends to be referred to by one or more of a series of stock adverbs or adjectives which are little more than an abbreviated way of suggesting the open-handed giving of feasts and distributions. In the west, a donor of Lucania in Italy was held to have sealed the services which he had rendered to his fatherland by his willing acceptance of the office of *duovir*, as a late second-century inscription records. In another inscription of roughly the same date the virtually compulsory gifts bestowed by Q. Avelius Priscus (D. 24) in respect of his various offices at Corfinium are given pride of place over gifts independent of any office. He was another of those donors who took upon himself the cost of the monument erected in his honour.[51]

Not unnaturally it was when corn or oil was in short supply, and therefore expensive, that it proved most difficult to find candidates for the offices serving the needs of the city. If it proved impossible, unqualified people, including both women and minors, or even gods, might be appointed—provided that they had resources which could be drawn upon. However, before such desperate measures were resorted to, a single individual, or group of individuals acting together, might agree to hold several offices in the same year, or to hold the same annual office consecutively year after year. Such devotion would again call for special mention in honorary inscriptions, according to the formula that X had accepted nomination for an office when no one else had been willing to stand. Thus, towards the middle of the first century three citizens of Akraephia in Boeotia were honoured because they undertook 'when called upon to do so' the office of *polemarch*, and in addition, 'observing the straits to which the city was reduced, accepted of their own free will the office of market-controller and that for the supply of oil' (D. 12). The acceptance of the latter offices obliged them to make gifts of corn or interest-free loans to the various tradesmen, apart from which it would have been impossible for their fellow citizens to enjoy 'unfailing cheap supplies'.[52]

The number of honorary statues and decrees eventually became so large that there arose both for Greeks and Romans the temptation to re-use old material by, for example, replacing the head of an old statue with another and erasing the original name in the inscription and substituting a new one. Hence we find Cicero writing as a provincial governor of Cilicia that he is utterly tired of '*falsas inscriptiones statuarum alienarum*', the lying inscriptions which really belong to somebody else's statue. From Tacitus we know that even the statues of deified emperors were not always immune from such an indignity; the head of a statue of Augustus gave way on at least one occasion to that of Tiberius when the latter succeeded to the Principate and the position of supreme patronage.[53]

Reference to the deified Augustus serves as a point of transition in our argument, for it is a reminder that the honours commonly sought by donors and benefactors were not simply those which might be enjoyed in life: they also sought honours which would continue after death and so gain them a measure of immortality. 'If we are not going to confer favours unless we get them back, we might as well die intestate,' said Seneca—a good debating point, but not in accordance with the facts. It is quite clear that those who conferred favours by bequest at death—and in Italy 'small gifts were more frequently made during the donors' lifetime than were large ones'—counted on receiving such immortality in return. Moreover, in many honorary decrees it is provided that the distinctions assigned to a particular benefactor should belong to his descendants for ever afterwards—as, for example, in the case of Eudemos of Miletus, whose place of honour in certain ceremonies was to pass after his death to the eldest of his descendants, as he had himself requested (D. 48; see also D. 2, 10, 40). Sometimes we find the formula that the honours voted to a person shall be such as are 'worthy of inheritance' by his descendants.[54]

But a second and more important basis for immortality was the continued commemoration of an honoured name by annual ceremonies, the cost of which could be provided for by a foundation. The best-known examples of this type of immortality are those associated with the 'ruler cult', an essential aspect of which is the obligation of the recipient of a favour to return a still larger favour to the person who has conferred it. When, therefore, an individual conferred a gift of almost superhuman proportions—and it was the monarch of a great kingdom who was best placed to do so— there seemed in a world where no clear distinction was made between the human and the divine, little alternative but to accord the donor the status of a god and to hold commemorative ceremonies in his honour. In the acquisition of 'divine' status the struggle for honour *via* giving and benevolence had reached its logical conclusion, as had the concept of 'friendship between unequals for the sake of the advantageous'.[55]

As we have seen, this development provided Hellenistic kings—and, later, Roman emperors—with a convenient moral basis for their rule. They claimed precedence in the state by virtue of their outstripping all others in terms of benefits conferred. The Hellenistic king was *Euergetes* (benefactor *par excellence*), or even *Soter* (Saviour)—so dependent were his subjects on his beneficence. It is generally agreed (against the emphasis of Bolkestein) that there is little need to look to oriental influences behind this cult, since theory supporting it can be found, for example, in Plato's *Politicus*. But, logically prior to any literary expression, it is inherent in the very attitude towards giving and receiving. So, in the familiar language of one of Menander's characters we find addressed to a man of quite modest means the dictum: 'To give aid to all men, to make as many as you can rich through your own generosity—this is immortal.' The Greeks came to express the same thought more epigrammatically in the maxim 'Man likens himself to god in doing good', which came to be rendered in Latin *'deus est mortali mortalem iuvare'*. The recognition of such 'divinity' is described by the elder Pliny as the 'most ancient manner of paying thanks to those who deserve them', while his younger namesake asks, 'What greater thing can be given to a man than glory and praise and these *for all eternity*?' (*'gloria et laus et aeternitas harum'*). Seneca observes of a certain act of favour that nobody could speak of it as calling forth love (*amabilis*) without also saying that it called forth worship (*venerabilis*). It is not surprising that we find Tertullian retorting, against those who scoffed at the Christian doctrine of eternal life: 'You pour forth statues and inscribe sculptured images and have your honorary epitaphs, reading "to the eternal memory of . . ." Why, as far as it lies in your power, you yourselves provide a kind of resurrection for the dead!'[56]

In the early history of Greek and Roman family life a person could rely upon a member of his family to carry out such rites as he deemed essential for the peace, if not the positive well-being, of his spirit beyond the grave. But eventually, both in the Greek world, especially after *c.* 300 BC, and in the Roman, early in the present era, family loyalties weakened and could no longer be relied upon for such services. It is true that at the same time religious feelings had changed, so that the same religious rites may no longer have been sought, having lost their original meaning. But, as Tertullian's exclamation implies, and as many inscriptions confirm, ordinary people were still concerned with life beyond the grave, if only in the sense that their memory should not pass away. Typical is the declaration of Zosimos, a benefactor at Priene, that through his benefaction he had acquired for himself 'riches' in the shape of 'praise from the living and of remembrance from those who were yet to live'. Even the philosopher Epicurus, whose philosophy taught that the gods do not care about men and that religious fear is vain, provided in his will (D. 80) that those to whom he bequeathed his property should devote certain moneys 'for the funeral offerings of my father and mother and brothers, for the customary celebration on the tenth day of Gamelion each year and also for the meeting of the members of my school held on each month in remembrance of me and Metrodorus'.[57]

The basic method adopted by Epicurus to secure his purpose was used with various modifications by many less famous and more materially minded benefactors, who left a certain amount of money or real property to friends or freedmen, or to the club or city to which they belonged, at the same time seeking to place upon the recipients the obligation to use some or all of the revenue deriving therefrom for the annual celebration of religious rites or of a sacred meal in their honour. Such 'gifts' with obligations attached, as we have seen, fell short of the status of independent foundations and involved a number of practical difficulties as far as the intentions of the donor were concerned. Briefly, however, the method was to give a limited group of people a material interest in undertaking the arrangements for the desired ceremonies, and, often, a larger group a more limited material interest in attending them. In a sense this was only an adaptation of the method followed as early as the fifth century by the Athenian general Nicias, who consecrated to the god at Delos a tract of land, which he had bought for ten thousand *drachmae*, the revenues from which the Delians were to expend on sacrificial banquets 'at which many blessings should be invoked upon Nicias from the gods'. It is probable that this was a more than usually successful application of the method, for payments were still being made under this endowment in the second century AD. In the same way Satyros of Tenos (D. 37) provided sums of money to secure a variety of religious and secular objectives, among them 6,000 *denarii*, 'so that from the interest each year, on the day fixed for the ceremony at the grave, there may be apportioned the sum appropriate to the number of those who come together'. Here it was a money distribution which was to attract attendance at the ceremony; often it would be a feast or games or an athletic contest, or a combination of these. In the second century BC Kritolaos of Amorgos (D. 5) left funds which were to be lent out in order to provide an annual revenue for a feast and public athletic contest, in this case for his dead son, Aleximachos; there was to be a sacrifice beside the statue of the latter, who was to be hailed as victor in the *pankration* (a contest combining both wrestling and boxing), for which event alone no prizes were to be offered—another commemorative device.[58]

Even where no specifically religious ceremonies are provided for, the choice of the birthday, as by Epicurus (compare D. 31, 34, 35, 40, 77), or the date of the donor's death (or of the death of the person in whose name the gift was given), for the public festival or distribution, or the choice of the statue or grave of the person as a venue, reveal the intention behind the gift. By variations of the same essential method, benefactors could hope for a prolonged period of remembrance after death; and the confident expressions, so familiar in the political sphere, such as Cicero's '*si non spiritu, at virtutis laude vivemus*' ('We may not draw the breath of life, yet we shall live through praise of our high worth'), find their parallel in not a few testamentary sentiments. For example, Phainia Aromation of Gytheion (D. 71) asserts that 'by this fitting and benevolent act my idea is to achieve immortality'.[59]

Our records of the same method being used by the Romans are late enough to suggest that they borrowed the idea from the

Greeks. Essentially parallel to the Greek model is the gift of Flavius Syntrophus, sometime after AD 200, of certain gardens, with buildings and enclosed vineyards, subject to the condition that the revenue therefrom be shared by Aithales and his fellow freedmen, and later by their descendants (one of the distributions, significantly, is to take place on the donor's birthday, another on the *Parentalia*). But once the device of the foundation came into use for this purpose, the concern with self-commemoration (in keeping with the Roman practical instinct) became more prominent, and to achieve this there were offered to those who would attend appropriate ceremonies, not merely feasts, but gladiatorial shows and other attractions of a mundane or even coarse character. Typical of this tendency is the testamentary gift of C. Titius Valentinus of Pisaurum (D. 32) who gave one million sesterces, the interest on 400,000 of which was to provide for a feast on the birthday of his son, while that on the remaining 600,000 was to meet the cost of a gladiatorial show every fifth year. It has been noted that even the enlightened Pliny's largest bequest (D. 36) provided income for the maintenance of a hundred freedmen and, after their death, for an annual feast for the whole populace at Comum—the largest known *priced* bequest in Italy for this latter purpose. Frequent, too, were distributions or feasts to commemorate the dedication of some building project, paid for by the donor, which might, but often did not, serve any social purpose. In Roman Africa there seems to have been a tendency to record in the appropriate inscription not only the amount given to meet the cost of such distributions, which was perhaps advisable for obvious reasons, but also the amount which had been spent on the building itself; and from this habit, since not infrequently the latter sum was the smaller of the two, it may be seen where the main interest of the donor lay. The smallest foundation known from this part of the Empire was the humble sum bequeathed by L. Aemilius Felix of Theveste, to provide his fellow tribesmen with a feast on his birthday. Inscriptions from Spain follow a similar pattern, thus L. Aemilius Daphnus (D. 78) provided a *denarius* for every citizen on the anniversary of the dedication of the public baths which he had given to his township.[60]

It was in keeping with the prime objective of Roman foundations that the associations of humble folk (*collegia tenuiorum*) concerned themselves almost exclusively with the provision of funeral
expenses for their members, and were approved by the imperial
authorities strictly on that basis; in this they differed from their
nearest Greek counterparts which counted this aim, if at all, only
as one among several. The existence of these associations removed
from such folk the incentive to resort to individual foundations,
supposing any could afford them, but provided the wealthier
element with yet another way of achieving 'immortality' by
generosity, for these could become patrons of such associations, so
securing annual feasts in their honour, as did L. Caesennius Rufus
at Lanuvium (D. 28), not merely (like the rank and file) decent
burial.[61]

So the beneficent of the ancient world could look upon their
generosity in a manner not unlike that attributed to some of their
modern counterparts, as a 'bargain in terms of perpetuity in this
world and the next'; and in this connexion it is noteworthy that
some of the early Christian Fathers found it difficult to avoid the
kind of language and ideas appropriate to the background of the
classical city-state, when they came to speak of the reward of
eternal life for those who showed Christian charity. Thus Basil,
as L. Robert has observed, seems to have in mind a scene familiar
in the city-state when he visualizes the reception of the faithful
before the Lord's judgment seat: 'the whole people standing
around you . . . will call you nourisher (*tropheus*) and benefactor
(*euergetes*) and all the other titles which are appropriate to *philanthropia*'. The term *tropheus* is simply one of the less common titles
(*euergetes* is the most common) invented with almost unlimited
ingenuity for benefactors in the Hellenistic age; it is found, for
example, linked with the title of 'king' (*basileus*) in an inscription
from Bithynia, *c*. AD 150, in honour of a certain P. Domitius, who
had given free distributions of corn, wine, oil and money to his
fellow citizens. The language of the Greek *polis* is thus transferred
to the heavenly city, however different the nature of the reward
itself, the one received of God, the other of men. In the same way
Gregory of Nyssa found it natural to urge the Christian to be

philotimos in coming to the aid of brethren in peril. John Chrysostom, on the other hand, was so conscious of the danger attaching to the conception of the Christian reward in the familiar terms of the city-state that he stressed that this reward must not be made the motive for giving—the motive must be pity. Subsequently, John Chrysostom came to adopt the extreme position that it is not the act of handing over a sum of money which constitutes the essence of Christian charity but the attitude of pity which motivates it. By contrast the classical preoccupation with *philotimia* left little room for any mention of pity—or of 'the poor' as peculiarly deserving of such pity.[62]

CHAPTER V

THE POOR

THE FREQUENCY WITH which 'the poor' are referred to in our sources as deserving of private benefactions or public assistance might lead one to suppose that Greek and Roman charity was to a considerable extent specifically directed towards those members of society whose material needs were the most acute. However, the Greek and Latin terms commonly translated as 'the poor' seldom imply absolute poverty or destitution. They were applied, in particular, to the vast majority of the people in any city-state who, having no claim to the income of a large estate, lacked that degree of leisure and independence regarded as essential to the life of a gentleman. In many instances such men would own small plots on which they would have to work themselves, though perhaps with the help of hired labourers or slaves. They could devote little or no time to the fuller life of the city. So Poverty, as personified in Aristophanes' *Ploutos*, airily distinguishes herself from Beggary (*Ptocheia*), declaring 'it is the beggar's life to live possessed of nothing, but the poor man's life to live frugally and by applying himself to work, with nothing to spare indeed, but not really in want'. Similarly, Demosthenes can claim that he has set to right the condition of 'the poor', to whom he has referred a moment earlier as those who 'are possessed of only a modest or small property'. In Latin, the father of the poet Horace is described as '*macro pauper agello*'—poor, with only a miserable plot of ground (he also, as we know, had a slave or two). Martial, a century later, re-echoes the theme of Aristophanes with the line '*non est paupertas, Nestor, habere nihil*'. Juvenal's poor are still better off: they always have 'just enough to keep them going in leisured indigence and their chief struggle is not to keep from starving, but to avoid the degradation of having to work'. In a political context, as a collective term, 'the poor' is commonly synonymous with the *demos/populus,* the general mass of the people, particularly those who have no more than the right of an occasional vote in political assemblies. Whenever, therefore, we find 'the poor' being referred to as the beneficiaries of any measure in this context, we can by no means assume that it is a completely impoverished minority element which is intended.[63]

Such language was, of course, appropriate to members of the upper class, from whom almost all of our classical literature comes. Their tone was usually disparaging, but if it was the small farmer whom the speaker had in mind, it might be otherwise, the farmer's status occasionally being idealized or even envied. Wherever the upper class tended towards luxurious living and the abuse of wealth, 'poverty' would be praised as the teacher of good and honest living, and equated with virtues such as *parsimonia.* Where the wealthy, just because of their wealth, were liable to vexatious prosecutions, the poor man's lot could be envied as immune from such perils. But the terms suggestive of complete destitution—or even of the lot of the class of labourers which possessed no land—are seldom idealized.[64]

Such was the Greek term *ptōchos,* a word suggesting 'one who crouches', and so a 'beggar'. Even here we must not over-generalize, for, although its more frequent appearance in Hellenistic and Greek-Oriental literature, as compared with classical, has been taken to reflect a higher incidence of dire poverty in this period, we have to allow for the inevitable devaluation of words —for the Greek tendency to hyperbole and variation of language for its own sake. In Menander's *Dyskolos,* Gorgias can describe himself as *ptochos,* in contrast with those who are 'men of means', though it turns out that he is possessed (rather like Horace's father) of a small plot of land (in this case described by a double diminutive) and a slave. Still earlier, Plato uses the same term of those who do not belong to the few exercising control in the oligarchical state. Even in Homer's *Odyssey,* Irus had found himself some sort of a job, running errands for the wealthy suitors; he is not a beggar in the sense of getting something for nothing. None the less, the common distinction between the 'poor' and the 'beggars' is illustrated, for example, by Plato's provision that in his ideal state 'beggars shall not be admitted', being described as those 'who make their livelihood by endless entreaties'; to have excluded 'the poor' from the state would have been impossible, for the state would have ceased to exist.[65]

The ban of the political philosopher finds a parallel in the attitude shown towards the beggar in the plays of Aristophanes: there Ehrenberg found that 'beggarly poverty is painted without love and almost without pity'. Yet the Athens of Aristophanes was an extreme exemplar of Greek democracy, and there (if anywhere) it might be expected that the poorest would find relatively good treatment. As for Rome, Bolkestein instanced the common attitude to real poverty by listing some of the adjectives with which words suggestive of such a condition are linked. In contrast with what is found in many Jewish texts, where the poor tend to be equated with the pious and deserving who are destined for happiness in the next world, if not in this, at Rome the poor are described as *leves, inquinati, improbi, scelerati*, etc., terms implying dishonesty. Indeed even those who work for their living but are without land of their own may be so described, as they are by Cicero (no true aristocrat himself, but with an aristocrat's contempt): 'Do you suppose that body of men to be the Roman people which consists of those whose services are hired out for pay? . . . a mass of men, a herd of slaves, of hired men, of rogues and destitutes?' This was the urban proletariate which Cicero felt it appropriate to describe as '*sordem urbis et faecem*', the poverty-stricken scum of the city, though ready to make political capital of those who carried the metaphor a little further by suggesting that this 'scum' should be 'drained off' to the colonies. Likewise the satirist Juvenal, so bitter about 'poverty', is not (as Highet has observed) really sorry for the very poor or working-class; he is sorry for the middle-class men like himself who cannot get advancement. Still less is there evidence of any really deep concern about those who had to toil in mines, such as those of Attica, Spain and Ethiopia, and whose condition of life was far worse than that of the working class. Diodorus, writing at the beginning of the present era, but perhaps reflecting the ideas of Posidonius a century earlier, alone among classical writers, it has been claimed, describes with human sympathy the lot of the miners themselves, instead of concerning himself with the profits and interests of those who exploited them. His account of the slaves who were provoked to rise against their masters on the large estates of Sicily shows the same sympathetic spirit.[66]

If those who worked for their living merited so little regard, it would be surprising if the beggar were viewed with any kindness. Yet while noting this, it might be added that the lack of sympathy for the beggar reflected a situation in which generally, as for long periods in English history, beggars represented no real social problem and unemployment could be equated with laziness. That, indeed, is the basic meaning of the Greek *aergos* and the Latin *iners*, both suggesting, not the lack of opportunity, but the lack of will to work. Plato's ban on beggars reflects what Madame de Romilly has spoken of as 'that optimistic outlook of much Greek political thought', in terms of which unemployment was regarded as an avoidable evil, which could be legislated against or banished on the strength of an expulsion order, should it begin to assume serious proportions. The beggar was, in Homer's language, *pandemios*, implying that one city after another could be expected to send him packing. It is in the same context that Solon's law directed against 'unemployment' is to be seen. It was aimed, probably, at those *without means* who did not work, rather than intended to protect the inherited property of those who had means. Again, there is the response of a Spartan to a beggar, quoted by Plutarch: 'But if I gave to you, you would proceed to beg all the more; it was the man who gave to you in the first place who made you idle and so is responsible for your disgraceful state.' Plautus makes the same point: 'To give to a beggar is to do him an ill service.'[67]

In Plato's political theory, the ban on beggars should be measured against the assumption that it was always possible to build an ideal state from scratch—a state in which there would be enough land to allow every full citizen a basic minimum for his livelihood, and in which the number of citizens would be controlled so as to prevent the fragmentation of this land, while strict regulations as to the bequest of property would prevent its

E

accumulation in the hands of a few. Thus, in Plato's *Laws* we find a regulation that no citizen shall be allowed to hold an amount of property more than five times the size of the smallest allotment; any bequests which might infringe this limit were to be null and void, and the amount in excess to be surrendered to the 'city and the gods of the city'. In this latter requirement there has been seen a religious as well as a political emphasis, reflecting the fact that the state and the 'church' were largely synonymous in classical antiquity. Since the excess property surrendered was to be made over to those citizens who otherwise might fall beneath the basic minimum, there may be seen here an antecedent for that 'portion for the soul' which was the lesser standard of charity required by the early Christian Fathers of those in the Christian community who felt unable to meet the idea of selling *all* and giving to the poor—but with this essential difference: that whereas the latter was seen primarily as in the interest of personal salvation, the chief purpose of the former was to secure the internal cohesion of the community.[68]

Aristotle is as much opposed as Plato to casual, hand-to-mouth help of the poor, but provides against any need for this in his theoretical state by making part of the land entirely public, so as to defray the expenses of worship and common meals for all the citizens. Parallel to Plato's demand for the surrender of excessive property to the 'city and the gods of the city' is his insistence that confiscations from the wealthy, where justified, should go to the city temples. (Here already is enough to explain why a writer such as Ruskin could regard himself as an apostle of Greek theory in calling for a greater moral and humanitarian emphasis in the approach to political economy.) Unfortunately, however, neither Plato and Aristotle have much to say about the large mass of people who serve the needs of the city, but are, *de iure* or *de facto*, largely excluded from its citizenship. How the welfare of these people is to be secured is not explained, an omission no doubt in part explicable once again on the optimistic assumption that, being largely foreign traders and artisans who had come to the city for their own private advantage, they could always go elsewhere if they find it impossible to make a living.[69]

The ideal of a minimum amount of property for each full citizen was, of course, greatly influenced by the rule for centuries followed, or aspired after, at Sparta; and it was the actual practice of that ideal with regard to full citizens that the Spartan kings Agis IV and Cleomenes III claimed to be re-asserting in the late third century BC. A similar claim was made by Tiberius Gracchus at Rome in the late second century, after social and economic changes had deprived many small farmers of their living. Both at Rome and in Sparta it was argued that, in the case of the 'public land' at any rate, there should be a return to an idealized *status quo ante* in which nobody had an excessive holding, this making it possible for everyone to enjoy a basic minimum. Their programme was, in fact, in accordance with the principle of Plato that 'in a city and under a constitution which is even moderately well organized, it is beyond belief that any man possessed of a modicum of worth could be allowed to fall into beggary'. This 'modicum of worth' was possessed by all those who were potential soldiers, possession of land being a qualification for military service. It is significant that the argument had to be based essentially on the rights of the soldier–citizen rather than on those of a human being. Also significant is the contrast of the proposed solution with, for example, that implemented in sixteenth-century England after new farming methods, comparable in their effect to those introduced in the Hellenistic world, had given rise to a similar large-scale displacement of previously useful citizens within a comparatively short period. The Elizabethan solution—which, it has been argued, arose (not unlike that at Rome and Sparta) from the recognition of a social threat, rather than from any new ethical or religious insight—involved the admission that there *was* such a condition as unavoidable unemployment, which could be met neither by casual alms–giving nor by any radical and immediate reform. Elizabethan realism led to the development of the Poor Law and encouraged the growth of private charities. At Sparta and Rome, however, reformers optimistically assumed that it was possible to revert to an over-idealized situation in the past, and that a legislative act could permanently eradicate the current poverty.[70]

Such proposals come within our purview only in so far as they help to explain why in the classical world there was seldom proposed or adopted anything like a Poor Law—especially since attempts to revert to the *status quo ante* invariably broke down in practice. Yet, even if it was impossible to restore the 'original system' within an existing city, it *was* possible, during the greater part of our period, to resort to what Plato called 'the ancient device'—to found a *new* state, a colony, elsewhere. For the Greeks especially, geographical factors encouraged the outflow of surplus population and it is not improbable that in the great wave of colonization which began in the eighth century BC 'it was the poor and the landless who began to compete among the Greeks first'. In these colonies, it seems to have been the practice to assign to each participant an equal basic allotment of land—a practice which, perhaps even before Plato's time, underlined the sharp contrast between the actual inequality in the mother cities themselves and ideal equality which was supposed once to have obtained in them. Even in the heyday of the Athenian Empire, the colony (*cleruchy*) was seen as the answer to the problem of surplus citizens without means of livelihood. The decree relating to Brea in Thrace, admitting both the *Zeugitae* (traditionally, the small-farmer class) and the *Thetes* (the lowest class) to a colonial venture, was probably an exception to the rule. For Romans, too, opportunities of acquiring land in the colonies increased enormously as the Empire expanded. Tenney Frank therefore saw little need for state charity until Cato's last years, since until that time there was plenty of public land available. Even later, within little more than a generation of Tiberius Gracchus' reforms, we know that there still existed opportunities of participating in colonial ventures, though admittedly in the more distant and less fertile parts of Italy to which few would be attracted.[71]

Another means of livelihood available to the very poor man was to become a mercenary soldier. Thus, in the fourth century thousands of Greeks enlisted in the service of Persian kings or satraps. Driven out of their own cities by catastrophic economic depression or internal strife, men who had temporarily become *ptochoi* (beggars) found in the east, as *xenoi*, a kind of hospitality and a source of income which might eventually enable them to acquire land. (As in the case of emigrating to a colony, however, becoming a mercenary did not depend entirely on the initiative of the poverty-stricken, since it was not uncommon for an officer from the upper strata of society, such as Xenophon, to act as leader.) Similarly in the late Roman Republic the *proletarii* might gain material rewards by serving ambitious Roman generals or, with the advent of the Principate, by becoming professional soldiers in the legions—the acquisition of land again, perhaps, being the ultimate aim of most. After the establishment of the *pax Romana*, however, there would have been little booty to supplement the soldier's meagre pay and pension, so rendering this alternative to poverty progressively less attractive.[72]

There were also negative methods of controlling poverty, notably by regulating the birth-rate. 'Fear of poverty and war will make them keep the numbers of their families within their means,' wrote Plato of his citizens in the *Republic*. Contraception or abortion (which tended to be confused in medical writings) and exposure of the newly born were the obvious expedients. As to the former, all we need say here is that there is evidence that in certain sections of society a variety of methods were known and practised. As to the latter method, the extent of its application at different periods and the motives behind it have been widely debated. Its use in fifth-century Athens has been overestimated by scholars lending undue weight to certain references in Aristophanes and to the legal right of fathers to repudiate offspring at birth. And Gomme pointed out that exposure of infants in Greek drama is due not to pressure of poverty, but to the demands of an oracle, or to illegitimacy and that the rescue of such infants is almost invariably undertaken by poor people! None the less, there can be little doubt that the Hellenistic age, with its high incidence of poverty, witnessed infant-exposure on a large scale; for we have not only the implications of New Comedy—which, it has been said, seems to be *'peuplée de petites filles abandonées'*— but also epigraphical evidence. From the latter, Tarn concluded that in the third and second centuries BC the one-child family was commonest and that, although there was a certain desire for two sons (to allow for a death, say in war), more than one daughter was very rare. If this evidence is reliable and representative, it is difficult to explain, except in terms of exposure.[73]

A whole series of quotations gathered by Stobaeus suggests that the 'cruelty' shown to those children who were exposed was viewed by parents rather as a loving concern that those who *were* allowed to survive should not have to endure poverty. The political theorists for their part were concerned with the interests of the state as a whole. 'If no restriction is imposed on the rate of reproduction (and this is the case in most of our states) poverty is the inevitable result,' maintains Aristotle, who later adds that 'there should certainly be a law to prevent the rearing of deformed children'. These passages seem to indicate that in practice the state did *not* normally impose a limit on the size of families, and that it was not uncommon for deformed children to be reared. Again, other remarks of Aristotle imply that there was in his day a growing feeling that abortion was preferable to exposure as a method of control. 'There should be a law', he says, 'in all states where the system of social habits is opposed to unrestricted increase, to prevent the exposure of children to death *merely* in order to restrict the population. The proper thing to do is to limit the size of each family, and if children are then conceived in excess of the limit so fixed, to have a miscarriage induced before sense and life have begun in the embryo' (my italics). But how far Aristotle was conscious (as Gomme argued) that most people would oppose abortion as such, as distinct from opposing the right of the state to decide when it was or was not to be carried out, it is scarcely possible to determine. All we can suggest is that for Aristotle any such opposition would have appeared (to borrow words critical of an aspect of Victorian charity) a matter of being 'kind to everyone except society'.[74]

Infant exposure continued to be practised in Greece under the Roman Empire. A letter of Pliny to the Emperor Trajan discusses, as a question which any provincial governor might frequently have to consider, the rights of those who had rescued and brought up abandoned children in cases where the latter were subsequently claimed by their parents. At Rome itself and in the Latin-speaking provinces evidence of the practice is less full and clear (though the *right* of the father under Roman law to exercise his *patria potestas* in this way is plain enough); and it is possible that for the Romans at certain stages territorial expansion made it less necessary. But it is significant that Musonius Rufus, commonly regarded as one of the most humane thinkers of the first century AD, seems to have had no better argument against infant exposure than that 'it is better for a child to have many brothers than much material wealth'—an argument in which the child is valued relatively rather than in its own right. Although we should note his almost New Testament answer to the poor man's question as to how he would feed his children, were he to have many: 'But from where do the little birds, so much more helpless than you, the swallows and nightingales and larks and blackbirds, feed their young? . . . Do they lay aside and store up food?' A possible index to the attitude of Romans of Stoic persuasion to the idea of sparing a child for a life in penury is the doctrine prescribing suicide should a man, once prosperous, find himself reduced to a state in which it is 'more in keeping with nature' to die than live. Significant, too, is the fact that after the Emperors Constantine and Theodosius I had, under Christian influence, forbidden the practice of infant exposure, it became necessary to admit instead the parents' right in cases of extreme poverty to sell a new-born child.[75]

It is true that this latter practice belongs to a time of abnormal economic stress. But, we may ask, was the general condition of 'the poor' in the city-state very much better in comparatively prosperous periods? Take fifth-century Athens: she was probably as prosperous—and as democratic—as any Greek city-state ever was, and according to Ehrenberg, could boast the 'unity of a middle class embracing town and country, including craftsmen, peasants, shopkeepers and traders'. But the term 'middle class' could well be misleading; so, more recently, it has been held that in spite of the alleged profits of empire 'the life of the ordinary Athenian was characterized by extreme frugality together with meanness and avarice which are born of a miserable struggle for existence' and that 'Athens never in fact banished the poverty which the Greeks had come to accept as a fact of life'. It is possible that too much may have been read into the fact that in public-building accounts we find the same wage being paid to the free citizen of the fifth century and the slave who worked beside him —since the slave's wage was his master's fee—but there are other references implying the assimilation of the material condition of the poor to that of the slave. For example, there must have been some basis in fact for the allegation of the satirical pamphleteer that in the city streets one could not distinguish between the free and the enslaved. In the fourth century taxation evidence shows a heavy concentration of wealth in the hands of no more than three hundred families. Moreover, Aristotle observes that in most city-states the middle class was small, and refers to its enlargement as a theoretical method of achieving greater political stability. In less prosperous cities and periods the assimilation of the poor man to the slave, rather than the enhancement of the latter's status, is suggested by their participating on equal terms in public banquets and distributions. It is also worth noting that where, as in fifth-century Athens, special conditions led to great commercial expansion, it would often be the non-citizen class possessed of capital which benefited most.[76]

At Rome, too, the wealth of empire brought fortunes to men of capital, but did not penetrate beyond a comparatively narrow class; and, again, the merchants, as distinct from the big financiers, were commonly non-Roman. The assimilation of free workers, who hired out their labour, to slaves within the Roman *familia* has been described by de Robertis, who emphasized the tendency, not only to give no preference to freemen in a labour force but even to assign positions of control to the slave. It is not surprising, therefore, that both are found as members on equal terms of the *collegia tenuiorum* (the societies of humble folk largely concerned with ensuring a decent burial for deceased members). And it is, no doubt, against this background that the upper-class aversion to paid work is largely to be seen. Throughout the Roman west the same general pattern held good. Thus, in the Roman Africa of the first and second centuries AD epigraphical evidence confirms the impression given by our literary sources that the available wealth was almost wholly monopolized by a small group of families which were also the source of most of the income of the cities in which they lived. It is probably no coincidence that in Africa, as compared with Italy, there is little evidence of modest foundations. As to the pattern in the Roman east W. M. Ramsay wrote of 'those great families possessed of immense estates which adapted themselves to every change in circumstances, floating on the currents of history'. The members of these families, though perhaps deprived of their priestly powers, acted as magistrates in 'autonomous cities' which maintained little more than the forms of Greco-Roman democracy. In southern Asia Minor, for example, Menodora of Sillyon was able to make an impressive series of benefactions, for herself and for her son and daughter, as each in turn was elected to a magistracy or priesthood (D. 41); while enormous wealth must also have been at the disposal of Opramoas of Lycia, who was commemorated by a great monument on which were inscribed copies of scores of documents, letters from emperors and government officials and resolutions of public bodies, all honouring the remarkable munificence which he had extended to many cities.[77]

As a result of this imbalance of wealth a relatively narrow margin must have separated the many 'poor' from the destitute, so encouraging the majority of citizens to limit their families by any method not wholly inimical to ethical or religious feelings. Perhaps it is significant that Polybius should have attributed the decline of Greece in the third and second century BC to *oliganthropia* (a shortage of manpower); while shortly afterwards Romans began to voice the fear that Rome might decline for the same reason. In any event, it is unlikely that an upper class which could openly recommend and itself practise infant exposure and abortion, to the extent of arousing the deepest indignation of Musonius Rufus, would be pre-disposed to discourage such practices among the poor. In this context we might also notice that provisions relating to orphans and adoption, of which there is a fair amount of evidence, in both the Greek and Roman worlds, dealt mainly with the protection of property-rights and so concerned only orphans of the propertied class; they had little or nothing to do with the welfare of orphans as such, except in the case of war-orphans whom the state might feel obliged to care for. Indeed, it was the absence of public orphanages and foundling hospitals (hospitals themselves were foreign to ancient Greece) which Gomme singled out as the most distinctive feature of ancient, as compared with modern, social thought and practice in this sphere.[78]

Certainly the emphasis in classical literature is not 'give to the penniless', but 'give to the good when they ask you'—words of Theognis in the sixth century BC, echoed in the fourth-century treatise *ad Demonicum*, attributed to Isocrates, by 'do good to the good', and again two centuries later in Cato's 'bono benefacito'. Give to those who are 'worthy' (*idonei*), urges Cicero; give to the 'most deserving' (*dignissimi*), declares Seneca—to the 'good' or to those who are 'capable of being made good'. 'It is a mistake', Seneca continues, 'if anyone thinks that it is an easy thing to give. . . . To certain people I shall not give, even though there is a need, because there will still be a need, even if I do give.' Aristotle had said the same; the generous man would not give to 'any Tom, Dick or Harry'.[79]

What did this demand for 'goodness' or 'worth' amount to? Generally speaking, since these are the precepts of the educated upper class, it amounted to those qualities of mind or character which could either serve or be appreciated by that class, qualities which could scarcely be possessed unless the approved recipient had at some time enjoyed comfortable circumstances and the education which these made possible. Thus, Cicero speaks of the need to take into account a man's 'sympathetic and co-operative attitude towards our (the benefactor's) way of life, and the contribution which he has already made to our well-being'. In Aristotle's *Ethics* the good and 'happy' man will consider worthy of his love and friendship above all the person who is the closest counterpart of himself; but, just as it will have been impossible for the former to have achieved his state of 'virtue' and 'happiness' in the absence of a certain *choregia* (material assets), so it follows that any 'friend' should not be totally without these, or at least should not *always* have lacked them. Hence the educated slave or freedman would normally be regarded as more worthy of 'friend-

ship' (and its material expression) than the freeman who had
always been poor. The number of Roman legal texts relating to
legacies to freedmen, which exceeds those relating to children
or fellow-citizens, points in the same direction. Right through the
history of subsequent moralizing on giving, therefore, it is seldom
possible to accept in its most obvious sense even so generalized an
injunction as that of Seneca: 'Wherever there is a man, there is an
opportunity for doing a good turn', the apparent universality of
which contrasts sharply with what a recent writer has called its
author's contempt for the common people, arising from his
'deeply rooted consciousness of his own intellectual aristocracy'.
The same sort of doubt may be felt about the younger Pliny's
simple exhortation to give especially to 'poor friends'; for the
term *amici* may be at least as operative as its epithet, while the
latter may be taken in a strictly comparative sense.[80]

Indeed, there arose, even on the part of some of the Christian
Fathers, a demand for a certain worth (*dignitas*) in the case of those
who asked for alms or who were adjudged fit to receive them.
Not all agreed with John Chrysostom that it was of no consequence to the Christian to discover whether a poor man who
begged for his help really required or deserved it, and that the
onus was rather on the poor not to accept without need. Many
followed Seneca in thinking that it was no such easy a matter to
give; but the 'worthiness' now demanded did not require any
material assets as its basis, although in contrast with the classical
demand, it might involve an expectation that the indigent would
accept *any* work offered.[81]

At its most stringent, however, the Christian demand involved
the surrender by the wealthy of *all* their wealth to the poor. That
there was so little suggestion of any such extreme sacrifice by the
wealthy Greek or Roman may in part be attributable to the fact
that the 'poor' who were considered to be worthy of gifts in
classical times did not exist in utter destitution. Certainly such
evidence as we have suggests that classical benefactors normally
gave out of regular income deriving from their estates or from
past savings, rarely out of capital. This seems to have been true
even of such a man as the younger Pliny, though rightly adjudged

one of the most enlightened and generous philanthropists of the classical world. Indeed, it is well known that at certain periods the wealthy were extremely reluctant to realize the value of their estates even to pay off debts, preferring to associate themselves with revolutionary programmes for the cancellation of debts instead. Some of these debts, however, may have been incurred as a result of over-ambitious attempts to help their own city (as well as to secure self-advancement); Rostovtzeff accepted Plutarch's assertion that in his time many were ruined in such attempts.[82]

Apart from these, there were a few, in the Cynic tradition especially, who did anticipate the Christian ethic, both in urging the total renunciation of material possessions by the wealthy and in advancing as a prime motive for doing so the opportunity which it provided for the contemplation of real and lasting values. In this way, it was claimed, the soul might become independent of the material world (the term which they used of this independence, *autarkeia*, was to be used by St Paul) and, by assimilation to the immortal and immaterial itself, might achieve immortality. But, as Tarn observed, unfortunately for the poorest element of society the parallel ended there, and the few who applied this ethic did not anticipate the Christian insistence that the possessions so renounced should go to those most in need. They apparently failed to distinguish between their own situation and that of those who had never known any wealth which they *could* give up—or the leisure which it afforded for reflection on non-material values. In general, therefore, the conditions of the poor were little ameliorated by the rich; the poor man's hope of better circumstances depended for its fulfilment rather upon his willingness to seize any opportunity of resorting to 'the ancient device', of making a new beginning elsewhere.[83]

CHAPTER VI

PITY FOR THE DESTITUTE

'WHEN YOU DO some act of charity, do not announce it with a flourish of trumpets.' Such is the New English Bible translation of some familiar words in St Matthew's gospel. The Authorized Version, with its more archaic language—'when thou doest thine alms'—underlines more effectively for the classical mind the narrow sense of 'charity' originally intended. The Greek which lies behind the English version means literally no more than 'when thou doest thine [act of] pity', the abstract term *eleēmosunē* (pity) being used, not merely of the motive inspiring a gift, but of the gift itself. This usage is quite foreign to classical Greek, as is the parallel use of *misericordia* to classical Latin. (Often the Greek term is merely transliterated.) It was, as we have seen, terms like *philotimia* and *philodoxia*, which classical Greek used in a precisely analogous way in the case of the gifts which come to our notice. Thus, the wealthy are called upon, or themselves claim, to display 'love-of-honour', a disposition finding concrete expression in 'acts-of-love-of-honour'.[84]

This bare statement of terminology pinpoints the sharp contrast between the *dominant* motive which it was thought appropriate to emphasize in the case of classical giving, on the one hand, and of Christian, on the other. But how far are we entitled to deny that some classical 'acts-of-love-of-honour'—which extended to the lower classes, even though not confined to them—were motivated by a degree of pity? How far should we assume that the classical donor would himself have repudiated such a motive? Behind the Christian emphasis is a long tradition of a God of pity, not only in the Old Testament, but also in Egyptian literature, a God who looks with mercy on the 'poor', in the absolute sense of the term. We may begin by asking whether in classical literature there is any suggestion that the Greek and

Roman gods adopted a similar attitude towards the poor and were concerned to inspire the same in their worshippers. At first sight, Homer might seem to offer an affirmative answer in, for instance, the claim of Odysseus to kindly treatment on the grounds that 'strangers and beggars are under the protection of· Zeus'. Yet (as Bolkestein urged) doubts arise; for even if we pass over the possibility that at such a point a fairy-tale element is to be detected in the story, Odysseus' claim seems to rest essentially upon the fact that he is a stranger, a traveller seeking hospitality, rather than upon the fact that he is a beggar, utterly without means. The reader is expected to bear in mind that Odysseus is a beggar only *per accidens*, that he belongs by birth to a class of men who are very well aware of the reciprocal implications of a claim to hospitality, and that he will be in a position to meet his obligations in the end. The father of the gods was never known as *Zeus Ptochios*, god of beggars, but as *Zeus Xenios*, god of strangers; thus, the normal attitude towards beggars was to send them packing (unless, like Irus, they could make themselves temporarily useful), an attitude untroubled by religious scruples. 'Those closest to the god in Homer', it has been observed, 'are not the poor and the meek, but the stronger and the powerful'; hence the occasional suggestion in his work that the poor, so far from receiving better treatment from the gods according to their needs and deserts, will receive worse because of their inability to offer adequate gifts and sacrifices. This was an argument rejected at an early date, as by Socrates in Xenophon's *Memorabilia*, on the grounds that it would involve a divine prejudice in favour of the wicked who were rich over the good who were 'poor'; but we have already seen how difficult it was for any Greek of the upper class to conceive of 'goodness' being compatible with absolute poverty, so that here, too, we may be justified in taking the term 'poor' in a comparative sense.[85]

    In Greek drama the claims of pity not infrequently urged upon the great and the wealthy are connected, not with the gods' pity for the poor as such, but with their envy of the prosperous—an envy by which the latter are lured into presumption and so to their downfall. The prosperous therefore had special reason to regard themselves as liable to a catastrophic change of fortune by which (in the words of the dramatist Philemon) 'the wealthy of today becomes the beggar of the morrow' and to ensure pity for themselves in the hour of need by a readiness to extend it to their fellows. So looking upon the downfall of Ajax, in Sophocles' play, Odysseus declares: 'I pity him, for I see his lot as mine no less than his.' The words of Homer which Scipio Aemilianus, the conqueror of Carthage (146 BC), is said to have repeated as he watched the flames destroy it, 'There shall come a day when holy Troy shall perish', so foreshadowing the time when Rome would look in vain for pity from her enemies, illustrate how the Roman *nobiles* had imbibed the lesson of many a Greek tragedy. Such a disregard (or belated regard) of the claims of pity was sheer imprudence, as Seneca was to re-emphasize: 'So many instances of wealthy men becoming beggars overnight, and yet never a thought on our part for the slippery slope on which our own prosperity is set.' The prudent would be more concerned to see that in case of misfortune there would be (to return to Philemon) 'comrades and friends and associates to contribute their aid'.[86]

The Greek term used by Philemon for this contribution of aid is of interest, for it was used of subscriptions paid into a club whose members shared in certain mutual benefits only so long as they continued to subscribe. We find Demosthenes using exactly the same metaphor in relation to the appropriate behaviour of the wealthy man in the life of the city-state. Addressing a popular court, in whose hands lie the fortunes of the wealthy Meidias, he philosophizes thus: 'I consider that all men make contributions over the whole of their life towards their own fortunes, not merely those contributions which certain people collect and pay in, but others also; for instance, in the case of a man who shows moderation and decent feeling [*philanthropia*] and pity for the masses, it is right that he should receive the same treatment from all, should he ever be in need or peril.' The basic attitude is clearly the same; the only point of difference, as compared with many a scene in tragedy, is that here, in an actual democracy, 'pity' must be shown not merely to other individual men of wealth, but to the *demos* collectively. Both on the stage and in real life, therefore, pity is seen as an attitude to be adopted on an essentially *quid-pro-quo* basis, just as *philanthropia* itself. Thucydides makes Cleon express the same view of pity without equivocation: 'Pity is appropriately given on an exchange basis to men of like character, and not to those who are not going to show pity in return.' Demosthenes is prepared to be no less blunt on occasion: 'Nobody is entitled to meet with pity who does not display pity, nor with sympathetic consideration who does not show such consideration.' Rather more gently, Xenophon makes the same point: 'Men need each other and so they pity and help each other, working in co-operation.' Accordingly, as applied to the popular law courts, this meant that the people could show 'pity' by resisting the temptation to condemn the wealthy man with a view to their own advantage (through the confiscation of his property); while the wealthy man could point out that he had earned their 'pity', by reference to his own show of pity in having voluntarily allowed the people to benefit materially from his prosperity. In the language of the Roman Republic this exchange between defendant and jury was just one type of exchange of *beneficia* between an individual and a larger group.[87]

The failure of a wealthy individual to show 'pity' to the people could, however, only marginally affect the condition of life of the ordinary citizen. It was the people's withdrawal of pity from that individual which could be catastrophic. So, when occasionally a city erected an Altar of Pity (a rare occurrence), it was clearly intended as a place of refuge for the wealthy faced with calamity, especially that arising from political strife; there was no altar or sanctuary to which the poor and weak could flee (as was possible for a long time in Egypt) to draw attention to their permanent condition of life. Homer Thomson has described the sculptures which probably belonged to the altar set up in the *agora* at Athens: it had four panels, each representing a 'piteous situation induced by a reversal of fortune'. We are reminded of Aristotle's view of tragedy, as arousing pity and fear through a sudden change of fortune befalling its hero, who had to be a man of fame or wealth. The poor, by definition, could not experience the reversal from prosperity to misfortune which called forth these emotions. Still less could the general mass of slaves, who, in their occasional revolts—particularly in the seventy years after *c.* 140 BC —looked to no Greek or Roman god for protection or inspiration. Aristonicus, who called out the slaves of Pergamum *c.* 133 BC, has been thought by some to have given to his projected new state the name 'Heliopolis' to suggest—under the influence of Greek philosophic, if not religious, ideas of equality—a city where everything would be shared, as is the sun, by all alike. But it is more likely that the bulk of his followers, if not he himself, took this name as suggestive of a city where worship would be directed towards an oriental baal, a god more appropriate to their origins and more likely to be seen as interested in their fate, since *his* justice was equated with pity. When, a generation later, the slaves revolted in Sicily, it was a Syrian goddess to whom they turned.[88]

The pity to which we find the wealthy challenged, both on the stage and in real life, was thus essentially linked with fear; the philosopher Anaximenes had himself observed that 'the wealthy are not accustomed to pity the unfortunate in the same way as do the poor. It is fear for themselves that engenders their pity for the misfortunes of others.' And it is through recognizing this that we are to understand the well-known Stoic attitude to pity which, taken out of context, might well seem inconsistent with their doctrine of 'well-doing'. They repudiated pity because they saw it as an essentially self-regarding emotion; like fear it was a *pathos*, a feeling which a person suffered by imagining himself the victim of a catastrophe which had befallen another. As such, pity was seen, not as a liberating emotion necessary to inspire the selfless service of others, but as an emotion which enslaved a man's mind and spirit, and undermined the good man's claim to self-sufficiency and self-command (*autarkeia*). Before the Stoics, Plato had banned drama from his ideal state precisely because it stirred up the emotions of pity and fear; while Aristotle only assented to the expression of these emotions on the stage the better to suppress them in real life. For the Stoic, a pity linked with fear was doubly objectionable: firstly, in that it questioned the wisdom of the universe, implying that a particular turn of events should never

F

have been 'allowed' to happen; and secondly, in that it implied an instability of character in the pitier, suggestive of the person who maintains the view that nothing happens *contra naturam* (contrary to nature) until it happens or seems likely to happen to him. So the Stoic caricatured by Cicero declares that no one is given to pity except the man who is without wisdom or stability—a doctrine which perhaps came easily to the typical Roman aristocrat, who was given to making a virtue of *gravitas*.[89]

For the Stoic, then, pity was not necessary to inspire generous action. 'Are we not able to be generous without pity?' asks Cicero, who himself answers: 'Surely we can, for our obligation is not to take upon ourselves bitterness and pain for the sake of others; it is simply, where possible, to relieve others of their pain.' A Stoic was by definition *phusei koinonikos kai praktikos* 'possessed of a social conscience and given to act upon it', but expected to make a rational rather than an emotional response to any situation —and to be moved no more by love of fame than by pity, such love and pity being regarded as diseases of the mind. Thus, Seneca can claim that 'there is no sect more gentle and kindly, none more full of love for mankind or more concerned for the common good.' His Stoic prince will 'rush to the aid of another in response to the latter's tears, but will not join in them; he will give help to the shipwrecked, refuge to the exile, and a copper to the penniless; nor will it be that disdainful help offered by the majority, who wish to appear given to pity, that help which is offered with contempt and loathing by men reluctant to come into contact with the unfortunate; rather will he give as man to man out of that which is common to man [*ex communi*]. He will give a son to a mother's tears, will bid his chains be loosed and save him from the arena; he will bury even the body of a criminal, but will do so unperturbed in mind and countenance'. The attitude is summed up in two lines quoted by Stobaeus: 'If I being a man do not aid man's lot, how shall I appear of right mind?' (where we might have said 'of sympathetic heart'). Similarly, the 'clemency' of Seneca's prince, *rationi accedit*, comes close to 'right thinking'.[90]

These few quotations are enough to show that, as far as theory was concerned, the Stoics could claim a high ethical ideal by which the wise man will do everything that the man of compassion might do, but without thinking of, or being afraid for, himself. (*'Es besser ist, mit zu helfen als mit zu leiden'*.) Their rejection of pity arose from a typically Greek awareness of the degree of self-interest which may lie behind even those attitudes and actions which are commonly taken as non-self-regarding; from a psychology which, as Cochrane put it, saw morality *either* as reason *or* as emotion, a dichotomy which was only later to be cut across by the *bona voluntas* of Christian ethics. And if it appears that the Stoic remains self-concerned, intent on his own composure of mind rather than interested in the plight of others, he might have replied to the Christian moralist that this concentration on the eternal reality, resulting in an assimilation to it, was not wholly unlike the latter's 'laying hold of eternal life' in this present world, by identification with Christ in 'charity'.[91]

The cold, rational nature of the Stoic doctrine as originally expounded had in fact been modified, perhaps especially by the influence of Posidonius in the early first century DC, and certainly some time before it found expression in the Latin of Cicero. By the time of Seneca, while it is still denied that the Stoic sage will experience actual pain even at the loss of his own children or friends, it is admitted that he may undergo something like an emotional disturbance (*aliquid simile perturbationi*) which is no longer regarded as a fault or evil, though it still cannot be accorded positive approval as good or praiseworthy. This greater allowance for human, personal feelings represents just one aspect of a change, very clearly seen in Seneca, whereby the wise man's adherence to an impersonal eternal principle of justice and benevolence comes nearer to the response to a personal and indwelling god. It was a change which encouraged the attempt (through bogus correspondence) to establish a link between the philosopher and St Paul, the contemporary expositor of Christianity to the classical world.[92]

In this connection, Seneca's insistence that the Stoic prince will 'avoid all disdain' in his ready response to the needs of others is particularly worthy of note, for it reappears in the teaching of the Christian Fathers, being carried to an extreme by John

Chrysostom, who asserts that where one has nothing to give, the mere utterance of a kindly word (that is, almost, the mere avoidance of disdain) may be accounted 'charity'. But the same insistence is found prior to both Seneca and Christianity in the writings of Hellenized Jews at Alexandria; and it was because Bolkestein linked the Stoic prince's 'copper for the penniless' and two other Senecan passages, in which a 'crust for the starving' and 'a coin for the beggar' are added to the traditional human obligations which fell under the *arai Bouzygeiai*, with parallel demands found in the writings of Josephus and Philo, that he concluded that at Rome also oriental influences were beginning to create a new attitude of pity for the poor in this period. There had certainly long been scope for such syncretism at Alexandria, and in Philo we find the significant addition that all such giving should be 'out of respect for God'. At Rome, however, the additional obligations may reflect the more urban life of Seneca's day, and to judge from its context, the action of his Stoic prince seems to relate to persons *suddenly reduced* to poverty or destitution rather than to those poor 'whom always you have with you'. It appears to resemble the attitude adopted towards war-captives by the upper class of the Hellenistic world, which readily ransomed men of their own class but left to their fate the proletarians of the towns or the peasants, once sold on the slave market' The philosophy with which such giving is connected, namely that 'our gift is not to a man but to mankind', repeats a dictum familiar to the Greeks (Diogenes Laertius was to put it into the mouth of Aristotle), the very generality of which, as has been noticed, is in sharp contrast with the particularity, for instance, of the parable of the Good Samaritan: 'the idea of humanity is not a motive for love in the New Testament'.[93]

Some of the very passages quoted to illustrate the basis of the Stoic attack on pity make it clear that not all of the wealthier class would have been anxious to deny pity as a motive for their beneficence (nor did all shrink from appealing to it when charged with a crime, since it was customary for defendants who had no *beneficia* to rely on, to parade their wives and children in court.) As to the vast unphilosophical majority, an analysis of prose epitaphs has indicated that among the Greeks at any rate there was little desire to record of the departed that they were given to pity. It was apparently sufficient to say of a man that 'he was the friend of all and *caused pain* to none'. The element of pity involved in the response to the needs of the beggar and penniless, when brought under the scope of the *arai Bouzygeiai*, might therefore be identified with that which even the Christian apologist John Chrysostom recognized as a natural human reaction (as Plassman puts it, '*aus reinem Naturtrieb*'), and therefore of no special 'merit' to the Christian.[94]

In the more democratic type of city, however, it was not always politic for the ruling class in their dealings with the rank and file to lay undue stress on pity, except on the *quid-pro-quo* basis noticed; for such an emphasis would have implied that the material benefits which they conferred were something to which the recipients had no moral claim, thus denying the whole basis of the bargain which we have seen to be implicit in the concept of the *polis*. If mentioned at all, pity tended to be linked with terms like 'fraternization', 'co-operation', and 'civil concord'—as it was by the philosopher Democritus in talking of the loans which the upper classes sometimes made to the poor. The Rhodians, described by Strabo as having 'cared for their poor, although not operating a democratic constitution', would have claimed to be more just and prudent than other ruling oligarchies rather than more given to pity, recognizing, with Aristotle, that 'it is in the interest of the prosperous themselves to distribute surplus revenue to the poor'. Moreover, the attitude of a man admitting to acts of pity or clemency might even have been taken by his fellow citizens as an admission of his 'tyrannical' status: in a 'free state' justice could not be identified with pity or mercy, as in the Hebrew or Egyptian languages. In Dittenberger's collection of Greek inscriptions reference to pity occurs but once and then only as a motive denied by Nero in announcing his benefactions to the Greeks, lest their 'freedom' might seem to be questioned.[95]

It has also been suggested that the institution of slavery made it natural for the wealthy to think of their dealings with the lower class in terms of self-interest rather than sympathy. They were accustomed to seeing the poor free man and the slave at work together, so it would be easy for them to think of their dealings with both in much the same way. The influence of slavery, however, worked two ways; thus, there were certain slaves of high education, employed mainly in the households of the wealthy, whose masters could not fail to recognize that in culture and ability they were more advanced, not merely than the average free man, but than themselves. Such slaves, above all, were capable of becoming the 'friends' of their masters *qua* men, as Aristotle emphasized (although it is more commonly remembered against him that *qua* slaves they could only be regarded as 'tools which have life'). Even those who performed for their masters personal services which called for qualities of character rather than intellect might be seen as 'friends' in some sense; such were the '*humiles amici*' noted in a letter of Seneca. It is this kind of relationship between master and slave which in fact again illustrates and confirms that the classical estimate of the 'worthiness' of a person to receive acts of beneficence, and so, in some sense, the sympathy with which he was viewed, tended to depend in practice, not on his legal status, but on his *disciplina et mores* (education and character), even if the latter had been achieved during a period of freedom and reasonable affluence which misfortune had ended.[96]

At this point it is appropriate to introduce the Latin concept of *humanitas* which, in its original usage, more than any other is expressive of this mutual appreciation of a common culture, irrespective of barriers of race or legal status. Gellius tells us that the term was originally used to express what the Greeks called *paideia* (education), and so it came to convey that kindly or humane attitude which one educated person might be expected to feel for another. Later, however, the term became assimilated in meaning rather to the Greek *philanthropia* (as not infrequently in Cicero's letters), which had itself, by the Hellenistic period (or even earlier, according to one view which sees it as expressive of the ideals of fourth-century Attic society), come to indicate something like a feeling of human decency. But the term *philanthropia*, by reason of its very derivation, tended to suggest the relationship between social inferior and social superior: it could be used in a clearly derogatory sense and applied to beings other than human, for instance, to the fawning of a dog in response to the kindness of his master. *Humanitas* was not naturally used in the same way, and some have suggested that by the late first century AD it may have conveyed the idea of a warm, human sympathy for the weak and helpless in a measure which *philanthropia* never did.[97]

It has been suggested that this wider sympathy had its origins and found expression in Rome's dealings with many different peoples as her empire expanded, leading her to see these peoples as deserving of individual treatment and yet also as possessed of a certain common worth enabling them to be grouped eventually under a single citizenship—something which the Greeks, perhaps because of their too coldly logical concept of 'friendship' or *philanthropia* between man and man, failed to achieve in practice. In another sense it might be seen as the extension of that attitude of *pietas* (is there a Greek word suggestive of the same depth of personal feeling?) from the narrow sphere of the Roman family to that of a family of provinces and peoples. In the cultural sphere this deeper emotional feeling perhaps finds expression in the more personal character (the limited evidence may be deceptive) of Latin elegy, as compared with Greek, or in that quality in Virgil which gives rise to such lines as the famous and untranslatable '*sunt lacrimae rerum*'. In philosophy it may be found in Cicero's call for the display of *reverentia*, rather than merely of *amicitia*, towards *all* men, not only the best, foreshadowing Seneca's '*homo sacra res homini*' and the religious expression of Stoic philosophy already noticed in Seneca. The same attitude of 'reverence' is demanded of the teacher towards the child by Juvenal, and Quintilian's whole discourse on education breathes the same spirit, as indeed much earlier do certain passages of Lucretius' poetry with their 'very Roman love of children and feeling for the family'. In the realm of law we see this *humanitas* inspiring the laws of the second-century Roman Empire in the interests of slaves vis-à-vis their masters, a trend running parallel to the development of administrative provision for the needs of children which reached its peak in the same period.[98]

Yet before we ascribe to Roman civilization, on the basis of the word *humanitas*, the development of what Dill called a 'pure human charity . . . a feeling of duty to the helpless, whether young or old' greater than anything which the Greeks had known, two notes of caution need be sounded. Firstly, there are many who believe that if our evidence for the Hellenistic age were fuller, we should find there a charity no less (if no more) purely human. Thus, a recent investigation of the term *benignitas* led to the conclusion that its development belonged to the evolution of charitable thought in the second century with its 'triple current, Greek, Stoic and perhaps Christian'. Already in Hellenistic comedy we see represented that kindly relationship between master and slave which seems to represent the ideal at which Roman legislation hinted; and from inscriptions we see slaves and freed men participating in certain public feasts and distributions on equal terms with the free citizens—though there was more than one side to this development. Secondly, we must certainly emphasize that any such distinctive sympathy was narrowly confined and 'Roman' only in the sense that it finds expression in the Latin-speaking west rather than in the Greek east. In general it would probably not be disputed that there was in the Roman character a coarse and even brutal element which it needed the graces of Hellenism to refine—an element expressed in the love of the arena show rather than of the cultural or athletic festival, even though it may be true that under Roman influence the Greeks, too, eventually acquired a similar preference. There were those who protested their dislike of such amusements, but rarely through a sense of sympathy with the victims; and the protestors seem to have been few and come notably from the country towns of Italy, such as Comum, or from the provinces—the home background of most of the paternalistic emperors (and not a few of their advisers) in the second century AD. It is therefore among a comparatively few rare spirits, even within the cultured Latin-speaking class of the Empire, that this distinctive humanity is, if anywhere, to be sought.[99]

CHAPTER VII

THE PROVISION OF
BASIC COMMODITIES

CORN, OIL AND CASH were the commodities most commonly distributed in the classical world, and since cash must normally have been used, even where not officially intended, for the purchase of food, it is convenient to treat all three together. We have evidence of a very large number of such private gifts, whether given during life or at death, whether recurrent (provided for by foundations) or non-recurrent. In this giving, however, we may safely generalize that the poorest class of society was never singled out for specially favourable treatment, although where the amount to be distributed by the donor was large enough, they might be treated on an equal footing with the more well-to-do, more especially when the occasion was of a religious character. Wealthy men who accepted supposedly civil magistracies often found themselves presiding over at least one popular religious occasion, perhaps involving a sacrificial feast, the whole or partial cost of which they would bear themselves. Those who accepted priesthoods or who, as private individuals, undertook the maintenance or revival of religious festivals—acts more apparently falling into the category of charity which Lord Macnaghten labelled 'the advancement of religion'—were likely to involve themselves in still greater expenditure; and while personal, political or social distinction was usually thereby achieved, Rostovtzeff regarded the devotion of the Greek bourgeoisie to the Pan-Hellenic and city gods as a 'genuine reflection of their religious sentiment'.[100]

For the common people, whenever food was distributed to all alike, as L. Robert wrote, '*l'essentiel dans le sacrifice est le banquet qui le suit*'. Robert provided a good example, that of Epaminondas of Akraephia in Boeotia, who in the mid-first century AD gained great popularity through his revival of the sacrifice and festival for Apollo (since this was associated with the Emperor cult at the time, it would also have gained the Emperor's approval). A lengthy inscription records of his five-year presidency of the revived festival that ' he neglected no expenditure or sacrifice' and, not satisfied with that, 'at the beginning of the festival in the sixth year he made a distribution throughout the city to all citizens, residents and slaves, giving to each man a measure of corn and half a measure of wine'. The inscription goes on to describe how, 'out of reverence for the gods', he sacrificed a bull to the gods and to the deified Emperors, 'being unfailing in his due provision of distributions of meat and meals and sweetmeats and dinners, while his wife, from the twentieth to the thirtieth day, provided in turn at all meals for the children of the citizens, the slaves who had reached manhood, the wives of the citizens, the young women and the adult women slaves; he did not even pass over the booth-holders and those who were putting on the festival, but gave them a meal at his own expense by public invitation, something which none of his predecessors had done' (the last phrase was one in which benefactors seem particularly to have revelled). The people, not unnaturally, were grateful and when a number of them met him, as he came down from the temple, to express that gratitude, he responded by making yet another sacrifice to Zeus and a feast for all those who had so gathered; and so the sequence might continue almost indefinitely.[101]

A more famous example, as benefactor at Athens about a century later, was T. Claudius Atticus, 'who would often sacrifice one hundred oxen to the goddess in a single day and entertain at a sacrificial feast the whole population of Athens by tribes and families', while the annual celebration of the Dionysia would provoke similar generosity (D. 80). It was on such occasions especially that women and children, non-citizens and slaves frequently seem to have been included during and after the late Hellenistic period. Thus, an inscription of the first century BC mentions the children of slaves who, following a sacrifice to all the gods, had shared in more than one banquet given by Soteles of Pegae (D. 10), near Megara. And in certain cities of Asia Minor particularly, such as Stratonicea (D. 33), with her two great temples of Panamarus and Lagina, a picture emerges from inscriptions of men, women, children, foreigners and slaves of every age and condition constantly participating in such feasts, whether within or without the sanctuaries—although in this area we must allow for non-Greek and perhaps Jewish influences. But the extent to which religious festivals might depend on the continuing readiness of affluent citizens to pay for them is evident in our example of Akraephia (D. 12), for only a generation after the revival of the Apolline festival by Epaminondas the celebrations were once more threatened by lack of money, causing the town to turn to the generosity of three of her citizens acting in concert, as it did also for other services essential to the general well-being.[102]

However, where the amount which a person had to give was on a lesser scale (and it was only a few men who could give a really worthwhile gift to everyone, as did T. Claudius Atticus (D. 80) in bequeathing a sum sufficient to provide every Athenian with a *mina* annually) the money was likely to go to the town-councillors or to that particular section of the upper class to which the donor himself belonged. This was true not only of a few gifts which might be regarded as mainly religious in character, but particularly of those where the emphasis was social rather than religious (in so far as these two aspects can be distinguished). The distribution was thus confined to those held 'worthy of honour' or, if spread over the whole population, was received in larger proportions by the former. This tendency has been noted both in Greek Asia Minor and in the Roman west; and most recently in Italy itself—Duncan-Jones has collected the evidence (D. 40, 42, 43). Here in fifty-eight inscriptions relating to multiple distributions (distributions in which different sections of the populace receive different amounts) the town-councillors never fail to appear as recipients and usually appear as the most privileged class. It is the next most affluent class, the *Augustales*, who receive at the second-highest rate, gaining special consideration in forty-four instances. In extreme cases the discrimination against the common people is in the ratio of fifty to one, and discrimination by factors of three or five is quite normal. Again, where children or wives are specifically mentioned as eligible (where they receive no mention, the presumption is that they did not qualify) it is usually those of the higher social classes who are so favoured. Certain multiple distributions in the Greek east (D. 41) seem at first sight rather more equitable, in granting almost equal amounts to members of both assembly and council, but the almost certain explanation is that in these cities there was a property qualification for membership of the assembly, which would not therefore represent the common people. It may be that the rarity of donations to cities for the relief of the burden of poll taxes, such as are known at Tenos and Ibiza under the Roman Empire (D. 37, 38), is to be seen in this context, for such donations would go against the normal trend in benefiting all classes equally, the tax being at a flat rate.[103]

Are we then simply to say that the regulation of the Italian *sportulae* (and of other comparable multiple distributions) was governed by honorific, not philanthropic, considerations? Such a generalization may perhaps be upheld, but we should be careful to make two qualifications. Firstly, we need to emphasize that, had there not been some degree of philanthropic feeling motivating the donors, the lowest class might have been excluded from the distribution altogether. This point becomes the more interesting in the case of Italy when we learn, unless our inscriptions are very unrepresentative, that multiple distributions were much commoner in the more depressed areas of central Italy and the urban south than they were in the prosperous north; for this might be taken to mean that members of the upper class *did* feel that money, which otherwise might have been distributed solely within their own class or expended on projects of pure self-glorification, should to a small degree at any rate be shared by the lower class on the grounds of sheer need. A certain element of *pietas* could be allowed for, a sense of duty towards the extended family of the city, assuming a form which perhaps did not seem as compelling in northern Italy.[104]

Secondly, there did clearly come a stage in the history of all municipalities when certain donors felt that by such special inducements men, otherwise unwilling, might be persuaded to stand for the offices essential to the life of the city, and not least to the material well-being of the lower class, calling as they did for so much private expenditure. Thus, a donor at Petelia in Italy left a sum of money for the acquisition of certain equipment for the priests of the cult of Augustus, considering that 'men will more readily take upon themselves the burden of the priest of Augustus as long as they have this asset before their eyes'. Looking eastwards we may quote the donation of Tiberius Piso Mithridatianus towards the liturgical expenses of officials connected with the gymnasiarchy at Apamea in Phrygia, or a similar attempt to be 'both philanthropic and useful' by a donor at Oxyrhynchus in Egypt (D. 44). Into the same context fits evidence from Athens, from the first half of the second century onwards, where inscriptions show that the expenses faced by the presiding committee of the Council (holding office for a month only) were commonly met by wealthy citizens who did not belong, as was once required, to the tribe which provided that committee; and so their name appeared, sometimes with that of Athena Polias (if her treasury had also helped), and sometimes alone, as 'eponymous' (official leader) of the 'prytanizing' tribe. By the third century the city itself is reinforcing the piety or patriotism of her citizens acting in such ways, by extending to them, as to a certain Eubiotos and his sons, a double portion in feasts at the town hall and council chamber and tax exemptions into the bargain. It may be that most of the inscriptions relating to multiple distributions in Italy and elsewhere antedate the stage where such enticements had become necessary, but the matter is scarcely open to proof in each particular instance.[105]

Even if a distribution for all equally was provided by a donor, this would of course mean, as is often stated, especially in the case of endowments with a strong funerary purpose, all who were willing and able to turn up at the appropriate place and time. How far can we suppose that in fact only the poorest class would turn up for a gift which was bound to be comparatively small because of the large number of those eligible to receive it? There is good reason to be cautious of such an assumption. As we have seen, in most city-states the large majority of the population, though not penniless, could not afford to disregard even small material benefits, particularly if the occasion happened to be a public holiday offering no opportunity for material gain by work. On such occasions the 'poor' will have been glad to rub shoulders with the poorest. As for the wealthy, the evidence of multiple distributions is a fair indication of their readiness to receive amounts which to them were still trifling, even when greater than those received by the general populace. And we might take account of their reaction at Rome when in 58 BC the tribune Clodius established a free public ration of corn. According to Cassius Dio they proceeded to manumit their slaves in order that as freedmen (and as such scarcely less useful to their late masters) the latter might receive the corn ration—even though they, the masters, were quite capable of supplying such corn themselves. Not that we should suppose that this meanness obtained among all members of the upper class, though the over-readiness of the Roman to receive from wealthy patrons, matching his un-readiness to give, is amply documented in the satires of Juvenal (where the wealthy slave-owners elbow out 'the poor' when the patron's gifts are being dispensed) and in certain passages of Pliny's letters some two centuries after Clodius. We may reasonably suspect that the tendency, apparent from the Hellenistic period, to make private distributions of corn, oil and, more commonly, sacrificial feasts, accessible to slaves was as much in the interests of their masters as of the slaves themselves, and that it was in fact contrary to the interests of the really poor among the free popu-lation who now had a larger number of rivals to contend with.[106]

But even if we allow for a mixture of motives behind private giving, these various factors should certainly give us pause before we assume, when we turn to the regular public provision of food or cash in the city state, that these distributions are to be seen as 'doles' for those particularly in need; especially as the financial resources sustaining them must generally have derived, directly or indirectly, from the class providing private benefactions. It has been with regard to the distribution of corn by the state that the 'dole' interpretation has occasionally been advanced, and it is for this reason that we shall argue in terms of corn distributions, although our argument will apply in general to other commodities distributed.[107]

The regular public distribution of corn in Greek cities is to be seen in the context of the constant resort to *epidoseis* (subscriptions), one of the most common purposes of which was to meet emergencies relating to the food supply. Even though special officers were appointed to maintain adequate supplies of corn and control its price, the very frequency of the need to rely upon their generosity or that of wealthy subscribers led in the Hellenistic period to the recognition in many cities that it would be better to establish a permanent fund producing an annual revenue sufficient to provide in advance against such emergencies. Our most detailed evidence as to such a fund comes from Samos in a lengthy, though incomplete, inscription (D. 6). Had the inscription been complete we might have known more than merely the names of those who combined to establish this fund and the amounts contributed. But we may safely presume that it came from the same class of wealthy men who were always expected to subscribe to *epidoseis* or even found schemes of their own, as did Euphrosynus at Mantinea (D. 13), who left to the city an amount of land, the revenue from which was to be used to 'provide an unfailing supply of food in perpetuity'.[108]

The Samian decree provides us with a great deal of detail as to the administration of the fund. We note the great care with which one set of officers is appointed to attend to the lending out of the money, another to receive the revenue with which the corn is to be purchased, the provisions regarding securities to be obtained from those who borrow and the fining of officials who fail to perform their duties satisfactorily, and the instructions as to where corn is to be bought (the district of Anaia on the mainland opposite, a convenient source, since it was temple land and the money paid became in fact a kind of financial reserve for the city, as it was understood that the money of a god could always be borrowed!). We notice, too, the very emphatic and detailed veto against any misapplication of the fund: 'Let no one have the right to use this money for anything else, nor the revenue deriving from it, except for the provision of corn etc.' Then there is the special provision made for those travelling or ill at the time of distribution. But among all these provisions and safeguards we find none whereby only those who were in genuine need should benefit; nor is there any suggestion of more generous provision being made for the fathers of large families. The wording of the decree, in fact, makes it extremely difficult to assume (as did Francotte) that 'it was understood' that the fund was intended for the poor: 'Let them measure out all the corn that has been bought individually to the citizens in residence by *chiliastys* (subdivisions of the tribes) giving *to each* a ration of two measures a month free.' The distribution was to 'begin in the month of Pelusion and to continue as long as the supply lasts'; thus, even though it was foreseen that such a distribution could not be maintained throughout the year, there was no attempt to disqualify the well-to-do so as to enable benefit to the poor to extend further.[109]

More fragmentary or shorter inscriptions have been found relating to other funds. One of the more recent comes from Samothrace (D. 8), and relates to the early or middle years of the second century BC. As its editor, P. M. Fraser, suggests, it may be significant that half a century earlier Samothrace had had to make special request to one of King Ptolemy of Egypt's generals stationed in the Hellespont and Thraceward regions, for permission to import corn tax-free from the Pontic Chersonese. Clearly, then, Samothrace had found difficulty in maintaining her food supply and presumably the emergencies became so frequent that something more reliable than a series of *ad hoc* remedies was felt to be essential. The matter was also seen as affecting the island as a whole, and it was in the interests of all, not simply of any one section of the populace, that the fund was established.[110]

No doubt, once a permanent revenue had been made available for this purpose, further supplementary gifts were always acceptable, whether or not called forth by an *epidosis*. Such may have been the context of an inscription from Iasos, dating *c.* 150 BC, which refers to certain citizens who had given a sum of money 'so that the people might ever live prosperously with ample supplies of corn, there being established for all the citizens from the public funds the principle of equal-rations'. The last word, *sitometria*, conveys something like the idea of a 'fair share for all', *to ison kai dikaion*, as applied to the corn supply in particular. The concept was to find a close parallel at Rome under the Empire, when on coins representing corn distributions there appeared the symbol 'equality' (*aequitas*), while in Galatia, in the period of the early Empire, an inscription speaks of a nobleman who 'gave *sitometria*', at the level of 5 *modii* per head.[111]

From Messene in the Peloponnese, too, we have epigraphical evidence for the existence of a permanent fund for the supply of corn, though in this case the inscription appears to deal not (as was once thought) with the arrangements for issuing each citizen with his proper share; rather it is concerned with the most advantageous exploitation of a glut of corn which had come into the hands of corn-commissioners, whereby the amount in excess of the year's need was to be handed over to any person who could use it, on condition that he returned its value with interest in the subsequent year. But there is no reason to doubt that these arrangements were being made for the benefit of the citizen-body as a whole.[112]

For Athens we have no evidence of a permanent public fund for free distribution, but it is consistent with the general picture that, on the occasion of the gift of a large quantity of corn to the Athenians by Psammetichos of Egypt in the mid-fifth century, there was no attempt to allocate it to those most in need. There is indeed reliable evidence of an attempt to limit the number of recipients, but the reduction was achieved only by an investigation of the citizen list with a view to removing non-citizens whose names had no right to appear there. Again, a century and more later, when a subscription was established to enable corn to be sold at the normal price in a period of widespread shortage (329–324 BC), this was in the interest of the citizen body as a whole; and, in keeping with the principle of *sitometria*, a corn rationing system was applied at the same time.[113]

In such cases the advantage to the poor is not to be overlooked. Were it not for such schemes the well-to-do might have been prepared to pay an exorbitant price for corn in times of shortage, so leaving the poor with nothing at all. Yet, undoubtedly another important factor in a city such as Athens was that the profits from the selling of corn at a black-market price would not ordinarily go to the well-to-do citizens but to the merchant of non-citizen (*metic*) status. Against him the rich and poor alike had a common interest in *sitometria*, and schemes to establish it were seen as providing a positive safeguard against the ever suspected attempts of the merchant class to cause artificial shortages of commodities which had to be imported in some quantity. So *sitometria* balanced the negative safeguard represented by the heavy penalties imposed on those who infringed the stringent regulations relating to a commodity's import and marketing.[114]

The Athenian method of distributing gifts of corn had an early precedent. In 483 BC, it was planned to distribute to each citizen an equal share of silver—a windfall of some hundred talents deriving from the mines in the Laurium district—since, like the windfall of corn, it was regarded as belonging to all alike (in the event, however, with Xerxes threatening invasion, Themistocles had the money spent on defence). This leads us on to consider two kinds of periodic money distribution at Athens: the *theorikon*, which comes into prominence in the fourth century BC, though it may have existed in some form in the fifth; and the *diobelia*, which belongs to the late fifth century.[115]

In a sense the *theorikon* was an assertion of the principle that the profits of the 'society' of all Athenians should be shared. Its official purpose, so Libanius tells us, was (as its name suggests) to provide the cost of a theatre ticket, so enabling the poorer classes in particular to attend the dramatic festival at a time when admission to the theatre still had to be paid for. But there is the clear implication in Libanius' account that *all* citizens were entitled to receive it. Part of the explanation for this lies in the fact that the dramatic festival was not merely a state religious occasion but, in the Periclean period (if it is accepted that the institution already existed in some form by then), an occasion for parading before the people the material evidence of their empire, the tribute of its member states—a moment of national pride in which it might be felt that all should share. In the fourth century, however, the 'theatre-money' was seen by Eubulus and his supporters as a means of giving the people as a whole a material interest in the maintenance of peace at a time when Athenian finances were in constant difficulties owing to allegedly unnecessary military and naval adventures. For the people could now be discouraged from approving such adventures—which were themselves attractive mainly because they offered hope of material gain—by an arrangement whereby any saving through cuts in military expenditure would be made available each year for distribution among the people. The actual amounts which were distributed is one of several points still in doubt. There is certainly no reason to believe that the increasing sums which passed through the hands of the commissioners of the theoric fund were all intended .for distributions, and one estimate suggests that a sum greater than 12 *drachmae* per citizen per year—less than a week's pay for a heavily armed soldier at fifth-century rates—was rare. But however large or small the amount distributed, again it appears that all citizens were eligible to receive it, though doubtless the *demos*, in the sense of the mass of ordinary citizens (rather than as also including the wealthy few—the word was conveniently elastic), had the greater interest in the scheme. It would be in recognition of this fact that a fourth-century politician called the *theorikon* the 'cement of democracy'; while Aristotle, by going on to discuss more positive and permanent methods of dealing with poverty after rejecting such distributions in principle, also makes it clear that herein lay their advertised purpose. For Aristotle himself it was clear that the purpose would never be achieved in that way, for 'the people, in the act of taking, ask for the same again. . . . To help the poor [a clear case where the latter term is synonymous with 'the people'] in this way is to fill a leaky jar'.[116]

In the case of the *diobelia*, the two-obol payment, there is more doubt as to the intended recipients. The payment has been identified by some scholars with the 'theatre money'; by others with the juryman's pay, as reintroduced by Cleophon in the later years of the Peloponnesian War, the disasters of which had caused these payments to be dropped after 413 BC. If the *diobelia* was in fact equivalent to the first, then presumably it went to all citizens; if to the second, it cannot be strictly regarded as a dole, but as the payment rendered by the state for the typical service of the small man in a radical democracy (although some have seen the establishment of large, paid juries as little more than a device for meeting the needs of older men oppressed by poverty even in the greater prosperity of the mid-fifth century). But a third possibility is that the *diobelia* was a payment specifically intended for needy citizens, irrespective of any services or attendances at state festivals, and its introduction may belong to the period when the principle asserted by the revolutionary government of 411 BC, that no one should receive payment for any kind of civil office, was still being maintained, even after that government had been overthrown. In this period it would be that section of the populace which had previously *relied upon* the juryman's pay for subsistence, perhaps a thousand or so 'drastically unemployed citizens', who would suffer most, especially under wartime conditions; and the years of ascendancy of men of moderate outlook, like Theramenes, might have provided the right political climate for such a provision as a temporary expedient. We may recall that Aristotle, who admired Theramenes, recognized that it was the duty of a 'genuine democrat' to ensure that the masses are not excessively poor. One cannot indeed deny the force of the observation of recent commentators that it is 'perhaps more in accordance with Athenian traditions' to interpret the *diobelia* as a re-introduction of fees for *everybody* at a lower level. Yet, were the Athenians unique in this respect? They are the only Greek people *known to us* who made special provision for their poorer disabled citizens—perhaps originally those disabled in war (D. 61). It could therefore be surmised that they made special provision for those suffering acutely from the economic effects of war as well. Such a measure would come nearer to poor relief in the modern sense than almost any other of which we have evidence; but it could not long have outlived the crisis which gave it birth.[117]

At Rome the great influx of population into the city and the need to import vast quantities of corn to feed it, especially in the last two centuries of the Republic, eventually gave rise to the same sort of permanent problem which had faced many Greek states. The traditional assistance of clients by patrons, even when

supplemented by the casual gifts of friendly kings, or by the
occasional abundance resulting from success in war or the 'public
spirit' of the *aediles* (which could cause the price of corn to fall as
low as one *as*) was quite inadequate. In the tribunate of Gaius
Gracchus, therefore, a permanent scheme was introduced (123
BC) whereby corn was to be provided monthly, not free (as at
Samos), but at a fixed and moderate price, presumably throughout the year. The capital sum required to provide the revenue for
this subsidy may have brought Rome a step nearer to the idea of the
'foundation', but in this case it was not drawn directly from the
wealth of the upper class, in the way that the Samian fund had
been, but rather from the profits of empire. There is a famous
story concerning one of the chief opponents of the law of 123,
L. Piso, who explained his presence at a subsequent distribution by
saying: 'I would prefer that you were not of a mind to divide my
property among the citizens individually, but seeing that you are
dividing it, then I shall ask for my share.' But Piso could claim
that it was *his* property which was being divided only in the sense
that it was part of the *publica*, the people's funds, which were his as
much as anybody else's—it was a stock criticism of any such law
that it was a drain upon public funds. Piso's answer, however,
makes it quite clear that the Gracchan scheme resembled that at
Samos in making the subsidized corn available to every citizen,
thus serving as a corrective against any literal interpretation of
Plutarch's statement that the scheme provided cheap corn for 'the
poor'. Gaius' surprise at Piso's appearance at the distribution was
due, not to the fact that he was wealthy and so had no right to
attend, but simply to his inconsistency in seeking to benefit from a
a law which he had opposed. Appian speaks quite clearly of the
law's 'fixing for *each of the citizens* a monthly ration of corn',
though less accurately in suggesting that the ration was already
free. Again, we observe, there is no provision for an extra supply
for the fathers of large families, such as a welfare scheme might
demand.[118]

On the other hand, we should not discount the disproportionate real value of cheap corn to the poor man as compared with the
wealthy; it is this (rather than the legal situation) which Plutarch

was concerned to bring out, as did Cicero, though with obvious
political bias, when he spoke of such measures being welcome to
the poor 'because food was supplied in free measure without
their needing to work for it'; and while the scheme undoubtedly
owed much to Greek precedent, it may be regarded in part as an
extension, on a more impersonal basis, of the Roman client-
patron relationship, whereby the upper class was being called upon
to admit a degree of collective responsibility for the lower
classes.[119]

Provision of corn at a moderate price did eventually lead on to
its free provision as a result of a law of the famous P. Clodius,
tribune of 58 BC, whose whole career, however, makes it unlikely
that he regarded it anything more than a vote-catching device (not
that we need suppose that Gaius Gracchus was unmindful of this
aspect of his original scheme, especially if we accept Appian's
chronology of his tribunates). Between the tribunates of Gaius
Gracchus and Clodius, yet another tribune, Saturninus, had
attempted (in 103 or 100 BC) to reduce the price payable to five-
sixths of an *as*, but it is very doubtful whether he succeeded. Some
scholars, indeed, have supposed that he passed a law re-introducing
the scheme of Gaius Gracchus, on the assumption that the
latter's law had already been replaced by a more moderate measure
of a certain M. Octavius. This suggestion, however, requires us
not only to emend the price as given in our sole source for
Saturninus' proposal—an odd price, admittedly, for what could
only have been a nominal charge—but also to pass over a remark
of Cicero which seems to make Octavius a contemporary of
young men who were coming into political prominence in the
early decades of the first century BC. It is better, then, to regard
the Gracchan law as remaining in force until the time of Sulla's
ascendancy, about 80 BC, and to suppose that Octavius was acting
in accordance with Sullan ideas in limiting the original scheme in
some way. Whether Sulla himself ever totally abolished the corn
distribution, as is commonly affirmed, the very poor evidence
scarcely entitles us to say. If he did, then this was one of the areas
in which Sulla most obviously failed to move with the times, and
by about 75 BC the tribunes were once again assuming their

traditional role in protesting about the inadequacy of the current arrangements, whatever these may have been. A law passed in 73 BC may have restored the Gracchan price but provided only a limited amount of corn, in practice, therefore, restricting either the number of citizens who could benefit under it or the amount of corn which each could buy. Public agitation continued, but the words put by Sallust into the mouth of Licinius Macer, who was active in arousing the agitation, are worthy of notice: 'The people responsible for this law have valued the liberty of all of you at five bushels per head.' It was in the name of *libertas* that the protest was made, not in that of *humanitas* (in its wider sense), with the emphasis on the *rights* of free men *qua* citizens rather than on the special *needs* of the destitute *qua* men. This emphasis foreshadowed that of the imperial coinage where the representation of a state corn distribution is accompanied by the legend '*libertas*', or attended by *Libertas* personified.[120]

The emphasis on *libertas* also implied, of course, that slaves were not included among the recipients of Clodius' free corn. But now, as we have already noticed, the masters of slaves in many cases took the hint and freed their slaves in order to make them eligible for a ration. Not only that, but there was a further difficulty in limiting the distribution to those normally resident in the city: Appian tells us that 'idlers and beggars throughout Italy' flocked to Rome in order to benefit. As a result of this, the need to draw up a list of those entitled to receive on grounds of domicile at Rome quickly became apparent, and Caesar, during his dictatorship (49–44 BC), did eventually reduce the number of beneficiaries to 150,000, as compared with the 320,000 said to have been receiving corn in the immediately preceding period.[121]

But was domicile at Rome the criterion which Caesar followed in so reducing the number of beneficiaries? Mommsen held that the criterion had now come to be that of need, Caesar converting what had been a general distribution into a genuine dole for the poor. This view was based in part on certain paragraphs of the *Lex Tabulae Heracleensis*, a municipal charter (or the raw material for one) apparently representing regulations introduced at Rome relating to the registration of those who were to receive a corn ration. Penalties are laid down to deter magistrates from giving corn to any person whose name does not appear on the list, and the assumption is that on this list there appeared only those whose property fell below a certain minimum. A certain plausibility may be lent to this suggestion in that in his agrarian law of 59 BC Caesar had shown readiness to regulate public assistance according to need, when it was fathers of three or more children who were offered allotments. None the less, Bolkestein came independently to the same conclusion as Van Berchem in a study specifically devoted to corn and cash distributions at Rome, namely that no 'means test' was introduced. Their views differed only in that, whereas Bolkestein emphasized the introduction of domicile as a criterion, Van Berchem insisted that this had always been the legal requirement and explained the reduction in numbers by reference to the extensive emigration encouraged by Caesar (according to Suetonius 80,000 colonists went overseas) and to the effects of civil war. The reduction of those admitted to the corn ration might even have been intended to act as a spur to colonization. It is pertinent, however, to observe with Van Berchem that the resort to lot, also ascribed to Caesar, in order to fill up the gaps in the list caused by death, does not argue for a careful determination of the recipients on the basis of need, though it does not necessarily exclude a means test; nor significantly is anything known of a provision whereby the *living* might be replaced in case they rose above the supposed minimum on which eligibility turned. But one may wonder, too, whether there ever was a list, prior to Caesar, with 320,000 names upon it; the figure is suspect as being precisely that of the largest number of people ever to receive *congiaria* from Augustus Caesar, with which it could easily—and perhaps conveniently—have been confused.[122]

As with so much of Caesar's legislation, the intention behind this particular measure must be left in doubt. In any case, after his death, the maximum number of recipients which he had set was ignored, and we have no certain evidence of the use of *subsortitio in demortuorum locum*. Cassius Dio describes the number of those receiving corn in 2 BC as unlimited; three years earlier it may have reached 320,000, on the assumption that the same number of people were entitled to regular distributions of corn as were admitted to the occasional *congiaria* of the Emperor Augustus. The imperial *congiaria* themselves may be dealt with briefly in passing, since they represented merely the continuation through the Emperor—'the first and foremost and universal benefactor', as Philo described him—of the distributions of corn or oil which had once been offered, especially by the *aediles*, to the people under the Republic. Just as the *aediles* had been accustomed to confirm the people in their goodwill by lavish distributions—originally of wine or oil, later of money—so the Emperor, though commonly holding no annual civil magistracy, did likewise on a vaster scale, especially on the occasion of his accession or of the introduction of his intended successor to public life. The most extensive distribution belongs to the occasion of Augustus' introduction of his grandson (and adopted son) Gaius, as heir apparent to the Principate. The Emperor's *congiaria*, unlike the monthly corn rations, represented '*un acte que le prince accomplit à titre personnel et gracieux*' —and as such they are referred to on the coinage by the legend *liberalitas*, which may be accompanied by an ordinal number to indicate the number of such distributions to date in the current reign. These *congiaria*, in accordance with their past history, naturally went to all citizens alike, the only change being that in the reign of Augustus boys under the age of eleven were included among the recipients, an extension which may be seen as a precedent for the institution of regular maintenance allowances for children by the end of the first century AD. But Augustus found it difficult to confine the *congiaria* even to this extended number of recipients, for the wealthy, repeating the manœuvre which they had adopted in order to benefit from Clodius' free-corn bill, again proceeded to manumit their slaves. The Emperor was provoked to declare that he would not give to those who had been freed after the announcement of a distribution, and that those who had been freed in anticipation of the announcement would in any case only cause a reduction in the ration for the individual recipient.[123]

With regard to the regular corn ration, the same problems arose as under the Republic, necessitating the occasional expulsion of foreigners from the city, together with some slaves, in face of food shortages. Indeed, Suetonius tells us that Augustus seriously thought of abolishing the public distributions once and for all, and credits him with no loftier motive for abandoning the idea than his belief that 'someone would restore them sooner or later through the desire to win favour (*ambitio*)'. Eventually, by 2 BC, he fixed the number of recipients at 200,000, though there may have been a subsequent reduction to 150,000, the number known to have benefited from Augustus' legacy to the people. There is still, however, no evidence that this reduction was based on any means test, and there is some evidence to the contrary. Thus, the implications of Suetonius' statements already quoted may be supported by the scholiast's comment on a line of Persius that all who became Roman citizens by manumission were automatically included in the number of those who received *frumentum publicum*. Furthermore, we have inscriptions in which certain individuals specifically claim that they were in receipt of *frumentum* or *frumentum publicum*; and, with a few possible exceptions, these are most easily explained as claims to Roman citizenship where there was no other ready way of proving it. On the hypothesis that mere citizenship and residence at Rome remained the only qualification, we are faced, indeed, with the conclusion that the *citizen* population of Rome may not have amounted to much more than a fifth of the total resident population of the city; but such a conclusion is by no means out of harmony with the general impression of the populace of Rome derived from literary sources.[124]

Augustus may accordingly have limited himself mainly to changes in organization, in particular to the issue of *tesserae*, tokens or 'coupons'. At first, apparently, these had actual purchasing power (hence the adjective 'nummariae' applied to them by Suetonius), but they came to be mere ration-cards, taking the form of wooden tablets (represented on the coinage) and indicated the eligibility of the holder to receive his ration, the day of the month on which he was to collect it, and the door of the *Porticus Minucia* at which he was to apply. A change by which the issue of corn was to take place at four-monthly intervals was also considered but not put into effect. Otherwise, the essential tradition of the Republic was maintained, particularly in that the actual distributions, although remaining under the general supervision of the Emperor, were effected through the *praefecti frumenti dandi*, appointed from the Senate, a procedure which was probably not significantly altered by a further reorganization under Claudius. Such propaganda devices, however, as the grouping of the distributions of *frumentum publicum* with the handing-out of personal largess (*congiaria*) in the official record of Augustus' achievements (*Res Gestae*), and the later representation of the Emperor at the corn-distribution scenes portrayed on the coinage, served to remind the recipient of the real source of his ration. Still more effective reminders would have been those occasions of special stress when Augustus showed that he understood his tenure of the *cura annonae* to carry with it the moral duty to override the normal official limits. In AD 6, for example, he gave 'free of cost to those who were in receipt of rations of corn as much again as they regularly received'—perhaps the occasion when Suetonius records that he '*tesserasque nummarias duplicavit*'—while at the same time he set a limit on the amount which anyone could buy on the market. Here we have an instance where it is practically impossible to disentangle the public and private aspects of the Emperor's activity. A coin issued in the reign of the Emperor Nerva bearing the legend '*plebei urbanae frumento constituto S.C.*' may best be understood as pointing to another instance of an extraordinary imperial distribution, though still advertising—through S(enatus) C(onsultum)—the nominal control of the Senate. In the next reign the special intervention of Trajan caused 5,000 boys, as it appears from the vague terms of Pliny's panegyric, to be included among the recipients of *frumentum publicum* from infancy. It was only with the advent of the Severi that the replacement of the *praefecti frumenti dandi* by an equestrian *curator aquarum et Minuciae* tore away the last suggestion of the Senate's nominal control of distributions. At the same time the references to the *origo* and *domus* of the recipients on documents cease, probably betraying the effect of the extension of Roman citizenship by the famous *constitutio* of 212, and more especially of the Severan tendency to deprive Italy of her privileged position in relation to the rest of the Empire.[125]

Apart, then, from the ultimate origin of the funds which provided for these large distributions, the corn ration at Rome, on the present interpretation, remained in principle essentially the same as that at other cities of the classical world; and the special provision of individual emperors, whether through separate *congiaria* or through subventions to an existing corn fund, was not essentially different from that of many a municipal benefactor, such as Q. Avelius Priscus at Corfinium (D. 24), or Haterius Claudius Summus at Salzburg (D. 29). The provision of Trajan in favour of boys *ab infantia*, however, leads us a step further, to an institution specifically concerned with the needs of children, the *alimenta*, which from Trajan's time, if not before, was organized at 'government' level (D. 18, 19), but which had precedents in private schemes going back at least as far as the reign of Nero. It was not later than Nero's reign that T. Helvius Basila left to the people of Atina 400,000 sesterces, the revenue from which was to be used to provide corn for their children until their coming of age, upon which day they were to receive the sum of 1,000 sesterces (D. 16). The regular revenue necessary for this scheme was provided by investing money in land, as in the case of many Greek foundations directed to different purposes. It was only the emphasis on the needs of children that was new. As to this, we have already seen that Augustus had pointed the way by including *minores pueri* among the recipients of his occasional *congiaria*; and Helvius Basila, who had been a *legatus Augusti*, would have known the mind of the emperor of the day no less than did Pliny that of Trajan when he established a private scheme at Comum (D. 17)— and perhaps celebrated its tenth anniversary by the publication of a letter to match Trajan's celebration of the government scheme by a special commemorative coin issue. In this respect it is not a point of much practical importance whether the original idea is regarded as imperial or private in origin. Clearly, however, the Emperor's role was given special prominence from Trajan's time, not only on the coinage or in public panegyric, such as that directed to Trajan by Pliny, but also in works of sculpture. One extant example from the Roman forum, representing the Emperor seated on a platform in a *toga*, with the personified *Italia* and two children before him, corresponds closely with the scene represented on certain coins of the period.[126]

The imperial scheme has occasionally been seen as designed, not merely to provide subsistence for children, but also to aid small farmers in need of capital to develop their land—an interpretation based not least on the fact that an essential part of the scheme involved the advancing of loans to farmers at a comparatively low rate of interest. But such loans, as we have noticed, were the common basis for *any* scheme designed to provide a permanent revenue, and the rate of interest was probably kept low in deference to those who were 'invited' to accept loans which were not repayable when no longer required by the borrower—a point in which the scheme again followed Greek precedent. A recent investigation of the distribution of loans under the government scheme at Veleia (Liguria) has in fact led to the conclusion that the aim was not to provide an amenity for farmers but to spread the load of state investment. This is most obvious in the case of the preliminary limited scheme initiated by the consular Gallicanus, for which the *largest* landholders were chosen, apparently on the ground that upon them the burden of such unwanted loans would rest the most lightly. In the main scheme, property worth the considerable sum of 50,000 sesterces was the minimum for eligibility, and this security had to be twelve times or more the amount of the sum borrowed. The fact that the *curiales* (town councillors), though invariably large landholders, are scarcely represented among the borrowers suggests that, in view of the other calls upon their pockets in their permanent official capacity, they were possibly protected from what was regarded by the upper class as just another public burden.[127]

From one of Pliny's letters we know that Trajan deprecated the imposition of non-repayable forced loans in the provinces; but such loans provided the simplest means of ensuring that the annual revenue essential to a fund did not fail, and here they could be justified as being in the public interest. Pliny himself had financed a similar scheme for the maintenance of boys and girls— by making over a piece of land to the *actor publicus* of Comum and then renting it back for 30,000 sesterces a year. Since the annual yield on the land amounted to a considerably larger sum Pliny felt confident that the land would 'always find an owner to work it', and that the revenue for *his* scheme was therefore assured (D. 17). The emperor, however, could not employ such a method, for at this time imperial land was not sufficiently extensive. The opening words of the inscription from Veleia (D. 19) may be taken as stating the one and only objective of the government scheme: 'Mortgages on properties to the amount of 1,044,000 sesterces, whereby in accordance with the kindly purpose of the best and greatest *princeps*, the Emperor Caesar Nerva Trajan Augustus Germanicus Dacicus, boys and girls may receive maintenance allowances.' The numbers of children to benefit follow; there is no hint that the farmer-mortgagees are receiving anything through the Emperor's *indulgentia*.[128]

There is evidence that the government scheme was extended by Trajan's successor, Hadrian, and then by Antoninus Pius, Marcus Aurelius and, in the third century, by Alexander Severus. Hadrian's action, however, may have been limited to raising the upper age limit of beneficiaries. But the appearance of the legend *libertas restituta* accompanying distribution scenes on coins of his reign, almost identical with those of his predecessor, recalls that equation of freedom with 'freedom from want' already noticed in a speech attributed to the late Republican tribune, Licinius Macer, and symbolized later by the representation of *Libertas* on coins advertizing regular *frumentationes*. Apart from this, only for Antoninus Pius is there any substantial epigraphical or numismatic evidence: namely, dedications to him by *pueri* and *puellae alimentarii*, and the legend *puellae Faustinianae* on coins relating to the fund established by Pius to commemorate his wife Faustina. But while the government *alimenta* spread to many parts of Italy, if only to a minority of its four hundred towns, many private schemes were established in the Latin speaking provinces (only two are known in the Greek east, and one of these was personally established by Hadrian). In Italy a growing imperial bureaucracy was directed to supervise the payments under the various funds (originally private schemes could also gain imperial protection), though the routine administration of particular schemes may have remained partly under local control. The chief officials, operating in some nine districts of Italy, the *praefecti alimentorum*, usually men of senatorial status acting as *curatores viarum* or equestrian *procuratores alimentorum*, are frequently referred to in inscriptions, as are their subordinates; and there is no doubt that the general scheme continued until the reign of Aurelian, with an interruption, rather than a deliberate cessation, of payments under Commodus. It has been doubted, however, whether the government organization was altogether beneficial; it seems to have had the effect of discouraging private schemes, unless it is merely coincidental that after Trajan's reign the evidence for private schemes comes largely from the provinces, where government competition was less formidable.[129]

But what caused the government to take an interest in such schemes? In so far as the personal initiative of the emperor was involved, Bolkestein saw here something closely approaching the 'oriental' type of non-reciprocal philanthropy, on the grounds that neither the children themselves, as the recipients, nor their parents, could have claimed that they had earned or were entitled to any such consideration. The days in which the common people had played any significant part in legislation or elections had long since passed. It might be added that the alimentary schemes initiated by the Emperors were, unlike the *frumentationes*, not confined to the urban populace of Rome, which had in large measure continued to provide the electorate on which high office depended, even in the period when citizenship was widely extended. Henderson offered a similarly idealized interpretation, though without the same emphasis on oriental influences. In the mounting of such schemes he discerned 'the obligation of wealth to supply the luxuries for the poor—a splendid feature of ancient civilization', and 'a characteristically Roman virtue'.[130]

Others have offered more cynical interpretations. Laum, for instance, saw the government scheme as '*mehr ein Akt der Politik als der reinen Menschenliebe*'; and it is, indeed, relevant to keep in mind that in the very process of establishing his power, Augustus (or Octavian as he then was) recognized the importance of an extra-constitutional appeal to 'all Italy', on which he relied for the greater part of his military backing. Moreover, in Pliny's references to Trajan's special provision for children on the occasion of distributions of corn, if not to the alimentary scheme as such, there is the strong suggestion that, although the recipients had not yet performed any service on the Emperor's behalf, it could be confidently anticipated that they *would* eventually make a return by way of military service, at a time when it was difficult to find willing recruits in Italy. Thus, in the *Panegyric*, Pliny addresses to Trajan the hope that through the *alimenta* these new recipients may be brought into the Emperor's service: 'these are being brought up at public expense as a source of strength in war and to adorn our name in peace' (some thirty legions, it should be remembered, were needed to maintain the Roman peace); 'from these our camps, from these our tribes will be replenished'. His more humanely expressed doctrine, 'for poor people the one means of bringing up their children is a good Emperor', only carries a small step further that expressed by Livy in the Augustan age (but projected back to the earliest Republic by the historian) that 'poor people make sufficient contribution [to the state] if they bring up their children'.[131]

Henderson doubted this less idealized interpretation on the grounds that from the Flavian period onwards Italy was seldom called upon to supply legionary recruits, and yet it is to Italy that almost all the records of government alimentary schemes belong. He therefore preferred to see here the latest expression of Roman *pietas*. However, although it is true that recruitment to existing legions, which were exclusively stationed in the provinces in this period, was normally done locally, mainly for reasons of administrative convenience and economy, it was not out of the question for new legions to be raised in Italy, as Marcus Aurelius was to make clear; nor can we assume that Trajan himself approved entirely of the dwindling Italian element in the legions of his day. *Pietas*, for the Roman, moreover, usually had a practical rather than sentimental mode of expression, as it did for the heroic exponent of this virtue in Virgil's epic. For Aeneas, *pietas* was essentially connected with a belief in and a self-dedication to

the idea of the eternity of Rome, which took precedence over all
other considerations. In the early Empire this *aeternitas* was
represented as depending not a little on the emperor's care and
foresight, his *providentia*, applied, *inter alia*, to the maintenance of
the number and quality of the Roman citizen body. Here, indeed,
we find the continued expression of that concern for a dwindling
population (or for its 'best' elements) which had lain behind the
famous proposal of the censor of 131 BC, Q. Metellus, for compulsory marriage, the agrarian reforms of Tiberius Gracchus, and
the land law of Julius Caesar giving special consideration to
fathers of three or more children. Augustus himself—although it
is his concern for the decline in the birth-rate of the upper class and
his attempt to counteract it by a policy of rewards and penalties
which is usually emphasized—also introduced measures relating
to the manumission of slaves. These gave legal access to full
citizenship to a considerable number of the more reliable of the
slave population, who had previously been left in an uncertain
position following unofficial manumission. In the Trajanic period
itself we find Pliny, on hearing of the many manumissions of a
certain Fabatus, writing that he welcomes the news, 'for I desire
our fatherland to be increased in anything, but above all in the
number of its citizen body'.[132]

How far, if at all, there was in fact during the Trajanic period,
or earlier, a serious decline in the population is a question much
disputed, and perhaps beyond certain answer. But we need only
posit a *belief* in such a decline, or the likelihood of it, in order to
provide one explanation of the *alimenta*, if the encouragement of
philanthropy in seventeenth- and early eighteenth-century
England by statesmen (and by men prominent in trade and
commerce) 'haunted by the spectre of a declining population' on
the very eve of a population explosion, is allowed to provide a
parallel. Some scholars, such as Sirago, have gone still further
and supposed that owing to a concern to swell his legions Trajan
discriminated numerically in favour of boys as against girls in his
alimentary programme. Certainly at Veleia the relevant inscription shows that in the main scheme 246 boys received allowances
as against 35 girls, while in the earlier scheme the ratio is 18 boys

H

to 1 girl. The problem here is whether this inequality was foreseen and intended by the author of the scheme or whether it was accidental. Inevitably, some scholars have regarded these figures as reflecting the more frequent exposure of girls than boys. Duncan-Jones, however, has suggested that the disparity may have been due to a limitation on the number of children who could benefit in any one family, which caused fathers of large families to register their sons rather than their daughters for allowances which were larger, as in many private schemes, for boys than for girls. If that were so, it would mean that, as in the corn distributions to citizens, large families received less favourable treatment than those not as large, which would again undermine an attempt to see any pure concept of 'welfare' attaching to the scheme. It could be argued, too, that the explicit provision normally made in private schemes for an equal number of boys and girls as recipients reinforces the suggestion that the Emperor evidently had military requirements in mind. And yet it might be that such provision had been made by these private benefactors only because of their knowledge of how the scheme at Veleia had, unintentionally, turned out. The question must probably remain open, as must another, still more fundamental and already implicit in a previous argument: Was it the case, even now, that the *poorest* children in any community were specified and *deliberately* picked out as recipients? There is no sure evidence to support any such assertion, beyond the statement of Victor that the *alimenta* were designed to aid 'boys and girls born to poor parents'. If Pliny's example is at all typical, it may be noteworthy that his other benefaction concerned with the welfare of children (D. 51) clearly supported those whose parents were of sufficient means to send their sons from Comum to Milan for their schooling. Again, the applicant, known from a papyrus, under Hadrian's scheme at Antinoöpolis in Egypt (D. 22), shows no consciousness of a need to attest his limited means—indeed he describes himself as 'living in his own house'—but simply the genuineness of the details of his birth and parentage. It may be prudent then to place the main emphasis of the *alimenta* on children, without further definition, taking the institution perhaps as the practical expression of that deeper regard for the child which we have seen reflected in the literature of the early and middle Empire. And we may wonder whether it might not have been men like Pliny, (childless himself, as far as we know) who would in particular be conscious not only of the desire but also of the wisdom of setting up such funds, so showing themselves worthy of exemption from the penalties and political hindrances which since the time of Augustus had been imposed on those who did not undertake the burdens of parenthood.[133]

Almost as essential a commodity as corn in the classical world was oil—useful not only as a comestible but also as a washing agent and as a fuel for lighting. In addition, particularly in the *gymnasia* of Greek cities, oil was regarded, in the words of an inscription, as 'most essential for the bodies of men and above all for those of old men'. 'Bread and oil' therefore came to be expected of public benefactors among the Greeks just as 'bread and circuses' was the cry at Rome under the Empire. But in so far as the distribution of oil in the gymnasia was intended for use there alone—and it was probably an act of unusual generosity for oil to be distributed there for consumption by recipients at home—we may appropriately defer the discussion of such benefactions to a later chapter. As for the distribution of oil for more general purposes, we need say only that private distributions followed the same pattern as those of corn (and other food-stuffs); once again there is no indication that any private donor discriminated in favour of the lower classes nor has there been any tendency to regard public distributions as doles instituted primarily to aid the destitute.[134]

CHAPTER VIII

EDUCATION AND CULTURE

THAT 'THE ADVANCEMENT OF EDUCATION' was one of the three specific categories put forward by Lord Macnaghten, in his attempt to tidy up the Elizabethan Act of Charitable Uses, is in itself a sufficient indication of the importance of education among charitable objectives in the modern world. But what evidence is there to suggest that education was seen in the classical world as an appropriate field for private giving or public support? In taking up this question it will be convenient—though un-Hellenic in spirit!—to consider academic and physical education separately. In this chapter we shall concentrate on the former and turn first to that final stage of education in the Greek city-state which most obviously called forth both public and private subventions, namely that associated with the institution of the *ephebeia*. This institution, as inaugurated, or re-established on a broader basis, probably under the influence of the Athenian statesman Lycurgus, *c.* 335 BC, was mainly, if not exclusively, concerned with physical and military training. It provided all young men of eighteen with a two-year period of 'national service', during which they were taught what it was to be an Athenian citizen, the course having to be completed before they could enter into that citizenship. But because the poorer elements of Athenian society could not afford to attend for such a period, the state provided a subsidy of some 40 talents a year, which probably (the matter has been disputed) enabled even those of the lowest class, the *Thetes*, to participate.[135]

This system was a limited application of that principle of compulsory and universal 'education' for all of citizen status which had long since been practised at Sparta in the case of children from the age of six upwards. But the Spartan *agoge* had remained essentially military in its nature and objectives, being designed to make each

Spartan permanently fit and available as a soldier, and little, if at all, concerned with his intellectual development. For that very reason it was criticized in the fourth century by Plato and Aristotle, who were otherwise clearly much impressed and influenced by it in their thinking. What was needed, the philosophers urged, was to follow the Spartan example but include in this long period of training by the state intellectual as well as physical education. At Athens the military aspect of the *ephebeia* very gradually withered away and by the early first century BC inscriptions suggest that it had become 'permanently, if not absolutely, demilitarized'; and in this form, entailing a varied (though not very systematic) intellectual training, it spread to most cities of the Hellenistic world, and so requires a prominent place in any study of classical education.[136]

Who, then, was in a position to enjoy the opportunities offered by the *ephebeia* in its developed form? Certainly not, at Athens, all who had originally been compulsorily enrolled for training. By 322 BC (perhaps before the academic side of the course had been established), a property qualification of 2,000 drachmae introduced by an oligarchic government, backed by Antipater, had already cut down the number of young men entitled to enter, and only a few decades later the course was reduced to a year and made no longer compulsory for those entitled to attend, whereupon the numbers of ephebes dropped sharply. The reason for this drop was almost certainly that not even the democracy, when restored, found it possible to re-institute the subsidy, so that many of those eligible found the financial burden of devoting as little as a year to the course beyond their means. The actual cost of such academic instruction as had been so far introduced was probably not a decisive factor, however, for this came largely to be met by magistrates and other generous individuals, even if the state withdrew or limited financial support. Not merely were lecture courses provided by these individuals, but competitions (both gymnastic and academic) and prizes for those who excelled in them. It is the gymnasiarchs, in particular, who are commended for this kind of generosity. One of them was Elpinikos of Eretria, who about 100 BC, among much else to the advantage of the physical training of the gymnasium, 'provided from his own funds a teacher of rhetoric' (D. 56); another was Mantidoros, who met the salary of a Homeric scholar, an Athenian named Philotas who 'gave a course in the gymnasium for the young men and the boys and for all others who were suitably disposed for education' (D. 57). At Priene, shortly afterwards, Zosimus (a Roman by birth who became first a citizen and then a magistrate of Priene), provided for the ephebes an instructor in grammar and philology, in accordance with his declared aim to make them, not only energetic in body (as proved by other generous donations), but 'to arouse in their minds the quality and feelings proper to men'. At Pergamum the gymnasiarch, Straton, continued 'to secure the publicly maintained teachers by the appropriate rewards [*philanthropiai*—the term is significant] and introduced, besides, another two, meeting the expense out of his own pocket, so that nothing of the instruction which was necessary should be lacking' (D. 54). Another gymnasiarch in the same city, in addition to meeting the salary of a teacher, established prizes for every field of instruction and a supply of equipment of every kind (the latter presumably for gymnastics). It is noticeable that *permanent* funds established by individuals tend on the whole to be directed rather to the provision of oil, to suit the gymnastic rather than the academic aspects of the *ephebeia*, although it is likely enough that such funds as existed at Pergamum for the latter originated from private endowments which had come to be publicly administered; the same bias may be noticed in the inscription for Menas of Sestos (D. 55).[137]

However, even where the costs of salaries and equipment were met by private benefactions, there was still a considerable amount of expenditure which the ephebe might be called upon to meet, both during his course and after 'graduation', when he would expect to join the *neoi*, who devoted themselves exclusively, it appears, to sports and gymnastics. At Athens, for instance, each ephebe was eventually expected to provide a certain number of books for the library attached to the gymnasium. More generally the ephebes were involved in various ceremonial and religious occasions, accompanied often by a public sacrifice. The extent of the expenses in which they thereby became involved is apparent from a number of inscriptions praising the ephebes as having met their obligations (liturgies) with devotion and enthusiasm. At Cibyra the oath of the *ephebes* included a clause whereby they undertook to 'safeguard the gymnasiarchy and its due income', the type of oath which in the classical world usually meant meeting any deficit out of one's own pocket. At Mytilene the *neoi* are found responding to 'the demand for contributions to the corn-purchase fund' with the large gift of 3,100 staters. In short, it is clear that the acceptance of this period of education came to be regarded, not so much as a privilege extended by the state, but rather as a burden undertaken in the interests of the state—the *ephebeia* being a kind of showpiece demonstrating the intellectual, religious and social aspects of a city's life in the persons of those few who were wealthy enough to afford to belong to it, and competing with its counterpart in other cities. So it became normal at Athens and elsewhere for decrees to be passed by council and people complimenting the ephebes and their instructors *en bloc* for their good discipline or serious application to the course. Athenian decrees award a wreath of olive to the ephebes, a crown of gold to the instructors, while the *kosmetes* (director of the ephebes) who served for glory alone, and not for pay, it seems, is also in some inscriptions awarded a crown of gold. Other inscriptions make specific reference to sacrifices carried out for the 'health and well-being of the city' or its component institutions. Such inscriptions were for a long time inscribed upon stone at public expense, though the stage did come at Athens (perhaps when it became increasingly difficult for the ephebes to claim that their institution had much to do with the safety of the state) when they had to seek an audience with the council and request permission to honour their *kosmetes* with a statue, presumably bearing the cost of this themselves.[138]

The number of ephebes at Athens would have decreased even more sharply, had not admission to the *ephebeia*, by the late second century BC, become virtually purchasable by wealthy young non-citizens, along with citizenship. Among the citizens it was not uncommon for the wealthiest indirectly to support the less wealthy, the *kosmetes* himself sometimes encouraging such generosity by his own example, in return for which the title of 'gymna-siarch' (of the ephebes, as distinct from that of city gymnasiarchy) was being conferred in some cities by the first century BC. But these subventions did not do more than maintain the number of ephebes at the low level which had so quickly established itself—essentially a matter of maintaining the privileged circle at its by now traditional dimensions.[139]

But it would in any case have been impossible to add greatly to the number of those benefitting from the higher education which the *ephebeia* offered, for the simple reason that most citizens could not afford to provide their sons with the required preliminary education, and in most states little was done, privately or publi-cally, to help them. There do exist inscriptions relating to generosity at this level, but they are very few compared with those concerned with gifts to the *ephebeia*, let alone those provid-ing for distributions of foodstuffs or cash. This perhaps did not prevent most citizens from learning to read and write—such at least has been argued of Athens in the fifth century, on the basis of our knowledge of the working of Athenian democracy, in which the institution of ostracism, for instance, implied the literacy of at least six thousand citizens. The same is implied by the kind of plays produced at Athens for a popular audience—Euripides' *Theseus* is especially notable for its inclusion of a spelling scene. This was, indeed, in a city whose radical democracy and cultural efflorescence gave to the average man a more than usual incentive to acquire a basic education. Much depended on whether one lived in town or country, however, and literary evidence suggests there was little emphasis on education for girls. Yet a passing reference by Thucydides to Mycalessus, a small town in Boeotia, may indicate that even there at least three schools were to be found in the same period.[140]

But if this was so—and of the Hellenistic period it has been as-serted that in fully Greek areas it was normal for the children (in some cases, as much for the daughters as for the sons) of all free men to go to school, *paidonomoi* (controllers of youth) being appointed to supervise their schooling—then the explanation must lie largely in the low fees which the elementary teacher could command, so low that even the poorer classes could afford to send their children to him, at least for a year or two. The possible character of such schooling and the upper class estimate of its value are well known from the unconcealed contempt with which the orator Demosthenes once spoke of the alleged association of Aeschines, his rival, with such an institution. Indeed, the social ethos according to which it was felt appropriate for a man of wealth to refer to another's education in public argument *ad hominem* has obvious significance for our study. Five centuries later a similar attitude is also evident at Prusa, birthplace of Dio Chrysostom. In part, the explanation of the apparently widespread evidence of 'basic education' will be that bare literacy may well have been achieved without any formal schooling; for there is certainly no evidence of, widespread private contributions towards the establishment of schools similar, for instance, to the Charity or Ragged Schools of eighteenth- and nineteenth-century England.[141]

Two inscriptions of the Hellenistic period, one from Teos and the other from Miletus, (D. 47, 48) are exceptions to the rule, relating as they do to private gifts for the support of the earlier, if not the earliest, stages of education, though otherwise true to type in their unequivocal assertion of the donors' concern for their own renown. Such renown is secured for Eudemos of Miletus through the public display of an honorary decree on two stone pillars, the stipulation of certain religious and ceremonial duties, and the naming of the fifth day of the month (presumably that of Eudemos' birth) as a holiday. This latter provision points towards, though it falls short of, the actual cult of the founders of *gymnasia*, which might involve burial within their walls. The inscriptions are also true to type in that they give no suggestion that the funds provided are to be used to assist those most in need, and in that they offer to teachers themselves little more than was earned in fifth-century Athens by common sailors.[142]

Both donors provide a capital sum, the interest from which is wholly or in part to be devoted to the payment of the salaries of the teachers, who are to be chosen by a vote of the people on an annual basis. The donors, we note, once having handed over their money to their city, can expect to have no further direct part in the administration of the fund, the gift being treated on exactly the same principles as those handed over for other purposes. The Teos inscription differs, however, from the Milesian, in that it is not exclusively concerned with elementary education but provides also for the appointment of military instructors by the 'controller of youth' (*paidonomos*) and the gymnasiarch. Although, therefore, all free boys are named as the intended beneficiaries of the fund, the implication is that the education to be provided would take place in the *gymnasia*, probably those maintained for the *ephebeia*, and would lead up to the type of course normally followed by the ephebes. It is possible, indeed, that there already existed endowments or state provision for all Tean youths to continue their education at this level too, as had originally been the case at Athens, but, if not, we may doubt whether those who had no prospects of following the latter course would be considered, or consider themselves, eligible to benefit from the fund which Polythrous had made available. In the same inscription there is a rather enigmatic reference to the likelihood of the elementary teachers 'disputing among themselves about the number of the children' (in which case the *paidonomos* was to decide the matter). We may wonder whether the disputes envisaged were expected to relate to too few, rather than too many children. Was it recognized that not all who were theoretically entitled to free education would in fact receive it, but that the parents of boys who *did* attend might supplement the teachers' pay (which, it appears, is to remain static) with *philanthropiai* of their own?[143]

Two other gifts, belonging to the second century BC, relate to the provision of elementary education, but both have an 'international' character, being the benefactions of Pergamene kings. The first of these, that of Eumenes II, in 162, took the form of a large quantity of corn, the proceeds from the sale of which were to be devoted to the 'provision of salaries for the teachers and instructors of the boys'. It is of interest not least because of Polybius, caustic comment upon the Rhodian acceptance of the gift: 'One might accept this from friends in case of financial embarrassment, as one might accept a gift in private life rather than allow children to remain uneducated for want of means.' He clearly implies that the Rhodians had demeaned themselves and surrendered something of their independent status by accepting a gift unnecessarily. The remark is of obvious relevance to the Greek concept of friendship and of giving in relation to friendship, but certainly does not justify any assumption that the fund was to be used specifically to help parents 'without means', in the absolute sense. Two or three years later Attalus II sent to the city of Delphi the sum of 18,000 Alexandrian silver *drachmae* 'in ready response' to a request for aid. The latter phrase suggests that there may have been already established some fund for this purpose at Delphi which had proved inadequate (as may well be true for Rhodes). But any such fund would probably derive from previous gifts handed over by private donors to be publicly administered, rather than from a regular revenue directly raised and allocated by the state for education; for in spite of the widespread appointment of officials such as the *paidonomoi*, in the cities of the Hellenistic world, it appears that their function was essentially supervisory, to regulate the education of those children whose parents could afford to meet the expense of their schooling rather than to insist on the same opportunities for the children of parents who could not. Plutarch may be quoted for a late first-century AD view as having urged that 'as far as possible' poor children and even slaves should receive an education; but the limited opportunity of the Hellenistic period is suggested by one of the mimes of Herondas in which the thirtieth of the month is represented as a bitter day, since it is the day on which the schoolmaster demands his fee.[144]

Since private individuals so seldom, it appears, saw fit to give for the furtherance of elementary education, we should hardly expect that collectively they would welcome the burden of public provision, and the occasional reference in our ancient sources which might seem to suggest otherwise may well be illusory. Thus, Diodorus records of the lawgiver Charondas of Catana that in drawing up laws for the colony of Thurii in Southern Italy 'he looked to that which was neglected by previous legislators in providing that *all* the sons of citizens should have an elementary education, the funds needed for teachers' salaries being provided

by the city; for he thought that those who were without means of
making a livelihood would be deprived of the noblest of pursuits'.
But a belief in the main statement is not encouraged by the obvious error of detail, by which the activities of a seventh-century
lawgiver are related to the foundation of a mid-fifth-century
Italian colony. The statement may simply reflect Diodorus'
awareness of proposals for publicly provided elementary education
in his own day (the late first century BC); but we have already
noticed the likely origin of the funds which would then be drawn
upon. If Charondas did make such a proposal for any colony, then
the explanation may be sought in connexion with those equali-
tarian tendencies evident in the establishment of a Greek colony,
by which each of the original settlers received his individual
allotment, and so would be able, as a 'man of means', to meet the
incidental expenses which the scheme would entail. Alternatively,
we may suspect that a property qualification kept the citizen body
narrowly defined and excluded from the privileges of citizenship
any who fell below it as mere residents, so leading to a situation
rather like that at Sparta, where all the true Spartans received their
peculiar type of public education from boyhood, but not the
large non-citizen population.[145]

Such a narrow definition of citizenship was certainly true of
Plato's and Aristotle's thinking in the fourth century. Both
declare the lack of any publicly provided education for Athenian
children in their period and protest loudly against it. 'No father',
so Plato would legislate, 'shall either send or keep away his son as a
pupil from school at his own whim, but every Tom, Dick and
Harry, so to speak, must as far as possible, be compelled to receive
education'. Aristotle argues similarly that 'the system of education
must also be one and the same for all . . . it cannot be left, as it is
at present, to private enterprise, with each parent making private
provision for his children and having them privately instructed as
he himself thinks fit'. But just as Plato's state excludes from the
citizenship traders and craftsmen, so in Aristotle the best form of
state will not admit 'mechanics' (or labourers) as citizens, on the
grounds that a man who lives the life of a mechanic or labourer
'cannot pursue the things which belong to excellence'. In neither

case, then, would children of these classes qualify for that education which Plato and Aristotle are discussing. There are suggestions in the *Republic* that a system of upgrading according to ability would allow the lower classes (who do appear there to be citizens of a sort) to enjoy an appropriate education, but the mechanism for this is left suspiciously vague. Moreover, these assertions are made not so much because a child has a right to be educated, but because an educated citizen is an asset to the state; for 'they are the children of the state even more than the children of their own parents'.[146]

The state of affairs against which Plato and Aristotle are found protesting in the fourth century implies a need for caution in drawing any wide conclusion from Plutarch's well-known report that in 480 BC the people of Troezen met the expense of teachers for Athenian boys evacuated there in the face of the Persian danger; or from a reference in Plato's *Crito* to a law of Solon calling upon each Athenian father to provide for his son's education—a 'law' which would at most represent the demands of social convention among those who could afford to heed it, rather than indicate that the state provided all citizens with the means of heeding it. Until recently, an inscription from Eleusis (D. 52) did seem at least to suggest that the state took some positive interest in the education of boys towards the end of Plato's lifetime, since it commends a certain Derkylos, a general, and records the award to him of a golden crown and other privileges because of his distinguished service (*philotimia*) on behalf of the deme of Eleusis 'especially with regard to the education of boys'. The generals are known to have been connected with the early history of the *ephebeia* at Athens (and elsewhere), so that, as long as this inscription was dated to *c.* 350 BC it appeared that they may have had some (though rather mysterious) connection with the education of boys as well, prior to the inception of the wider ephebic system. However, there has recently been offered a more satisfactory explanation, based on a dating to 319/18, a year in which a Derkylos was certainly general; at this date his service could have involved much more than the education of boys, as indeed the size of his reward suggests, namely the maintenance within his own deme of the ephebic course on an unofficial basis, after it had been severely cut down, if not abolished, by a pro-Macedonian oligarchy. His office as general would have made it easier for him to carry out this service, in view of the mainly military character of the *ephebeia* at this period; while the reference to 'boys' (a flexible term) rather than ephebes would have been determined simply by diplomatic considerations. If this interpretation is accepted, then Derkylos' gesture was much more patriotic and political than charitable in motivation.[147]

The number of people who could hope to benefit from the more advanced teaching which came to be available in the gymnasia must therefore have been very limited, even though in theory it was open to all equally. Peripatetic scholars in particular might give occasional lectures open to all, perhaps mainly to establish their reputation. Such a scholar was Epikrates, son of Demetrios (D. 53) who received public commendation and Samian citizenship, having remained at Samos for a considerable time, during which he not only served the needs of private individuals, but was well known for his generosity towards the people, 'in that for those of the common people who could not pay his normal fee he gave his time at no charge'.[148]

Epikrates belonged to a class of men of learning who did normally charge a fee. But some of the most famous schools of Greek philosophy followed the Socratic view that a fee should not be demanded by those whose function was conceived to be that merely of calling forth the knowledge of the truth already buried deep within the mind of the 'pupil', so that it was here above all that education at the highest level was offered without regard to material advantage. The schools of philosophy created by Plato and Aristotle, and later by Epicurus and others, were organized as religious brotherhoods, worshipping at the altar of the Muses (so, too, avoiding undue suspicion of being illegal political organizations), and offered no more to their founders than those honours which were felt appropriate to any founder, honours carrying the hope of 'immortality'. It was the spirit of free learning which Socrates, Plato and (more doubtfully) Aristotle established, rather than a school in the physical sense, for their teaching began in public gymnasia, the Academy and the Lyceum—though Plato eventually established, close to the Academy, his own school, with a sanctuary of the Muses and a lecture room, which bore the same name. But the will of Epicurus (D. 59), for instance, may be quoted to illustrate how the actual material possessions, as as well as the teaching, of such philosophers might become the common property of those who shared in the pursuit of truth: 'I give all my property to Amynomachos, son of Philokrates, of Bate, and to Timokrates, son of Demetrios, of Potamos . . . on condition that they shall make available the garden and its appurtenances to Hermarchos, son of Agemortos, of Mytilene, and to his fellow-philosophers and to whomsoever Hermarchos leaves it as his successors, to live and pursue philosophy therein; and I entrust the school in the garden in perpetuity to those who are its members, so that they may preserve it to the best of their ability, together with Amynomachos and Timokrates, and to their successors.' The will goes on to provide for those offerings and celebrations of a quasi-religious kind already noticed. Thus, Epicurus used for the perpetuation of his objective the same method that was followed by so many others for more mundane object-tives; and for some six hundred years the provisions were largely effective, though they passed through some perilous days, described in one of Cicero's letters, in the first century BC. The will of Theophrastus (D. 60), who took over the presidency of Aristotle's Lyceum, is very similar in style and spirit. Thus, the philosophic schools were the nearest pagan equivalent to those early Christian communities which held everything in common, while pursuing a different kind of truth. But inevitably it was mainly men of considerable means who shared in these brother-hoods; it is no coincidence that the earlier among them retained a distinctly aristocratic character in a period when the claims of aristocracy were passing out of favour.[149]

At Rome Polybius was amazed to find in the middle of the second century BC that even higher education was left in the hands of parents. There can then be little doubt that the same was true for the earlier stages of education—and so it remained for the most part, even under the Empire. Here, too, therefore, the low fees payable to elementary schoolmasters must provide the main basis for any claim that most children went to school. By the time of Pliny the Younger, at the end of the first century AD, we learn that in many places '*praeceptores publice conducuntur*', a fact which Pliny used in attempting to persuade parents at Comum to subscribe towards a similar arrangement there (D. 51). He also offered an incentive of a kind not uncommon in charitable appeals today, namely that he would add a third to whatever the parents thought fit to contribute, though he himself had no children. We need not doubt the sincerity of his assertion that he would have been willing to meet the total cost, were it not for the consideration that 'those who are perhaps irresponsible in handling the money of others will at least be careful with their own' (compare with D. 48). In a way Pliny's offer parallels that of Eudemos and Polythrous, yet the whole drift of the relevant letter makes it clear that it was parents of some means whom he was helping; for at the time of the offer these parents were educating their children in Milan, so involving themselves in both accommodation and travel expenses in addition to those for tuition, and Pliny's main argument is that it was more economical, as well as more in keeping with local municipal pride (an important factor in the acquisition of municipal amenities of any kind) that Comum should have a school of its own to which these children could go. There is nothing to indicate that it was intended that parents who failed to contribute would be allowed to send their children, supposing that they could meet the incidental expenses. Even if this was Pliny's intention, he clearly did not think that its declaration would serve as an incentive to those invited to subscribe. We may suspect that the same would be true of those other towns at which 'teachers were employed on a public basis'.[150]

For young men *collegia iuvenum* came into being in Italy and the Latin-speaking provinces, bearing a resemblance to the ephebeia, or perhaps to the clubs of *neoi*, in the Greek world, and, like them, attracting private benevolence. But, from the time of the earliest inscriptions relating to them, the *collegia* seem to have been 'fashionable clubs for the aristocracy where gilded youths could

learn how to live properly and how to enjoy their brand of sport'
—which, in view of the Roman aristocrats' distaste for the
athletic activities of the Greek gymnasia, meant that of the circus
or the amphitheatre rather than of the stadium. There is some
evidence of the admission of freedmen, and even of slaves; but
they had to be rich.[151]

Public funds to support higher education came to be given
under the Empire indirectly through an edict of Vespasian in AD
74, whereby doctors and teachers (but not primary teachers) were
granted exemptions from taxation. This encouraged the setting up
of secondary schools which, Ulpian implies, were to be found in
every village of the Empire in the second century. But it was only
at the highest level of learning and only at Rome that the Emperor
Vespasian provided direct support, by establishing two chairs, one
for Latin and one for Greek rhetoric, out of public funds—a step
which was followed up about a century later by Marcus Aurelius,
who established four chairs of philosophy at Athens. Clearly this
must have been of advantage to the sons of parents of modest
means, though scarcely to those who had never been able to
afford more than the rudiments of education. The same might be
said of the municipal libraries established through the generosity
of various benefactors, among whom again the younger Pliny is to
be numbered (D. 36). More famous, however, was the library
established by Tiberius Julius Celsus Polemacanus and his son at
Ephesus, later in the same century.[152]

Had there been any criticism of a situation in which private
and public funds were so largely directed to the advantage of the
wealthier element of society, it would have probably been met
along lines indicated by Plato—that these privileged few were
being trained for the task of administering (normally without pay)
the affairs of their city. Some have held that this was Plato's main
objective in establishing his Academy, and certainly the associations of ephebes and *neoi* modelled their organizations on the city-
state, with parallel magistracies and treasury. The considerable
element of self-interest on the part of those who subscribed
towards such an objective is not, of course, to be denied, en-
hancing as it did the claim of the sons of the upper class to inherit

I

their fathers' social status. But neither can we deny the benefactors' general conviction that in so doing they were providing their city with a governing class which would exercise control in accordance with certain standards of honesty and efficiency by which every class could benefit—a conviction which could be compared with that behind much of the 'charity' devoted to the advancement of education in England; Owen found it 'almost impossible to isolate the philanthropic component in the English school structure'.[153]

Nor should we regard as foreign to the thought of all but a Plato (or a Pericles) the consideration that the very environment of the *polis* might provide the ordinary citizen with a kind of informal education. Thus, it might be held that the poorer element in many a Greek city benefited more from the expenditure of those who (like Kritolaos and Parmenion at Amorgos—D. 23) accepted the public burden of staging the plays at dramatic festivals, than they could have done from the application of the same expenditure to formal education. Similarly, as the people (of Athens, especially) moved among great works of architecture and sculpture reflecting the 'love of glory' of the wealthy, they might have found, in Plato's words, that 'all the works of art they see influence them for good, like breezes from some healthy climate'. In so far as this was true, it is undeniable that the Greeks in particular were concerned in some sense with education for all.[154]

CHAPTER IX

HEALTH AND HYGIENE

THE EXTENT TO WHICH individual physicians of the classical world saw fit to tend the sick, and the state to provide general medical care, regardless of a patient's ability to pay a fee, is a possible measure of the extent to which we might expect to find evidence of pity or altruism in other spheres. The ethics of Greek medicine, as expressed in the *Maxims* of Hippocrates, parts of which may not post-date the lifetime of the famous doctor of that name by much more than a century, do not, however, venture significantly beyond the familiar terms of more general ethical writings. Accordingly rather than any emphasis on money as of *no* importance compared with the patient's need, we have the familiar suggestion that it is of *secondary* importance as compared with honour: 'the quickness of the disease . . . spurs on the good doctor not to seek his profit, but rather to lay hold on reputation', and when the maxim continues with the practical point that 'it is better to reproach a patient after you have saved him rather than extort money from those who are at death's door', it appears that the patient envisaged is not entirely without means of eventually making a material return. Another maxim, typically Hellenistic in expression, urges the doctor to avoid undue *apanthropia* (the negation of 'philanthropy') and to take into account the resources of the patient, and sometimes to be ready to give treatment without a fee. But this, too, is diluted by an apparent reference (the text is uncertain) to the 'memory of a former favour received or of present approval', leading us to wonder whether we are to take in an unqualified sense the following precept, that 'if the chance arises to serve a stranger who is without means [*aporein*] you should make a special point of giving treatment to such, since where *philanthropia* is to be seen there also is *philotechnia*, devotion to one's art'. How absolutely 'without means' is that stranger?

And others belonged to the empiric school of medicine, whose practitioners held less 'philanthropic' views, explicitly naming the making of money as their prime objective.[155]

Doctors did, indeed, commonly regard themselves as worshippers of the god of medicine, Asklepios, who was certainly a god of much greater gentleness than the Olympian deities—so much so that he was apparently singled out by Christian apologists as a more serious rival than the Olympians to the Christian God. Aristophanes might make Chremylus speak satirically of the 'patriotism and wisdom' of the god in causing Wealth (in the play of that name) to see; but centuries later, in the face of Christian claims, the Emperor Julian was to contend that Asklepios did not 'heal men with hope of a reward but everywhere gratifies his own loving concern (*philanthropeuma*) for mankind'. Bolkestein read into this, in conjunction with another passage from the same source, the provision of free medical treatment at his temples. There seems little or no evidence, however, to justify such a view or, indeed, a belief in any actual *medical* attention at these temples before at least the second century AD; and Edelstein concluded that there was no religious organization, any more than a moral or professional code, which obliged doctors to give their service freely to the poor. At most, it seems, the outbuildings or hostels attached to some of his sanctuaries were open to poor and rich alike, for accommodation, while they waited in hope of a cure of a non-medical kind. In this way they provided some precedent for the Christian hospital—which, as the name suggests, was for long a refuge for the poor and infirm, for travellers and unfortunates, 'an ecclesiastical, not a medical, institution'—especially where the Church took over these hostels together with the pagan temples themselves for its own purposes.[156]

Inscriptions, however, make it quite clear that for the sake of 'honour' not a few doctors were ready, as Hippocrates urged, to regard money as of secondary importance. Such was Menokritos of Samos (D. 67), who 'had saved many of the townsfolk of Brycous [Carpathus] when they were in a critical condition, accepting no fee, and continuing to display a proper sense of devotion in his attendance upon each of the residents in the suburbs of the city'. The doctor of Gytheion (D. 68), who was praised for 'being fair to all alike, both rich and poor, both slaves and free', presumably scaled his charges in accordance with the means of his clients, or made himself equally available to all at moderate cost, as did Xenotimos at Cos (D. 63), who accorded special favour to no one, but 'saved mens' lives by his ready service of all equally'. Diodoros (D. 65), who won a testimonial for service at Samos over many years, also followed a Hippocratic maxim, when he gave treatment not only to the Samians but to certain judges who had come to Samos and fallen ill, displaying an 'uncomplaining readiness to help all alike'. The same doctor is also commended for his exceptional services at a time of emergency following an earthquake, when again he did not discriminate between those in need. At Gortyn in Crete, Hermias of Cos (D. 64) also extended his services, after attending to those whom he had been called to serve, to many allies in time of war, 'displaying the same care for them and saving them from great dangers'. Inevitably they had their rewards of honour; these included such titles as *proxenos* and *euergetes*, the vote of a golden crown, and (more important, materially) the right to possess land and a house in the city of their residence, and even, in the case of Hermias, citizenship which was to be inherited by his descendants.

So far we have concerned ourselves with the actions of doctors acting in a private capacity, and it was as such that Menokritos, for instance, had foregone his fee in attending to the needs of people of Brycous resident at Rhodes. But the same inscription tells us that Menokritos thereafter became a doctor in public service (*iatros dēmosieuōn*), a position which he held for twenty years, and the recurrence of this title in a number of cities has led to the widespread view that the state came to appoint doctors who were contractually obliged to give free medical attention to all who might require it, the free gifts or service of individuals having led in this sphere, as in others, to free provision by the state.[157]

The evidence, however, as to any such obligation on the part of doctors bearing this title—or of doctors who were called to service in a particular city by a public decision, whatever their official title—to give treatment without charge is, at best, not very strong, as has been argued by Cohn-Haft in a recent monograph. It depends largely upon the testimony of a scholiast to a line from Aristophanes' play, the *Acharnians*, in which a farmer, who has 'cried his eyes out' over two oxen, says to Dikaiopolis: 'Come! ointment for my eyes! Set me at peace without delay', only to meet with the reply: 'But, you wretch, I am not acting as a man in public service [*demosieuon*].'

In explanation of this the scholiast informs us that 'the doctors chosen by the people to be public doctors, provided medical care at no charge'. What Dikaiopolis means, then, according to the scholiast, is that he is not going to supply the farmer with ointment for nothing. But is the scholiast right with regard to fifth-century Athens, or even to the practice of the Hellenistic period? Or is he reflecting institutions of his own day, perhaps no earlier than the fifth century AD?[158]

Another piece of literary evidence derives from Diodorus, who tells us that Charondas of Catana 'went beyond previous legislators who had provided that the sick among private citizens should be treated by doctors at public expense' when he made provision for elementary education for the sons of all citizens. Unfortunately this is the passage the latter part of which we have already felt it necessary to question. Can we trust the earlier part of it either, whether for the existence of such a medical service in Charondas' day or in that of Diodorus?[159]

Both these questions receive a negative answer from Cohn-Haft, who argues largely from the evidence of inscriptions. But he does not perhaps prove as much as he wishes by his argument that, because there is no confirmation, even in Hellenistic inscriptions, of Diodorus' suggestion of the allocation of public funds for education, we may suppose his reference to medical treatment at public expense to be equally out of touch with reality. For although Cohn-Haft may be right in regarding the Teos inscription, for instance, as evidence merely of the public administration of private endowments, rather than of a state-supported system of education, in practice this may have been largely a distinction without a difference. As we have seen, many of the city funds providing cheap or free corn probably derived originally, not from the revenue of direct taxation imposed specifically to meet the cost of such distributions, but from private endowments or subscriptions, and to that extent they also might be regarded as not wholly 'public' in character. It is by no means inconceivable that some cities had received gifts from private individuals with the request that they should be used to provide free medical care for all citizens, and, if that were so, these funds could be regarded as no less, if no more, public, than the others.

It is true, however, that as far as the inscriptions go, most of those which use the word 'freely' or 'as a gift' in relation to the activities of doctors *demosieuontes* can be interpreted as implying that these doctors forewent their salary rather than that they gave free medical attention. And where, rarely, the free provision of medical attention *is* clearly intended (the most certain case seems to relate to a veterinary doctor), we are faced with the simple logic that this free service must be the *outstanding and unusual action* which called forth the honorary decree, not something which was true of every doctor who bore the title. On the orthodox view, therefore, it is argued that the mention of free service in such decree is completely superfluous: 'the physician is being praised for having done simply what he was hired to do'.[160]

Even this argument is not as strong as might appear at first sight, in view of the fact, already noticed, that the honorary decree was the almost inevitable result of *any* public service, even though the honorand had done no more than it was his duty to do. Take, for instance, the many decrees in honour of ephebes for diligent attention to their training, or the decree passed in praise of a fourth-century Athenian councillor because he had shown himself 'not given to the acceptance of bribes' during his term of office (it was presumably not intended to imply that the latter had gone beyond the call of duty). Yet, there is, admittedly, a distinction between these cases and the *demosieuontes*, for the former had been providing unpaid services as citizens, while the latter seem normally to have been non-citizens and in receipt of pay.[161]

It is, in fact, the normal (though not invariable) foreign origin of the *demosieuon* which leads Cohn-Haft to his suggestion as to the significance of the appointment in many cities of doctors with this title; for this is taken to indicate that the skilled practitioner was something of a rarity in the Greek world and not readily available, so that the smaller Greek cities sought to guarantee the presence of at least one in their community by offering a public salary: 'that the town had a public doctor meant simply this: a doctor was available'. On this view, the salary was merely a retainer, and did not preclude its recipient from charging fees as well; and we may recognize that in some of the poorer and more remote cities a doctor might well find that, not merely his limited number of remedies, but the unreadiness of the sick—except in desperate need—to pay any fee, made it almost impossible for him to make a decent living, apart from the assurance of a basic minimum. The Greek physician, commonly trained at the medical school of Cos, was necessarily a man of some culture and social standing; he would not (it is reasonable to think) expect to live from hand to mouth, dependent on nothing but fees. Indeed, it could be that there was not simply an absolute shortage of skilled practitioners but a shortage of cities in which the latter could hope to make the kind of living which they felt was their due.[162]

If the title *demosieuon* implied a doctor receiving a retainer in smaller cities, did it mean the same thing in cities such as Athens and Cos as well? Cos, so far from being short of doctors, supplied them to other cities on request, while at Athens a passage in Plato's *Gorgias* may indicate that the people were able to choose between the claims of rival doctors, instead of simply requesting the Coans (as did the people of Gortyn in Crete, for instance) to send a doctor of their own choice. At Athens and Cos, therefore, it is suggested, the title indicated a 'doctor whose professional qualifications are publicly endorsed', without implying the payment of a retainer. Yet, if the payment of retainers is admitted for the smaller cities, it might be thought that the Athenians too would find it advisable to offer a similar financial inducement, if they wished to obtain the *best* doctors available. Thus, any degree of competition for appointment at Athens, in contrast with the lack of it at Gortyn, could be accounted for, if not simply by a higher retainer, then by the greater prestige which a doctor who had been appointed by the Athenians would almost certainly enjoy. Such an appointment might open up the way (if a famous story of the late sixth-century Demokedes of Croton is anything to go by) for a claim to higher fees at the next city to which he went, whether or not in the capacity of *demosieuon*.[163]

As to the nature of any payments by patients which such doctors may have received, Cohn-Haft perhaps discounts too readily the suggestion that these may have been regarded officially as gifts rather than fees. Indeed, in view of the social and cultural standing of the skilled physician, we may reasonably wonder whether the retainer itself would not have been politely styled as *philanthropon*, the term used for at least some of the rewards secured for publicly maintained teachers by Straton of Pergamum (D. 54). Particularly when such doctors came to attend to citizens of similar standing to themselves it would be entirely in keeping with what we have said of relationships within their class for the reward for their service to be offered (and expected) as a 'gift' rather than demanded as a fee. And since it would be upon upper-class patients that the financial success of his period in residence would largely depend, a doctor may have found it prudent to waive any payment which the 'poor' could afford, particularly in a city in which the appointment of the *demosieuon* depended on a popular vote. It is perhaps as likely as not that a polite silence was maintained as to whether the *demosieuon* might *contractually* demand a fee. If he could, then the humane doctor would have been the one who did not assign priority to his patients acording to the amount they were likely to be able to pay. By this test, if by no higher, doctors such as Damiadas of Sparta are credited with a proper sense of humanity —and if it is the humanity of a man *sōphrōn kai pepaideumenos* (as the inscription has it), more suggestive of the prudence necessary for the man who wished to be socially accepted than of any deep emotional feeling, it may be that the ascription of the less common *philostorgia* (rather than the conventional *eunoia*) with which it is linked, is meant to redress the balance.[164]

At Athens the hypothesis of free medical attention available to all would be in line with the provision made for the physically lame and incapable, whose property assessment was less than three *minae*. Such cripples received an allowance of two obols a day by the mid-fourth century (apparently only one obol at an earlier date). Our literary sources are not agreed as to whether the payment was introduced by Solon early in the sixth century, or by Peisistratus a generation later; while among modern scholars, Jacoby would regard it as one of the social measures of the radical democracy under Pericles, designed originally for those disabled by war, but extended almost immediately to all in this condition. But the point of particular interest here is the application of a 'means test', not found in other areas of private or public beneficence. If fees were payable to public doctors, there may be grounds for a belief in some similar arrangement with regard to medical attention for the poorer class, as well.[165]

Whatever the answer to this question, a well-known passage in Plato's *Republic* makes quite clear that for the ordinary Athenian of the early fourth century any lengthy cure was out of the question. 'When the carpenter is ill', we are told, 'he expects his doctor to give him medicine which will expel the disease by vomiting or purging, or to cauterize or cut the wound and set him right. If anyone prescribes him a long course of treatment . . . he says at once that he has not time to be ill and that it does not pay him to live like that, giving all his attention to his illness and neglecting his proper work. With this he bids his doctor good-day and goes back to his ordinary way of life, regains his health and lives on doing his work, or if his body is not strong enough to carry him through, he dies and is released from his troubles.' And Socrates approves of this state of affairs; he challenges only the common assumption that another standard applies in the case of the wealthy man who can afford to 'live, in the sense of pro-tracting his physical existence, through continual medical atten-tion; for unless the latter too can do his job (which meant, for Socrates, the practice of *aretē*: that sort of activity which promotes the good life both for state and individual), then he too should not be encouraged to 'live like that'. The whole question, like that of rearing deformed or surplus children, is seen mainly as a social rather than personal question; and to Asklepios, the god of healing himself, is attributed the view that 'it was not right to treat a man who could not live in his ordinary round of duties, such a man being useless to himself and to the state'.[166]

The view that a system of free public medicine was widespread has also been based to some extent on references in Greek documents of the Hellenistic period to a tax known as the *iatrikon*. These documents, however, are very narrowly distributed in time and space, most being Egyptian papyri of the third and early second century BC though three come from the Aegean area, Cos, Teos and Delos. It is difficult to give an entirely consistent explanation of all of them, but the balance of likelihood is that in Egypt this was a tax introduced by the Ptolemies, payable (normally in produce rather than money) only by Greek settlers in the Egyptian *chora*, which entitled them alone to 'free' treatment. No *necessary* connection with the 'doctors in public service' of our other documents can be posited.[167]

It is from Egyptian papyri, too, that we have a score of references to *demosioi iatroi*, ranging over a period from the late first century AD to the middle of the fifth century. But the failure to overlap with references to the *iatrikon* tax is noteworthy. The *demosioi iatroi* have been equated with *iatroi demosieuontes*, and the latter, again, with doctors bearing the title of *archiatroi* who are found both in the western and eastern parts of the Roman Empire by the second century AD, suggesting that a system of free public medicine became still more widespread in Roman times. The identifications on which the doctrine rests, however, are open to challenge, and it is to be observed that the documents (though they may, of course, be unrepresentative) seem mainly to relate to matters of forensic medicine—there is reference to violence in every document except one—where doctors or medical officers have been called upon to attest to such matters as a person's death or the illness of an employee. Indeed, it has been argued that the doctor was only a secondary figure in many cases, the expert called in by a superior civil servant for a particular purpose. Moreover, in the cases where the doctor does seem to be the chief figure involved, another possibility arises, namely that since these cases all fall after AD 173—shortly after the date at which Antoninus Pius introduced a limitation on the number of doctors within a municipality who could enjoy immunity from public obligations—the title was used to distinguish the privileged doctor from the unprivileged.[168]

In view of these various uncertainties it would be bold to assert categorically that the Greek world under Rome made any more progress towards a free public medical service than had independent Greek cities. The Romans themselves took over most of their medical ideas and practice from the Greeks, and it is perhaps indicative of a comparative lack of sensitivity towards the pain of others that, as Pliny the Elder tells us, the medical art was the last of the arts to be adopted by the Romans from the Greeks, Rome for long relying on Greek slaves and freedmen for her doctors. Although a really skilled physician needed to possess a considerable degree of culture and social standing, the Roman upper class apparently long felt that it was undignified for such a person, even in the practice of medicine, to be under any contractual obligation to serve the needs of another. Perhaps consistently with such an attitude, even under the Empire medicine was given rather indirect support through the offer of fiscal immunity to doctors, first by Vespasian and then on a larger scale by Hadrian. This may have been intended to carry with it a moral (rather than contractual) obligation in the interests of those who might not be able to afford a doctor's fee. But it was only with the reign of Antoninus Pius (in AD 161), as far as we know, in association with the restriction of the numbers of such privileged doctors in each municipality according to its size, that the enjoyment of the privilege was made to depend *inter alia* upon the doctors' performance of his duties with diligence. These duties, however, are unfortunately not defined in our sources, though it has commonly been assumed that free treatment of the poor was expected, on the analogy of the earlier practice supposed in Greek cities. The same principle is inherent in Libanius' declaration in the fourth century that 'the law demands of the doctors a single public obligation (*liturgy*), namely that which arises from their craft'. But that this did not mean that they were in fact equally at the service of poor and rich is suggested by one of the provisions introduced by Valentinian I for the *archiatri* of Rome, that they were 'honestly to attend to the poor rather than basely to serve the rich'. But within our chosen period there is no firm evidence of any *legal* obligation upon the doctor so to act, and since the 'public doctors' appointed under the Empire must have depended everywhere for their appointment upon the municipal councils rather than upon a popular assembly (just as it was upon enrolment by a decree of the council that a doctor depended, under Pius' ruling, for exemption from taxation), it would be the upper class which determined how far such doctors had lived up to their obligations and interpreted their nature.[169]

Still less can we suppose that the poorer classes would normally benefit from the development of hospitals (no longer merely hostels to receive the sick) under the later Empire. In agreement with the Roman's practical instinct, we learn of these first in connexion especially with provision for the sick and wounded of the legions, but *valetudinaria* and *sanatoria* spread to the households of the wealthy and to the imperial court. In the wealthy household indeed, medical care might on occasion be made available to the humbler members, judging by the generous concern of men like Cicero and Pliny for the well-being of their slaves or freedmen, or even to those of the household of an *amicus*, but scarcely in any case where no such personal relationship was involved.[170]

Perhaps more important to the health of the lower class than theoretically available public doctors, however, were institutions such as the gymnasia and the large public baths, and the aqueducts supplying the latter as well as the city as a whole. All acted as preventive measures against disease by encouraging exercise and cleanliness, so that in this context the view of Carnegie has been aptly quoted that 'the best means of benefiting the community is to place within its reach the ladders upon which the aspiring can rise—free libraries, parks and means of recreation; works of art . . . and public institutions of various kinds which will improve the condition of the people'. Clearly the baths and gymnasia were such institutions. The physical recreation offered by the latter was at least effectively open to a far greater proportion of the population of cities than the intellectual education could have been, and those who gave free supplies of oil for use in the gymnasia, whether as gymnasiarchs or as private individuals, were making available a commodity which was regarded almost as vital as corn itself. As in the case of corn, occasional gifts, or gifts in association with magistracies, gave rise to foundations assuring a permanent free supply. At Eretria, a certain Theopompos gave 40,000 *drachmae*, the interest on which was to be devoted to this purpose, so 'lightening the burden of the people' (D. 69). Across the Aegean, in Asia Minor, Attalus of Aphrodisias, a man of princely wealth, among many benefactions left a fund that 'the citizens might have no lack of oil for anointing, and that men might be found more easily to serve as official oil-purchasers'; and at Cibyra, Q. Veranius Philagrus permanently provided for the expenses of the gymnasiarchy (of which a free supply of oil was the chief), after holding twelve gymnasiarchies in his lifetime, with a fund of 400,000 Rhodian *drachmae*.[171] It has been argued, from the lack of archaeological evidence of oil-reservoirs in the buildings of the gymnasia, that until the beginning of our era it was normal for each person to bring his own supply, for which he would presumably have paid himself. If that was so, the poorest may until then in practice have been largely excluded from the gymnasia—a fact possibly reflected in an inscription from Priene which refers to the gymnasiarch Dioskurides 'making the place available even to those who, through evil fortune, were not sharing in it', though we may suspect that the reference is to men suffering from comparatively recent 'evil fortune'. Those, then who had in practice been excluded for so long would scarcely be expected suddenly to appear when supplies of oil were eventually made available to 'all'. And for many, lack of leisure would be the decisive factor: not all could be available at the hour fixed for distribution, as was recognized by one benefactor, Zosimos of Priene, who made arrangements to supply oil 'throughout the day, from sunrise to sunset', as well as other facilities, to those 'who were being prevented by the fixed hours laid down by the law'. To some distributions slaves as well as resident aliens came to be admitted in Hellenistic times, as under the terms of the donation of Phainia Aromation (though only on specified days) at Gytheion (D. 71), while at Dorylaeum in Phrygia we have evidence of a 'gymnasiarch for slaves and free'.

But this should not necessarily be taken as indicating a very wide enjoyment by slaves of the facilities of the gymnasia. It is at least in part another indication of the decline in the social status of the free, in part an application of the advice given long since by Aristotle, that masters of slaves should give to their slaves a training according to the purpose which they had in mind for them, on which basis, indeed, they might occasionally enjoy also the intellectual opportunities offered by the gymnasia.[172]

The gymnasia commonly had baths attached to them, which sometimes received the specific attention of benefactors, such as L. Vaccius Leo at Cyme in Asia Minor (another benefactor of Roman origin), in the early years of our era (D. 55 refers to an earlier example). But it was the Romans, who were little attracted to the traditional Greek gymnastic programme, who developed baths on a large scale in the Empire period. They also did this largely through the gifts of the wealthy. Among the latter were Gaius Torasius Severus of Spoletium (D. 35) and Pliny the Younger, and L. Aemilius Daphnus (D. 78) in southern Spain who involved themselves in very considerable expenditure. To provide free access to the baths, others gave sums for a limited period, or through permanent foundations. Well known among these is Augustus' right-hand man, M. Agrippa, as *aedile* in 33 BC at Rome; his example was followed by T. Aviasius Servandus at Bononia (D. 76), who made provision in perpetuity and specified that both sexes should be included, and by C. Aurunceius Cotta at Praeneste (D. 75), who included all temporary and permanent non-citizen residents and their slaves as well. At Novaria a woman benefactor provided both the baths themselves and free access, while others were far-sighted enough to provide for the upkeep of the baths, as did Pliny, or for the heating, as did Satyros of Tenos (D. 37), or for both, as did a generous donor at Altinum (D. 77). At the baths, as at the gymnasia, oil was also needed, and another donor at Comum (who has sometimes been identified with the father of Pliny the Younger) established a foundation for an annual distribution of oil in the local baths, as did others at Theveste and Gor in North Africa (D. 72, 73). In the latter province the town of Timgad may be quoted as evidence of the extent to which in some towns the baths must have been frequented, for there are traces of no less than twelve separate bathing establishments for a population of some fifteen thousand inhabitants. Inscriptions, if representative, suggest that some twelve per cent of the expenditure of benefactors for building projects in Rome's western provinces was devoted to baths. With regard to Rome herself it has been said that 'the emperors put personal hygiene on the daily agenda and within reach of the humblest; and the fabulous decoration lavished on the baths made the exercise and care of the body a pleasure for all, a refreshment accessible even to the very poor.' As such, the baths brought immense benefit to the people. It is of some interest to compare the situation in nineteenth-century England, when it was found prudent, in view of the lack of sanitary facilities in the cities, to set up a committee to provide baths and washhouses, with the result that in London the bathhouses 'were credited with the awesome total of two million baths a year'. This was essentially a method of meeting a parallel need at the individual rather than at the social level, and adopted very late in the day—long after that period when, because of the less salubrious aspect of the baths of classical times (hinted at in an inscription which refers to them as being 'essential not only for high living but for health and hygiene') the unwashed state could be equated with godliness! Yet, the more mundane needs were by no means totally neglected by classical benefactors, as indicated by an inscription relating, it seems, to the *destercoratio* (cleansing) of the public latrines, for which a Spanish benefactor provided a sum of money—following, on a smaller scale, the example of M. Agrippa at Rome, who during his *aedileship* had also met the expense of great improvements in the city's sewage system.[173]

To provide a town with its water supply could be a still more expensive gift. A donor at Aspendos in Asia Minor (D. 81) gave eight million sesterces to this end, while Tiberius Claudius Atticus, father of the famous Herodes Atticus of the mid-second century AD, did not limit his generosity to Athens but supplemented the cost of building an aqueduct at Troy (D. 80) to the tune of sixteen million sesterces. Such expenditure only the very wealthiest could afford, though at other towns more modest schemes were possible, as at Verona, where a donor provided some 600,000 sesterces. While such expenditure would undoubtedly display the magnanimity (in its true classical sense) of the donors, it also served the community by providing it with an amenity from which the poor might derive equal, or almost equal, benefit along with the rich. Probably most parts of the classical world, as men like the Emperor Antoninus Pius recognised, would have been better served by more benefactions of this type and less of those concerned with the 'largely frivolous provision of annual feasts and cash distributions, and a group of purely self-regarding foundations for rites in the memory of the donor'. But we already know something of why the latter retained their prominence.[174]

K

NOTES

BIBLIOGRAPHICAL ABBREVIATIONS

The following abbreviations will be used for references to books, periodicals and collections of inscriptions after the first (which will always be quoted in full):

A. Ant. Hung.	Acta Antiqua Academiae Scientiarium Hungaricae
Abbott and Johnson, MARE	F. F. Abbott and A. C. Johnson, Municipal Administration in the Roman Empire (1926)
ABSA	Annual of the British School at Athens
Adkins, MR	A. W. H. Adkins, Merit and Responsibility (1960)
AE	L'Année Epigraphique
AHR	American Historical Review
AJA	American Journal of Archaeology
AJPh.	American Journal of Philology
BCH	Bulletin de Correspondence Hellénique
Berchem, DBA	D. van Berchem, Les distributions de blé et d'argent à la plèbe romaine sous l'Empire (1939)
BMC, Imp.	H. Mattingly, ed., Coins of the Roman Empire in the British Museum (1923–)
Bolkestein	H. Bolkestein, Wohltätigkeit und Armenpflege in vorchristlichen Altertum (1939)
Broughton, MRR	T. R. S. Broughton, The Magistrates of the Roman Republic
Bruck, FM	E. F. Bruck, 'Les facteurs moteurs de l'origine et du développement des fondations grecques et romaines', RIDA, 1955, 159ff
Bruck, STR	E. F. Bruck, Der Stiftung für die Toten in Recht, Religion und politischen Denken der Römer (1954)
Bruck, TS	E. F. Bruck, Totenteil und Seelgerät (1926)
Bruns	C. G. Bruns et. al., Fontes Iuris Romani Antiqui, 7th edition (1909)
Buchanan, Theorika	J. J. Buchanan, Theorika: A Study of Monetary Distributions to the Athenian Citizenry during the

	Fifth and Fourth Centuries BC (1962)
CAH	*The Cambridge Ancient History*
Carcopino, *DLAR*	J. Carcopino, *Daily Life in Ancient Rome*, transl. E. O. Lorimer (1941)
CIL	*Corpus Inscriptionum Latinarum*
Cohn-Haft, *PPAG*	L. Cohn-Haft, *The Public Physicians of Ancient Greece* (1956)
CR	*Classical Review*
Crook, *LLR*	J. A. Crook, *Law and Life of Rome* (1967)
CSSH	*Comparative Studies in Society and History*
Day, *EHA*	John Day, *An Economic History of Athens under Roman Domination* (1942)
Delorme, *Gymnasium*	J. Delorme, *Gymnasium: Étude sur les monuments consacrées à l'éducation en Grèce* (1960)
Dessau	H. Dessau, ed., *Inscriptiones Latinae Selectae*
Dittenberger	W. Dittenberger, *Sylloge Inscriptionum Graecarum*, 3rd edition (1915–24)
Edmonds, *FAC*	J. M. Edmonds, *The Fragments of Attic Comedy* (1957–61)
Ehrenberg, *PA*	V. Ehrenberg, *The People of Aristophanes* (1951)
Francotte, *MN*	H. Francotte, 'Le pain à bon marché et le pain gratuit dans les cités grecques', *Mélanges Nicoles*, 1905, 135–57
Frank, *ESAR*	T. Frank, ed., *Economic Survey of Ancient Rome* (1933–40)
French, *GAE*	A. French, *The Growth of the Athenian Economy* (1964)
Gernet	L. Gernet, 'Droit et prédroit en Grèce ancienne', *L'Année sociologique* 1948–9
IBM	*Greek Inscriptions in the British Museum*
I. Cret.	M. Guarducci, ed., *Inscriptiones Creticae* (1935–50)
IG	*Inscriptiones Graecae*
IGRP	R. Cagnat *et al.*, *Inscriptiones Graecae ad Res Romanas pertinentes*, (1911–27)
IL Alg.	S. Gsell, ed., *Inscriptions latines de l' Algérie*, I (1922), II (1957)
Inschr. von Priene	Hiller von Gaertringen, *Inschriften von Priene* (1906)
IRT	J. M. Reynolds and J. B. Ward Perkins, ed., *The Inscriptions of Roman Tripolitania* (1952)
Jacoby, *FGH*	F. Jacoby, *Die Fragmente der Griechischen Historiker* (1923–)
JHS	*Journal of Hellenic Studies*

JOAI	*Jahreshefte des oesterreichischen archaeologischen Instituts in Wien*
Jones, *AD*	A. H. M. Jones, *Athenian Democracy* (1957)
Jones, *GC*	A. H. M. Jones, *The Greek City from Alexander to Justinian* (1940)
Jordan, *PE*	W. K. Jordan, *Philanthropy in England, 1480–1660* (1959)
JRS	*Journal of Roman Studies*
Kabiersch, *BPJ*	J. Kabiersch, *Untersuchungen zum Begriff der Philanthropia bei dem Kaiser Julian* (1960)
Laum	B. Laum, *Stiftungen in der griechischen und römischen Antike* (1914)
Le Bras, *SR*	G. Le Bras, 'Les fondations privées du haut empire', *Studi Riccobono III* (1936), 23ff
Lewis and Reinhold, *RC II*	N. Lewis and M. Reinhold, *Roman Civilization*, vol. II (1955)
Magie, *RRAM*	D. Magie, *Roman Rule in Asia Minor* (1950)
MAMA	*Monumenta Asiae Minoris Antiqua*
Marrou, *HEA*	H. I. Marrou, *History of Education in Antiquity*, transl. G. Lamb (1956)
MDAI (A)	*Mitteilungen des Deutschen Archäologischen Instituts (athenische Abt.)*
Michel, *GDR*	J. Michel, *Gratuité en Droit romain* (1962)
Nathan, *CA*	Lord Nathan, *The Charities Act, 1960* (1962)
Not. Scav.	*Notizie degli Scavi di Antichità*
OGIS	W. Dittenberger, ed., *Orientis Graeci Inscriptiones Selectae* (1903–5)
Owen, *EP*	D. E. Owen, *English Philanthropy, 1660–1960* (1965)
PBSR	*Papers of the British School at Rome*
Pélékidis, *Histoire*	C. Pélékidis, *Histoire de l'éphébie attique des origines à 31 av. J. C.* (1962)
Plassman, *AJC*	Otto Plassman, *Das Almosen bei Johannes Chrysostomus* (1961)
Pöhlmann, *GSF*	R. von Pöhlmann, *Geschichte der sozialen Frage und des Sozialismus in der antiken Welt* (1925)
Pouilloux, *Choix*	J. Pouilloux, *Choix d'Inscriptions Grecques* (1960)
RE	A. Pauly *et al.*, ed. *Real-Encyclopädie der classischen Altertumswissenschaft*
REA	*Revue des Études Anciennes*
REG	*Revue des Études Grecques*
REL	*Revue des Études Latines*
RHDFE	*Revue Historique de Droit français et étranger*
RIDA	*Revue Internationale des Droits de l'Antiquité*

Robert, *EA*	L. Robert, *Études Anatoliennes* (1937)
Rostovtzeff, *SEHHW*	M. Rostovtzeff, *The Social and Economic History of the Hellenistic World* (1941)
Rostovtzeff, *SEHRE*	M. Rostovtzeff, *The Social and Economic History of the Roman Empire*, 2nd edition, revised by P. M. Fraser (1957)
SEG	*Supplementum Epigraphicum Graecum*
Sherwin-White, *LP*	A. N. Sherwin-White, *Letters of Pliny: A Historical and Social Commentary* (1966)
Smallwood	E. Mary Smallwood, ed., *Documents Illustrating the Principates of Nerva, Trajan and Hadrian* (1966)
Snell, *DM*	B. Snell, *The Discovery of Mind* (1953)
STh	*Studia Theologica*
TAM	*Tituli Asiae Minoris*
Tarn and Griffith, *HC*	W. W. Tarn, *Hellenistic Civilization*, 3rd edition, revised with G. T. Griffith (1952)
Tijdschrift	*Tijdschrift voor Rechtsgeschiedenis*
Treves, *GET*	A. A. Treves, *A History of Greek Economic Thought* (1916)
Ziebarth, *GS*	E. Ziebarth, *Aus dem griechischen Schulwesen*, 2nd edition, enlarged (1913)

CHAPTER I

1 W. W. Tarn in *Hellenistic Civilization* 3rd edition, revised with G. T. Griffith (1952). Elizabethan Act, cited from W. K. Jordan, *Philanthropy in England, 1480–1660* (1959); his comment on the wording, 114; see also his article in *AHR* 1961, 401ff. The preamble is cited in modern English in Lord Nathan, *The Charities Act, 1960* (1962), 23; Lord Macnaghten's revision, 24–5; see also D. E. Owen, *English Philanthropy 1660–1960* (1965), 324. *Encyclopaedia Britannica*, XIth ed., V, 861

2 Pity, Tarn follows Bolkestein, 113ff. Motives, Jordan, *AHR*, 1961, 406, *PE*, 143ff; Owen, *EP*, 395 (Owen also notes 'antipathy to relatives' as an occasional motive); the particular testator, 322, cited from *Transactions of the Social Science Association, 1859*, 69

3 Owen, *EP*, 578, quotes Mr Justice Vaisey in explaining why, in the Charities Act of 1960, the Elizabethan enumeration remains the ultimate authority. For Rome, see T. Frank, *Aspects of Social Behaviour in Ancient Rome* (1932), 97

4 Bolkestein, 426ff, language; his whole argument summarized, 455ff, and the conclusion stated that Christian charity was in part 'die antike φιλανθρωπία in der eingeschrankten Bedeuting von φιλοπτωχία', a narrowing due to great impoverishment in the third century AD

5 *Humanitas*, see Chapter VI, n. 97. Private or public?—see the recent discussion of the donations of Augustus, P. M. Brunt and J. M. Moore, *Res Gestae Divi Augusti* (1967), 58. Public collections within the wider citizen body are perhaps best attested epigraphically in the case of sums raised to pay for statues in honour of public benefactors, J. S. Reid, *The Municipalities of the Roman Empire* (1913), 498, the public response to 'charity'; see, for example, D. 43

6 Tiberius Gracchus, a recent discussion in A. E. Astin, *Scipio Aemilianus* (1967), 190ff. The judgment of Plutarch (*Ti. Gracch.* 10, 2) reflects the outlook of his own day on this kind of measure as much as that of the Gracchan age

CHAPTER II

7 See Nathan, *CA*, 29, on the definition of 'charity trustees' for the purposes of the 1960 Act, and 25ff, 47ff, on some subtle legal distinctions between classes of charities

8 For a brief summary of the historical background, see Nathan, *CA*, 2f; for a fuller account, Jordan, *PE*, 113ff; *AHR* 1961, 404; Owen, *EP*, 70. On 'associated philanthropy', see Owen, *EP*, 3, 11f, 71f

9 Legal personality, B. Laum, *Stiftungen in der griechischen und römischen Antike* (1914), 168; J. Walter Jones, *The Law and Legal Theory of the Greeks* (1956), 162ff; P. W. Duff, *Personality in Roman Law* (1938), 168ff; M. Kaser, *Das römische Privatrecht* (1955) I, 265f. There is much recent literature on Greek and Roman foundations (*Stiftungen*): see, generally, R. Feenstra, 'L'histoire des fondations', *Tijdschrift* 1956, 381–448; *RIDA* 1956, 245ff; E. F. Bruck, 'Les facteurs moteurs de l'origine et du développement des donations grecques et romaines', *RIDA* 1955, 159ff. More especially for Rome (but against Greek background), E. F. Bruck, *Der Stiftung für die Toten in Recht, Religion und politischen Denken der Römer* (1954); G. Le Bras, 'Les fondations privées du haut empire', *Studi Riccobono* III (1936), 23ff; a sequence of gifts, Bruck, *STR*, 73ff; Le Bras, *SR*, 59; origin of foundations, Laum, 157ff, 163ff, 243ff; E. F. Bruck, *Totenteil und Seelgerät* (1926), 179ff; *STR*, 48ff; *FM*, 163; Le Bras, *SR*, 28ff; protective devices, Laum, 180ff; Bruck, *TS*, 197ff; *FM*, 164; compare the reversionary clauses and 'minute and binding instructions charged with suspicion' expressing distrust of the church in its capacity as an administrator of perpetual endowments for prayers for the dead in pre-Reformation England, see Jordan, *PE*, 51, 306. Greek unreliability, Polybius VI, 56, 13; Epikteta, Laum, No. 43, ll. 77ff; Bruck, *TS*, 196; Laum, 198ff, discusses the difficulties involved

10 Roman law, Bruck, *STR*, 79; J. Michel, *Gratuité en droit romain* (1962), 277; J. Crook, *Law and Life of Rome* (1967), 122ff. Bruck suggests that documents were drawn up by scribes and notaries (*tabelliones*), not by lawyers, to suit the inclinations of their clients rather than the requirements of the law. Titus Flavius Praxias, *IGRP* IV, 660/1; W. M. Ramsay, *REA* 1901, 273; de Visscher, *RIDA* 1965, 247ff; for another feast on 'happiness-day' D. 45. Flavius Syntrophus, *CIL* VI, 2, 10239; Bruns, 139; for similar documents, compare Bruns 117 and 118; Le Bras, *SR*, 32–3; Bruck, *STR*, 88–9; Laum, 198, 244

11 De Visscher, *RIDA* 1965, 247ff. Gifts to city, Bruck. *STR*, 88–9; Le Bras, *SR*, 32–3; Laum, 198, 244. Nerva, Ulpian, XXIV, 28, which le Bras, *SR*, 34, takes to mean that *some* towns had the right to receive legacies before Nerva; cf. Bruck, *STR*, 75–7; Crook, *LLR*, 126, 152; A. N. Sherwin-White, *Letters of Pliny: A Historical and Social Commentary* (1966), 663–4, doubts whether this right was now extended to peregrine communities

12 Laum, 217, cites the Teos inscription, No. 90 (D. 47), relating to a fund intended to provide education for children, but its range was extended to cover young men (*epheboi*)—possibly, however, with the donor's consent (as suggested by D. Magie, *Roman Rule in Asia Minor*, (1950), 1444, n. 43). The courts, Laum, 219; J. H. Oliver, 'The Ruling Power', *Transactions of the American Philosophical Society* 1953, 972ff

13 Vedius Pollio, K. M. T. Atkinson, *RIDA* 1962, 261–89; *SEG* IV, 516 A and B. Vibius Salutaris and Antioch endowments, *IBM*, III, 481 (Laum, no. 74), Malalas, 284 (Laum, 291): J. H. Oliver, *The Ruling Power*, 945ff, 975ff. Sanctions more impressive, but F. F. Abbott and A. C. Johnson, *Municipal Administration in the Roman Empire* (1926), 388, believe that the reference to the imperial authorities was introduced mainly for reasons of vanity on the part of the donor, not in real hope of greater security for the gift. Flavius Praxias' phrase 'during the unending rule of Rome' may then perhaps parallel an English donor's threat of eternal punishment 'so long as the world endureth', cited by Owen, *EP*, 325. Both Laum and Le Bras are pessimistic about the chances of long survival for the average foundation, though there were exceptions, see E. Ziebarth, *Hermes* 1917, 425ff. The final enemies were inflation, Le Bras, *SR*, 64, n. 268, and war, Laum, 255

14 Laum, 255; *cf.* R. Duncan-Jones, *PBSR* 1965, 206f

15 *Digest*, 50, 8, 6, income from bequests not to be used for gladiatorial fights, etc., even if designated for that purpose; Magie, *RRAM*, 656; note also *Digest* 12, 13, 1, decree of Antoninus and Verus: *condiciones donationibus adpositas quae in rem publicam fiunt, ita demum ratas esse, si utilitatis publicae interest: quod si damnosae sint, observari non debere'*. The latter is one of the principles on which in England the Charity Commission may think fit to revise the purpose of an endowment; see Nathan, *CA*, 3, 20f, 744ff, on the growing relaxation of the principle of cy pres; and Owen, *EP*, 207f, on the Charitable Trusts Act of 1860 as providing a kind of 'poor charity's Chancery' for trustees who wished to offer a new scheme but had not been able to meet the expense of the procedure previously involved (Owen quotes from *The Dead Hand*, 327). Flavius Syntrophus, Le Bras *SR*, 58; Bruck, *STR*, 87

16 Abbot and Johnson, *MARE*, 144, emphasize the 'intolerable drain on the public treasury when prosperity declined' caused by repair of theatres, colonnades, etc. See Jordan, *PE*, 46, 276, for the extent to which 'charitable uses' were relied upon for such repairs in Tudor-Stuart England; De Visscher, *RIDA* 1955, 200, comments on 'la médiocrité assez générale des objectifs poursuivis par les fondations romaines'. Not simply lack of machinery, Le Bras, *SR*, 31f

CHAPTER III

17 An article by Marcel Mauss, originally in *L' Année sociologique* (2nd series) i, 1923–4, then, as *The Gift* by Ian Cunnison (1954). Mauss urges that we should return to customs of this sort, too much generosity being harmful to man and society, 66. See also, with regard to these relationships, that 'there is either complete trust or complete mistrust, 73

18 Mauss, *The Gift*, 3, 51, 118, on the 'agonistic' attitude and on 'dependence'

for the loser; L. Gernet, 'Droit et prédroit en Grèce ancienne' *L' Année sociologique* 1948–9, 43–6; *cf.* Bolkestein, 443f

19 M. Fortes and E. E. Evans-Pritchard, *African Political Systems* (1940), 207; J. K. Campbell, *Honour, Family and Patronage* (1946), 144

20 Mauss, *The Gift*, 51ff; Gernet, 28ff; E. Benviste, *Problèmes de linguistique générale* (1966), 315ff. For the application to Rome, see J. Michel, *GDR*, 469ff. On slavery for debt, see M. I. Finley, *RHDFE* 1965, 159ff. For the significance of the term *nexus*, R. M. Ogilvie, *Livy I–V* (1965), 296ff

21 Homer, *Il.*, VI, 211ff; *Od.*, IV, 613ff; I, 307ff; M. I. Finley, *The World of Odysseus* (1956), 65f, 68ff, 106ff, 134ff; *RIDA* 1955, 165ff; see also W. K. Lacey, *JHS* 1966, 55ff, and *The Family in Classical Greece* (1968), 41; on meanness leading to ill-repute, Homer, *Od.* XIX, 325ff, XVII, 457ff

22 Evans-Pritchard, preface to Mauss, *The Gift*, *vii*; Thuc. II, 97, 3–4; Democritus, fr. 96 (its authenticity is doubted by W. K. C. Guthrie, *A History of Greek Philosophy* II (1965), 490); Lysias, 19, 59 (where the advocate apologizes for mentioning his client's good deeds); Demosth. *de cor.* 269; Aristotle, *E.N.* 1162 B36–7; comedy—J. M. Edmonds, *The Fragments of Attic Comedy* (1957–61), III, 749

23 Terence, *Andria* 43 (cf. M. Boas, *Disticha Catonis* (1952) I, 15); Cic. *de amic.* 20, 71 and 9, 31; also *de fin.* II, 35, 117; Sen. *de ben.* I, 2, 1; IV, 14, 1, IV, 21, 3; Aristotle, *E.N.* 1120 B7; cf. Sen. *de ben.* I 6, 1; I, 7, 1). Septuagint, *Proverbs*, 22, 8; *Eccles.* 35, 9; *Tobit* 4, 7. Hellenistic literature, Bruck, *STR*, 106ff; 2 *Cor.* 9, 7; Sen. *de ben.* II, 9

24 John Chrys. II, 126; Cic. *de off.* I, 15, 49; Sen. *de ben.* II, 35, 1 (cf. I, 1, 12); I, 1, 4; Cic. *de off.* I, 15, 48

25 Thuc. II, 40, 4; Aristotle, *E.N.* 1167 B17–18; Menander, Edmonds, *FAC*, IIIB, 917 (cf. Tac. *Ann.* IV, 18: '*beneficia laeta, dum videntur exsolvi posse*'); Dem. *de cor.* 269; Aristotle, *ep.* 3

26 Aristotle, *E.N.* 1178 A24ff (to have the will, but not the means (*choregia*) to give, provides no proof even as to the will); 1120 B27 (giving and receiving)

27 Friendships, Bolkestein, 84; Aristotle, *E.N.* 1155 A7; Cic. *de amic.* 51 (from Panaetius?; Fritz-Arthur Steinmetz, *Das Freundschaftslehre des Panaitios* (1967), 196; see also Michel, *GDR*, 503ff; J. Ferguson, *Moral Values in the Ancient World* (1958), 53ff

28 Michel, *GDR*, 552, 191, F. de Robertis, *Lavoro e Lavoratori nel mondo romano* (1963), 76–8. For the attitude of the lower class at Athens, see A. H. M. Jones, *Athenian Democracy* (1957), 11; Quintilian, *Inst. Orat.* XII, 7, 12. *Infamia*, Michel, *GDR*, 589

29 Cic. *pro Planc.* 81; *de amic.* 55; Xen. *Mem.* II, 4, 1; Aristotle, *E.N.* 1120 B16; *Rhet.* 1361 A28; Martial, V, 42, 7–8; Sen. *ad Lucil.* 119, 12. On Athenian society, see A. French, *The Growth of the Athenian Economy* (1964), 173; similarly, in a Roman context, R. Duncan-Jones, *PBSR* 1963, 161.

30 Aristotle, *E.N.* 1159 B12, 1163 B 1

31 *Philanthropia*, J. Ferguson, *Moral Values in the Ancient World* (1958), 102ff.
   Its development is traced by C. Spicq, *Agapè* (Paris, 1958–9), I, 170, n. 3, to
   the late fifth-century orator Antiphon. See also in *STh* XII (1958), 169–91.
   Cf. B. Snell, *The Discovery of Mind* (1953) 249ff; J. Kabiersch, *Untersuchun-
   gen zum Begriff der Philanthropia bei dem Kaiser Julian* (1960), 76ff; Bolkestein,
   110ff, and literature there cited. (Besides the abstract noun *philanthropia*
   (plural *-iai*), the adjective *philanthropos* (plural *-oi*), which is used in the
   neuter (*philanthropon*, plural *-a*) as a noun, the adverb *philanthropōs*, and
   less commonly, the verb *philanthropeuesthai* recur in inscriptions, etc. In the
   text the nominative form of the noun or adjective and the infinitive mood
   of the verb will be quoted)

32 Club and state, Aristotle, *E.N.* 1160 A; E. Barker, *Greek Political Theory*,
   1918, 235–6. Unpaid office, C. Hignett, *History of the Athenian Constitution*
   (1952), 220 (expresses some doubt about the office of *strategos*). Friendship
   and the state, Aristotle, *Pol.* 1321 A; *E.N.* 1160 B32–5, 1155 A23–5;
   Lucretius, V, 1392ff

33 Material gain, Aristotle *Pol.* 1279 A. Definition of liturgy, *E.N.* 1163 A29.
   On the number of liturgies at Athens in the mid-fourth century, see J. K.
   Davies, *JHS* 1967, 33ff; on the attitude to them in fifth century Athens, V.
   Ehrenberg, *The People of Aristophanes* (1943), 173, and, later, Jones, *AD*,
   56–8. At Athens there was the curious right of the citizen who had been
   assigned a liturgy to challenge another whom he believed to be wealthier
   than himself either to accept it himself or to agree to an exchange of
   properties (*antidosis*). See A. H. M. Jones, *The Greek City* (1940), 167, on the
   'tacit convention whereby the people elected rich men to magistracies and
   they as magistrates contributed freely to the public service under their
   charge'; so, too, in Asia Minor under the Romans, Magie, *RRAM*, 61.
   Summa honoraria, taken as the equivalent of the Greek liturgy, Abbott and
   Johnson, *MARE*, 144; particularly well attested in Roman Africa, R.
   Duncan-Jones, *PBSR* 1962, 64; Frank, *ESAR* IV, 76–8; not so well in Italy
   itself, Duncan-Jones, *PBSR* 1965, 226f; in the Greek world, Jones, *GC*,
   237, n. 25; J. Day, *An Economic History of Athens under Roman domination*
   (1942), 97; Frank, *ESAR* IV, 802; III, 149; V, 65ff

34 Graded honours, Aristotle, *Rhet.* 1361; G. Klaffenbach, *Griechische Epigraphik*, 2nd edition (1966), 77ff; E. Ziebarth, *Das griechische Vereinswesen*
   (1896), 164. *Aionios*, Laum, 46–53; Jones, *GC*, 175. Sale of citizenship,
   L. Robert, *Hellenica* I, 1940, 39ff. The device forbidden to the Athenians by
   Augustus (Dio Cassius LIV, 7), who thereupon accepted *gifts* on the same
   basis, J. Day, *EHA*, 170

35 E. Skard, *Euergetes-Concordia* (1932), 67ff. On coins, B. V. Head, *Historia
   Numorum* (1911), 77, fig. 38; Aristotle, *E.N.* 1167 A22ff (*homonoia* as
   politikē philia); 1155 A26–8 (*philia* and 'justice'); 1159 B 31 (Xen. *Mem.* I,
   4, 6; III, 11, 4); *Pol*, 1263 A31 (rejecting Plato, *Rep.* 462 C); see also A. W.
   H. Adkins, *Merit and Responsibility* (1960), 211

36 Voluntary basis, J. Walter Jones, *The Law and Legal Theory of the Greeks* (1956), 155; Frank, *ESAR* IV 802 (cf. M. Rostovtzeff, *Social and Economic History of the Hellenistic World* (1941) 621); Jones, *AD*, 58; Day, *EHA*, 12, 36, 90. *Epidosis*, A. Kuenzi, *Epidosis* (1923), relating to subscriptions for military needs, public buildings, religious objects, corn supplies, financial needs; on the method, A. M. Andreades, *A History of Greek Public Finance*, revised by C. N. Brown (1933), 349

37 H. Francotte commented on the system: '*Personne n'est forcé de souscrire, mais chacun comprend ce que cela veut dire*'. The English situation, Jordan, *AHR*, 1960, 404; Owen, *EP*, 70

38 See Lysias, 19, 56; 25, 13; Isaeus I, 45; A. W. H. Adkins, *MR*, 201–4

39 Xen. *Symp.* IV, 29; Isoc. *antidos.* 159; Aristotle, *Pol.* 1320 A; Plut. *Mor.* 821 F; Dio Chrys. *or.* 47, 3

40 Liberality, Aristotle, *Pol.* 1163 B10. Hellenistic monarchies, W. Schubert, 'Das hellenistische Königsideal nach Inschriften und Papyri', *Archiv für Papyrusforschung* XII (1936), 1ff, esp. 10, 20; E. R. Goodenough, *Yale Classical Studies* I (1928), 55ff; C. Spicq, *STh* 1958, 185ff; Rostovtzeff, *SEHHW*, 268–9, 434, 1078, 1359, 1379–80; Egypt, M. Th. Lengler, 'La notion de bienfait royal et les ordonnances de rois Lagides', *Studi in honore di V. Arangio-Ruiz* I (1952–3), 483ff; see also E. Skard, *Euergetes-Concordia* (1932), 56ff. To this context belongs the well-known dictum of the Emperor Titus, twenty-four hours having passed by without his having done anybody a favour, 'I have lost a day' (Suet. *Tit.* 8), which may originally have been attributed to Alexander the Great, (Kabiersch, *BPJ*, 11, 90ff)

41 These two terms have adjectival and adverbial forms, also related verbs, *philotimeisthai* and *philodoxein*, which are used in a way analogous to those connected with *philanthropia* (see note 31); they will be quoted in the same way. Plato, *Rep.*, trans. by H. D. P. Lee (1955) 184–5. Bolkestein quoted Anatole-France: '*cet égoisme qui inspire à l'homme tous les actes de générosité*'. Aristotle, *E.N.* 1159 B25ff; Owen, *EP*, 165; Jordan, *PE*, 228–9

42 Aristotle *E.N.* 1167 B17ff; *Pol.* 1263 B; Sen. *de ben.* I, 6, 1; *ad Lucil.* 9, 8 (see Aristotle, *E.N.* 1159 A26–7); *ad Lucil.* 48, 2 (Menander, Edmonds, *FAC*, IIIB, 755); *de ben.* II, 28, 2; Origen, *c. Cels.* 1, 4; 11, 5 (H. Chadwick, *Early Christian Thought and the Classical Tradition* (1966), 164)

43 Pliny, *ep.* I, 8, 10–13; Dio Chrys. *Or.* 47, 9. T. Claudius Atticus, J. S. Reid, *The Municipalities of the Roman Empire* (1913), 497; cf. C. S. Walton's suggestion (*JRS* 1929, 55ff) as to the motive behind the lavish gifts of Opramoas of Rhodiapolis (doubted by Magie, *RRAM*, 1395)

44 *Arai Bouzygeiai*, Bolkestein, 471; Michel, *GDR*, 585–6; Angelo Brelich, *Gli eroi Greci* (1958), 174ff; *Corpus Paroem. Graec.*, Appendix, 388; Sen. *de ben.* IV, 29, 2; cf. Cic. *de off.* I, 16, 51. A passage in Aristotle's *Rhetoric* (1361 A27) implies that such acts did obtain their reward of 'honour' often enough, because of their situation and timing (cf. Mark, 9, 41, Matthew, 10, 42). '*Do ut des*' interpretation, Snell, *DM*, 168; Kabiersch, *BPJ*, 30,

emphasizes Seneca's remark that no *gaudium* (joy) is associated with such gifts

45 See Note 4. Elections, Tac. *Ann.* I, 15. Lack of sense of social obligation, R. von Pöhlmann, *Geschichte der sozialen Frage und des Socialismus in der antiken Welt* (1925) II, 266. Concordia, E. Skard, *Concordia-Euergetes*, 81ff. Epigraphical evidence, A. Lussana, *Epigraphica* 1956, 86, and 1952, 106; cf. R. Duncan-Jones, *PBSR* 1963, 161

46 Le Bras, *STR*, 121–2; Polybius, XXXII, 12, 9 (Michel, *GDR*, 293, notes the consequence in the sphere of law: '*on peut admettre que la notion juridique de donation antèrieurement à 204 av. J. C. était complêtement étrangère aux Romains*', the *lex Cincia* of that year admitting it only the better to exclude it from the domain of juridical institutions); G. Highet, *Juvenal the Satirist* (1962), 7

CHAPTER IV

47 Aristotle, *E.N.* 1123 B20–1; Theophrastus, *ap.* Stobaeus, IV, 72; Demosth. XX, 10; Cic. *de off.* I, 14, 44; Pliny, *ep.* I, 8, 15

48 G. Klaffenbach, *Griechische Epigraphik* (1966), 77ff—hence the possibility of confident reconstructions of sections of quite fragmentary inscriptions. Rutilius Viator, *CIL* XI, 1681

49 Hera, *SEG* I, 367 (*MDAI(A)* 46, 14ff). Colony of Callatis, *Dacia* I (1924), 4–6. Kolophon, F. G. Maier, *Griechische Mauerbauinschriften* I (1959), 69 B, *ll.* 28ff; Oropus, F. G. Maier, *ibid.*, 26A, *ll.* 12ff, 23ff. Cibyra, *IGRP* III, 422 (see L. Robert, *Études Anatoliennes*, 378–80)

50 E. Ziebarth, *Das griechische Vereinswesen* (1896), 164; cf. Crook, *LLR*, 266. Expenses of priesthoods, L. Robert, *Hellenica* XIII (1965), 224–5. Corn distributions, Rostovtzeff, *SEHHW*, 393, 618–22, 951, 1124, 1248–51, 1314, 1464, 1520; *SEHRE* II, 599ff; H. Francotte, 'Le Pain à bon marché et le pain gratuit dans les cités grecques, *Mélanges Nicoles* 1905, 135–57; Jones, *GC*, 217, 350 n. 15; Magie, *RRAM*, 645, nn. 1511–3; L. Robert, *EA*, 319ff; Bolkestein, 255ff. Aediles, Cic. *de off.* II, 16, 58 (Bolkestein, 371ff)

51 Francotte, 143–4 (cf. D. 3, 9, 14, 15, 29). Aphrodisias, *MAMA* VIII, 408, *ll.* 7. Stock adverbs, Robert, *EA*, 343. Lucania (Tegianum), Dessau 5054 ('*ad honorem quoque duumviratus ad cumulanda munera patriae suae libenter accedit*').

52 Jones, *GC*, 167, 237 n. 25, 182ff, 342 n. 55; Magie, *RRAM* 839 n. 54, 1518 n. 50, 1519 n. 51. (The text of Pliny, *Ep.* X, 113, often cited as evidence of unwillingness to hold the office of town-councillor in the early second century AD, is dubious—see Sherwin-White, *LP*, on this letter.)

53 Cic. *ad Att.* VI, 1, 26; Tac. *Ann.* I, 74

54 Seneca, *de ben.* IV, 11, 6. It is relevant to note that only two of Pliny the Younger's numerous public benefactions were clearly non-testamentary (Sherwin-White, *LP*, 103), and to compare the doctrine of the Christian

apologist, John Chrysostom, that testamentary giving was less deserving of God's reward—see Otto Plassman, *Das Almosen bei Johannes Chrysostomus* (1961), 20. Italy—R. Duncan-Jones, *PBSR* 1965, 208–9. On the social function of the legacy at Rome, see L. Boyer, *RHDFE* 1965, 333ff. Honours for descendants, *MDAI (A)* 1907, 259; Polybius VI, 54, 1; Cic. *de off.* II, 18, 63

55 Tarn and Griffith, *HC*, 49ff; E. Skard, *Euergetes-Concordia*, 28ff; J. P. V. D. Balsdon, *Historia* 1952, 363ff, traced the tendency to ascribe 'divinity', though not divine cult, to great men in recognition of their services, long before Alexander the Great

56 Bolkestein, 393–400; cf. reviews of R. Meiggs, *CR* 1940, 106–7; A. J. Festugière, *REG* 1940, 237–41. W. Schubart, *Archiv. für Papyrusforschung* XII (1936), 1ff, shows that not even the Aristeas epistle, written by a Jew in Alexandria, is without its dominant Greek element in thought and expression (cf. A. Pelletier, *Lettre d' Aristée à Philocrate* (1962), 76). Plato's *Politicus*, see edition of J. B. Skemp (1952), 57: 'an absolutism based on the innate superiority of the ruler as a creature of a higher order is unacceptable; but it must have been a doctrine actually put forward at the time'. In general, C. Habicht, *Gottmenschentum und griechische Stadte* (1956), shows the direct relationship between the incidence of cult for individual Hellenistic kings and the actual benefactions of the latter to the cities, which established such a cult as a *legitimus honor.* Menander, *Dysk.* 805–9; *Anec. Gr.* II, 131, 11 (see L. Sternbach, *Wiener Studien* 1887, 199ff); Sen. *de ben.* III, 15, 4; Pliny, *ep.* III, 21, 6; Sen. *ad Lucil.* 115, 4 (cf. Cic. *pro Lig.* 38); Tertullian, *apol.* 50, 10–11

57 Laum, 221; Bruck, *TS*, 168ff; *STR*, 48ff; *FM*, 160ff. Zosimos, *Inschr. von Priene*, 112, *l.* 15. Epicurus, Bruck, *TS*, 204f

58 Plutarch, *Nikias*, 5, 3 (Laum, No. 53)

59 Bruck, *STR*, 62–7; Cic. *Phil.* XIII, 7

60 Bruck, *FM*, 170; de Visscher, *RIDA* 1965, 253. Flavius Syntrophus, Bruns, 139 (see Le Bras, *SR*, 58ff; Bruck, *STR*, 77ff). Funerary aspect, Le Bras, *SR*, 61; de Visscher, *RIDA* 1955, 200. Pliny, R. Duncan-Jones, *PBSR* 1965, 187. Roman Africa, *PBSR* 1962, 50–1. Theveste, *Inscriptions of Roman Tripolitania*, 268 (*IL Alg.* 3017)

61 P. Guiraud, *La main d'oeuvre industrielle dans l'ancienne Grèce* (1900), 206–7; M. N. Tod, *ABSA* 1906–7, 336, J. Crook, *LLR*, 263ff

62 Jordan's characterization of an aspect of English philanthropy, Jordan, *PE*, 229; Basil, *On Riches*, I, 14, 37; L. Robert, *Hellenica* X–XI (1955) 573, with n. 4 for a list of titles in Hellenistic inscriptions. P. Domitius, *SEG* XX, 25 (L. Robert, *Hellenica* VIII (1950) 76–7). Gregory of Nyssa, Migne, *PL* III, 457 C. John Chrysostom, LXIX, 166, 380 (Plassman, *AJC*, 92); Bruck, *STR*, 117ff, re. John Chrys., *in epist. II ad Cor. Hom. XIII.* Bruck, *STR*, 134–6, points out a resulting contrast in Roman and Byzantine law: for the latter the evidence of a 'gift' is the *animus donandi* (a subjective criterion),

for the former the undoubted transfer of an object without the payment of a price (an objective criterion)

CHAPTER V

63 Bolkestein, 181ff, 325ff; cf. V. Ehrenberg, *The People of Aristophanes* (1951) 178; Aristophanes, *Plut.* 551-4; Dem. XXI, 102; Horace, *Sat.* I, 6, 71-8; Martial, XI, 328; Juvenal, G. Highet, *Juvenal the Satirist* (1962), 68

64 F. de Robertis, *Lavoro e lavoratori nel mondo romano* (1963), 87ff; von Pöhlmann, *GSF* II, 457; Stobaeus IV, 72, collects a number of quotations 'concerning praise of poverty'

65 Bolkestein, 410; Menander, *Dysk.* 284-5, cf. 23-4; Plato, *Rep.* 552 D. Example of language variation, Dem. VIII, 66; Homer, *Od.* XVIII, 1ff; Plato, *Laws*, 936C

66 Ehrenberg, *PA*, 178; Bolkestein, 328, compare 52 (Israel); Cic. *de dom.* 33, 89; *ad Att.* I, 16, 11; *de leg. agr.* II, 26 70 ('*hoc enim verbo est usus, quasi de aliqua sentina ac non de optimorum civium genere loqueretur*'); Lucan, VII, 404; Juvenal, G. Highet, *Juvenal the Satirist*, 37, see also 51, 68 Mines, B. Farrington, *Diodoros Siculus, Universal Historian* (1937), 16-19; H. Strassburger, *JRS* 1965, 48-9 (*contra* M. Laffranque, *Poseidonios d'Apamée* (1964), 490); Diodorus V, 35-8

67 Owen, *EP*, 242, records how 'only with the greatest reluctance and then in qualified terms would the Charity Organization [founded in the 1860s] admit unemployment to be a fact'; cf. earlier statutes of the Tudor period relating to the 'professional poor'—vagabonds were to be 'whipped until bloody and then returned by a direct route to the parish of their birth or legal residence' (Jordan, *PE*, 94f; see also 41, on the *worthy* poor whom endowments were intended to benefit); de Romilly, *REG*, 1965, 575; Homer, *Od.* XVIII, 1; Plut. *Solon*, 17 (Bolkestein, 283-6; cf. A. R. W. Harrison, *The Law of Athens* (1968), 79f, for the opposite emphasis); Plut. *Moral.* 235 A; Plautus, *Trin.* 339

68 Plato, *Laws* 744 DE, 745 A (see A. A. Treves, *A History of Greek Economic Thought* (1916), 60); E. F. Bruck, *Kirchenväter und sozialen Erbrecht* (1956), 49-51. Bruck's thesis is that the Christian Fathers, through establishing a portion of property which should be given away, indirectly established the amount of property which a Christian might retain. Plassman, *AJC*, 53; according to the doctrine of John Chrysostom, the rich have *to thank the poor* for the chance of alms-giving. J. Leipoldt, *Der soziale Gedanke in der altchristlichen Kirche* (1952), 169ff

69 Aristotle, *Pol.* 1320 A6ff; Ruskin, Treves, *GET*, 46, 149

70 A. Passerini, *Athenaeum* 1930, 273ff, observes that these schemes, unlike so many others for redistribution in the classical world, did not simply involve giving to the 'poor' at the expense of proprietors or political enemies. On Sparta, see A. Fuks, *Athenaeum* 1962, 244ff, and T. W. Africa,

Phylarchus and the Spartan Revolution (1961), 16ff. Africa doubts whether Cercidas, to whom Tarn attributed 'the one expression of philanthropy in literature', voiced his support of the popular cause before that cause seemed already won. For the events of and background to 133 BC at Rome, see D. C. Earl, *Tiberius Gracchus* (Collection Latomus, LXVI, 1963), 30ff, Earl emphasizes the military motive behind Tiberius' law; Bolkestein, 349–57, emphasizes also the financial assistance provided by Tiberius for the re-established *coloni*, but this may have been intended (as Livy suggests) for those for whom land could not be found, and in any case seems to have been an afterthought. The Elizabethan period, Jordan, *AHR* 1961, 404, *PE*, 149

71 Plato, *Laws*, 740 E; F. M. Heichelheim, *An Ancient Economic History*, 2nd edition (1964), 240; D. Asheri, *Distribuzioni di terre nell' antica Grecia* (1966), 11–16, 65. Brea, Jones, *AD*, 168, against the implication of Bolkestein, 421–3. In Italy, G. Tibiletti, *Relazioni II, Storia dell' Antiquita* (1955), 249ff; T. Frank, *Aspects of Social Behaviour in Ancient Rome*, 97; A. Bernardi, *Nuova Rivista Storica* (1946), 285–8

72 Mercenaries, G. T. Griffith, *Mercenaries of the Hellenistic World* (1935). On the motives of Roman *proletarii*, P. A. Brunt, *JRS* 1962, 79–83 (against other recent views). Meagre pay, G. Forni, *Il reclutamento delle legioni da Augusto a Diocleziano* (1953), 120ff

73 Plato, *Rep.* 372 B; K. Hopkins, *CSSH* 1965, 3ff. Athens, H. Bolkestein, *CP* 1922, 222ff; A. Cameron, *CR* 1932, 105–14; A. W. Gomme, *Population of Athens* (1933), 79–82; J. K. Lacey, *The Family in Classical Greece* (1968), 164–7, 307 n. 83; A. R. W. Harrison, *The Law of Athens* (1968), 70–1. Hellenistic period, Tarn and Griffith, *HC*, 102; G. Humbert, *Dictionnaire Daremberg-Saglio* III, *s.v. expositio* (930–9); Rostovtzeff, *SEHHW*, 623.

74 Aristotle, *Pol.* 1265 B, 1335 B (transl. E. Barker, *The Politics of Aristotle* (1948)); Treves, *GET*, 74ff; Victorian critic—quoted by Owen, *EP*, 167–8

75 Pliny, *Ep.* X, 6, 2 (Sherwin-White, *LP*, 650–2, 654); Rostovtzeff, *SEHRE*, 476, 738, n. 15; U. Kahrstedt, *Kulturgeschichte des römischen Kaiserzeit* (1958), 57, 316, emphasizes the continuance of the practice in the period of the *alimenta*; Lewis and Reinhold, *RC* II, 404–5; see also Crook, *LLR*, 58, 299 n. 101; J. Carcopino (transl. E. O. Lorimer), *Daily Life in Ancient Rome* (1941), 77. Musonius Rufus, Cora E. Lutz, *Yale Classical Studies*, 1947, 3ff, collects the fragments and writes of a 'new spirit which he breathed into the old Stoic concept of *humanitas*' (perhaps overstated): see esp. XV, 19–22, 96–99. Suicide, Sen. *ad Lucil.* 70, 15; *cons. ad Marc.* 20, 3 ('*caram te, vita, beneficio mortis habeo*'); cf. Epictetus, 1245 D; *Theod. Code*, XI, 27, 1

76 Ehrenberg, *PA*, 183; A. French, *The Growth of the Athenian Economy* (1964), 159. Slaves' earnings, A. H. M. Jones (M. I. Finley ed.), *Slavery in the Ancient World* (1960), 6f; cf. Xen. *Mem*, II, 8, 4–5; ps-Xen, *A.P.* 1, 10; fourth century, A. H. M. Jones, *AD*, 87; Treves, *GET*, 74; Aristotle, *Pol.* 1295 A. Banquets and distributions, L. Robert, *EA*, 388 n. 2; W. L.

Westermann, *Slave Systems of Greek and Roman Antiquity* (1955), 41, 109, 120, 161

77 F. de Robertis, *Lavoro e lavoratori nel mondo romano* (1963), 108ff, 112ff. Africa, R. Duncan-Jones, *PBSR* 1963, 165ff. Asia Minor, W. M. Ramsay, *The Social Basis of Roman Power in Asia Minor* (1941), 2–4. Panamara and Lagina, Magie, *RRAM*, 587–8. Menodora, Laum, No. 150 (D. 41). Opramoas, *IGRP* III, 739 (C. S. Walton, *JRS*, 1929, 55ff; Magie, *RRAM*, 536–7). The adoption of 'democracy' in some of the colonies of modern western European nations may be regarded as similarly superficial

78 Polybius XXXVII, 9 (see A. W. Gomme, *Population of Athens*, 81, for a cautionary note; also D. Asheri, *Distribuzioni di terre nell' antica Grecia* (1966), 24, defining *oliganthropia* (invariably?). Sherwin-White, *LP*, 298 (re. Pliny, *ep.* IV, 21, 3) points to the apparent difficulty of ensuring the continuance of noble Roman families, even where no limitation was intended. Orphans, Bolkestein, 275–82; A. W. Gomme, *Population of Athens*, 82 n. 1; Crook, *LLR*, 111–3. War-orphans, Thuc. II, 46; Aristotle, *A.P.* 24, etc. In England, Owen, *EP*, 157ff (including provision for 'destitute children of middle-class parents')

79 Theognis, 1161; Isoc. *ad Demon.* 29; *Disticha Catonis* (M. Boas, 1952), 24, No. 39; Cic. *de off.* II, 15, 54; Sen. *de vit. beat.* 23–4; Aristotle, *E.N.* 1120 B3; cf. Plassman, *AJC*, 91

80 Cic. *de off.* I, 14, 45; Aristotle, *E.N.* 1098 Λ16, 1123 B17 (Cic. *de off.* I, 17, 56); Sen. *de vit. beat.* 24, 2 (cf. Cic. *de off.* III, 6, 27); Pliny, *ep.* IX, 30; J. N. Sevenster, *Paul and Seneca* (1961), 215

81 John Chrysostom, Plassman, *AJC*, 29ff, 83, 97. See also J. Leipoldt, *Der soziale Gedanke in der altchristlichen Kirche* (1952), 158f, with whom J. Kabiersch, *BPJ*, 43, disagrees as to the teaching of the *Didache*

82 Gifts out of income, Sherwin-White, *LP*, 149f (on Pliny, *ep.* II, 4, 3); R. Duncan-Jones, *PBSR* 1965, 178. Debts, A. Passerini, *Athenaeum* 1930, 299

83 Cynics: Tarn & Griffith, *HC*, 111; Rostovtzeff, *SEHHW*, 1129; cf. Plassman, *AJC* 92–4; Leipoldt, 167, 191. *Autarkeia*, 2 *Cor.* 9, 8 (cf. J. Moreau, *Epictetus* (1964), 80: 'le détachement est, pour le stoïcien la condition de l'autarcie . . . ce n'est pas le renoncement a soi-même, par quoi le chrétien est rendu entièrement disponible pour le dévoeument à autrui'.) Immortality through identification, Kabiersch, *BPJ*, 30, 49ff, traces it back to Plato, *Theaetetus* 176 A

CHAPTER VI

84 Matthew 6, 2. G. W. H. Lampe, *Patristic Greek Lexicon. s.v.* 'ἐλεημοσύνη. *Misericordia*, H. Petré, *Revue des Études Latines* 1934, 376ff; used by Tertullian of charity towards an infant exposed (*Apol.* 9, 17), towards a beggar in the street (*Apol.* 42, 8). *Philotimia*, Laum, 43

162 NOTES

85 Christian background, Bolkestein, 19ff, 47ff, 423ff, 179ff. Homer, Bolkestein, 423; B. Snell, *DM*, 33; Xen. *Mem.* I, 3, 3

86 Pity in Greek drama, E. B. Stevens, *AJPh* 1944 1ff; Philemon, *ap.* Stobaeus, IV, 30; Soph. *Ajax*, 121ff. Scipio, Polybius, XXXIX, 4, 2–3. Seneca, *ad Marc.* 9, 1; Philemon, *l.c.*

87 Demosthenes, *in Meid.* 184, cf. 99, 101. On the various meanings of *eranos*, see Bolkestein, 240. Thuc. III, 40, 3; Xen. *Mem.* II, 6, 22

88 Bolkestein, 141, 346, cf. 27–9; H. A. Thompson, *Hesperia*, 1952, 47ff. Epidaurus, *IG* IV, 1282, and C. Spicq, *STh* 1958, 189 (the altar probably belongs to the late second or early third century); Aristotle, *Poetics*, 1452 A, 1453 A (Pausanias, I, 17 1, describes the altar as 'of the greatest avail in face of changing circumstance'). Slaves, Bolkestein, 320–6; von Pöhlmann, *GSF*, I, 409; II, 305; J. Vogt, *Sklaverei und Humanität* (1965), 34, questioning the influence (and the implied dating) of Iambulus' Sun State (see Tarn and Griffith, *HC*, 122, 125, and E. Will, *Histoire Politique du Monde Hellénistique* (1967) 355f) and taking Diodorus' account, and still more the parody in Lucian over a century later, as a reflection of romantic rather than serious political ideals; von Pöhlmann argues that the late fifth-century comedies of Aristophanes were more in touch with political reality. See also, Rostovtzeff, *SEHHW*, 808, 1132, 1523–4, n. 81

89 Anaximenes, Stobaeus, *Concerning the reproach of poverty*, 21; Plato, *Rep.* 604ff; Aristotle, *Pol.* 1341 B33ff; *Poetics*, 1449 B28–9; Cic. *pro Mur.* 39, 61

90 Cicero, *Tusc.* IV, 26, 56; von Arnim, *Stoicorum Veterum Fragmenta* (1921–4), III, 109, 28, 110, 7; Sen. *de clem.* 2, 5, 1; Bolkestein, 143

91 C. N. Cochrane, *Christianity and Classical Culture* (1940), 507f. Self-composure, see Note 83 above

92 Posidonius, M. Laffranque, *Poseidonius d' Apamée* (1954) 474ff; Seneca, *ad Lucil.* 74, 30, and 82, 11. Personal emphasis, W. R. Halliday, *The Pagan Background of Early Christianity* (1925), Ch. 4

93 Disdain, Bruck, *STR*, 117ff; Plassman, *AJC*, 26; Bolkestein, 435ff, 471; Sen. *de ben.* IV, 29, 2; *ad Lucil.* 95, 5; Philo, *ap.* Eusebius, 358D; Josephus, *contra Apion.* II, 29, 1; cf. Cic. *pro Quinctio*, 97, 'obscravit . . . si non hominis, at humanitatis rationem haberet'; Diogenes Laertius V, 1, 21, 'it was not to the man that I gave help but to humanity' (the general philosophy implied is not inappropriate to Hellenistic thought, even though the other version of this tale in D.L. V, 1, 17, has the highly suspect *eleēmosunē* in place of *eranos*); Gellius IX, 26, attributes a similar reply to Herodes Atticus in the second century AD, and in the fourth century it re-appears in a letter of the Emperor Julian (290 D); see Kabiersch, *BPJ*, 70f. For the New Testament comparison, see J. N. Sevenster, *Paul and Seneca* (1961), 171; C. Spicq, *Agapè* (1958–9) I, 170f: Jesus '*choisit des exemples concrets où la méchanceté du prochain est si accusée qu' une prescription de l' aimer d' amitié ou humainement serait un nonsens*'. On war-captives, see Rostovtzeff, *SEHHW*, 202–4,

'charitable souls who saw respectable citizens' (the key-word is 'respectable')

94 Appeals via children, etc., Aristophanes, *Wasps*, 568; Demosth. *in Meid.* 186–8; but Socrates refused to follow the fashion, Plato, *Apol.* 23. On the defendant's use of the term 'pity' as equivalent to 'a decision in my favour', see Adkins, *MR*, 203, where it is pointed out that this appeal was not necessarily a confession of guilt. Epitaphs, M. N. Tod, *Annual of the British School at Athens*, 1951, 186. John Chrysostom, Plassman, *AJC*, 81, re. LXII, 210, LVIII 524, etc.

95 Bolkestein, 44, 133ff, 459; Democritus, *fr.* 255. Rhodians, Strabo, 652 F; cf. Aristotle, *Pol.* 1319 A8; Dittenberger, 814, *l*, 20

96 Bolkestein, 463f; Aristotle, *Pol.* 1253 B32; *E.N.* 1161 B2–4; see also Plato, *Laws* 777 D. On *excessive* care for slaves as property, and disregard of friends, Xen. *Mem* II, 4, 2–3. '*Humiles amici*', sen. *ad Lucil.* 47, 1

97 Gellius, XIII, 17; Sen. *de ben.* IV, 3, 1; Bolkestein, 305–7. There is an immense literature on the term: some recent work is discussed by H. Hafter, *Philologus*, 1956, 287ff. Athenian background, Snell, *DM*, 250ff (finds already in the fourth century a recognition of the individual's human dignity, irrespective of education, on the part of a stratum of cultured people, which was to find expression later in certain passages of Menander; Snell attributes the 'strong mixture of condescension' attaching to *philanthropia* to its 'admixture with the ancient view of the frailty of man'); see also, Kabiersch, *BPJ*, 76ff. On Cicero's usage, J. Mayer, *Humanitas bei Cicero* (Dissertation, Freiburg, 1951), emphasizing the *seelisch-gefuhlsbetonte* aspect of *humanitas* which he relates to Roman *pietas*. See A. E. Astin, *Scipio Aemilianus* (1967), 302–6

98 Rome, H. C. Baldry, *Fondation Hardt*, VIII (1961), 190ff. Elegy, G. Luck, *The Latin Love Elegy* (1959). Virgil, W. F. Jackson-Knight, *Roman Virgil* (1966), 396ff; Snell, *DM*, 288, 301. *Reverentia*, Cicero, *de off.* I, 99; Seneca, *ad Lucil.* 95, 33 (but giving the term a new application, see Note 99). Children, Juvenal XIV, 47–9; Lucretius, D. E. W. Wormell in *Lucretius*, ed. D. R. Dudley (1965), 57. Law, F. Schulz, *Classical Roman Law* (1951) 103ff; W. L. Westermann, *The Slave Systems of Classical Antiquity* (1955), 111ff; Pliny, *ep.* viii 16

99 S. Dill, *Roman Society from Nero to Marcus Aurelius* 2nd edition (1905), 191. *Benignitas*, RHDFE 1948, 137ff. Hellenistic comedy, e.g. Philemon, fr. 22 (*Kock* ii 484 = Edmonds, *FAC*, IIIA, 15): 'a slave or not, my lord, here is a man, if we suppose him of humanity'. Note, too, the new system of manumission developed under Delphic influence after *c.* 200 BC, described by Westermann, *The Slave Systems of Classical Antiquity* (1955), 34ff; more briefly, by Tarn and Griffith, *HC*, 104f. Roman brutality, M. Grant, *The World of Rome* (1960), 119–25, and *Gladiators* (1967), 117, where he notes that Seneca was the first to be shocked (*ad Lucil.* 95, 33), as distinct from merely bored, by these shows; L. Robert, *Les Gladiateurs dans*

l'Orient grec (1940), 244ff, 254ff; see also H. I. Marrou, *The History of Education in Antiquity*, trans. G. Lamb, (1956) 299–301; J. Delorme, *Gymnasium* (1960), 434–5, Magie, *RRAM*, 534, 655f

CHAPTER VII

100 Bolkestein, 321ff; Rostovtzeff, *SEHHW*, 1123; Magie, *RRAM*, 59, notes that in Asia Minor under Rome the original powers of the eponymous official were reduced to sacrifices, often at his own expense

101 L. Robert, *Hellenica XIII* (1965), 224ff; Epaminondas, *IG* VII, 2712; L. Robert, *BCH* 1935, 438ff; for a similar kind of benefaction, see D. 23

102 Stratonicea, J. Hatzfeld, *BCH* 1927, 57ff, 123ff, emphasizes the apparently wide reach of the god's invitations, suggests Jewish influence and compares Christian 'love-feasts'; but the date of the documents is uncertain. See also Magie, *RRAM*, 587f; Frank, *ESAR* IV, 804–6

103 T. Claudius Atticus; it is fair to note that the bulk of the Athenian populace never received their *mina* annually, for his son Herodes Atticus (for all his own generosity) largely invalidated the will by making a final cash payment of five *minae* instead—a mere 'paper' transaction, since he simply deducted this amount from the sums owed to himself by many citizens. They were probably bad debts, like those cancelled at Rome by Hadrian (*SHA Hadr.* 7, 6; Dessau, 309). See P. Graindor, *Un Milliadaire Antique* (1930) 71–9; Philostratus, *V.S.* II, 1, 3–4. Asia Minor, Magie, *RRAM*, 658, 1523–5, n. 58; L. Robert, *Études Anatoliennes* (1937), 347–8. The West, R. Duncan-Jones, 'An Epigraphic Survey of Costs in Roman Italy', *PBSR* 1965, 189ff. Africa, 'Wealth and Munificence in Roman Africa', *PBSR* 1963, 163. Property qualification, Jones, *GC*, 174; Magie, *RRAM*, 640, 1503, n. 26. Poll-taxes, R. Duncan-Jones, *Historia* 1964, 201; Jordan, PE, 46. Jordan notes the 'very substantial endowments' for a similar purpose in Tudor-Stuart England, as well as others to defray the costs of the elaborate dinners bestowed upon the municipal officers and their successors

104 See Duncan-Jones, *PBSR* 1965, 214–5, 220 n. 3

105 Petelia, Dessau 6469 (the donor was M.' Megonius Leo, D. 31). Apamea, *IGRP* IV, 788 (Abbott and Johnson, *MARE*, No. 123). Athens, J. H. Oliver, *AJPh* 1949, 299ff; *IG* II, 2064 (J. H. Oliver, *Hesperia* 1951, 350–4; B. D. Meritt, *Hesperia* 1962, 26ff and *Suppl.* V 126)

106 Clodius, Cassius Dio XXXIX, 24; Dion. Hal. IV, 24; D. van Berchem, *Les distributions de blé et d'argent à la plèbe romaine sous l'Empire* (1939), 19

107 *e.g.*, Francotte, *MN*, 151)

108 Samos inscription, Bolkestein, 259ff. *Euphrosynus*, W. Liebenam, *Städteverwaltung im römischen Kaiserreiche* (1900), 109

109 Anaia, Jones, *GC*, 350 n. 13

110 P. M. Fraser and G. E. Bean, *Samothrace* II, i, 26ff

111 *Sitometria*, A. Wilhelm, *Mélanges Glotz*, II (1932) 904. *Aequitas, BMC Imp* II, 254, No. 152; II, lxvii. Galatia, *OGIS* 533

112 Messene, *IG* V, i, 1379 (L. Robert, *BCH* 1928, 426ff; Tarn and Griffith, *HC*, 108)

113 Athens, Plutarch, *Per.* 37, 4; Schol., Aristoph. *Wasps*, 718. C. Hignett, *History of the Athenian Constitution*, 343ff rejects the view that Pericles' citizenship law of 451 was only applied in 445/4, the date of this gift. G. Nenci, *Rivista di Filologia e di Istruzione Classica*, 1964, 173ff, holds that Aristophanes refers to a distribution of 424/3, not to that of 445/4, but that each was preceded by a revision of the citizen roll, *contra* F. Jacoby, *Die Fragmente der griechischen Historiker* IIIB Suppl. II 573 n. 3; A. French, *The Growth of the Athenian Economy* (1964), 146. Athens, 329–4 BC, Demosth. XXXIV, 37–9; XLII, 21, 31; Tarn & Griffith, *HC*, 107; D. 2

114 Attitude to corn-merchants at Athens, R. Seager, *Historia* 1966, 172ff; at Rome, Bolkestein, 366–9. Under the Republic penalties for attempts to corner the market (*annonam comprimere, attentare, vexare*) tended to be less severe than in fourth-century Athens. Treves, *GET*, 47: 'Greek theories of distribution are, on the whole, not the outgrowth of human sympathy for the poor and the common labourer. . . . The purpose seems to be to guard against dishonesty.'

115 Laurium, Aristotle, *A.P.* 22, 7; Herod. VII, 144

116 *Theorikon*, Libanius, *Hypoth.*, Demosth. i *Olynth.*, Ch. 4. In general, see J. J. Buchanan, *Theorika: A Study of Monetary Distributions to the Athenian Citizenry during the fifth and fourth Centuries B.C.* (1962). In Periclean period? —not mentioned by Aristotle, *A.P.* 27, 4; but perhaps implied in some form by Plutarch, *Per.* 9, 3–4, 11, 4; Thuc. II, 38, 1. See also, Jacoby on Philochorus, fr. 33 (*FGH* IIIB *Suppl.* I, 563), placing *theorikon* probably in 'first half of the 40s'; Buchanan, 28ff; French, *GAE*, 152, 197 n. 38. Parade of tribute, B. D. Meritt, H. T. Wade-Gery, M. F. McGregor, *The Athenian Tribute Lists* (1939–53) III, 16–7. Fourth century, G. L. Cawkwell, *JHS* 1963, esp. 53ff; Jones, *AD*, 33ff. Cement of democracy, Plutarch, *N.Q.* 1011 B, Aristotle, *Pol.* 1320 A8

117 *Diobelia*, Aristotle, *A.P.* 28, 3. Equiv. to *theorikon*, Aristotle, *A.P.* (J. E. Sandys, 2nd edition (1912)), 119ff; A. E. Haigh, *Attic Theatre*, 3rd edition (1907), 330ff; see also Aristotle, *Pol.* 1267 B1ff; M. N. Tod, *Greek Historical Inscriptions* (2nd edition) I, No. 83 (six talents spent on one festival alone in 410 BC). Equiv. to *dikastikon?*—K. J. Beloch, *Rheinisches Museum für Philologie* (1884), 239–44; see also *IG* II (2nd edition) 1686B *l.* 59 (grain doled out to jurors in lieu of money in 405 BC); but *A.P.* 28, shows that *diobelia* was something *new*. Equiv. to dole for needy?—Buchanan, 41ff ('a strong array of epigraphical evidence'); W. S. Ferguson, *CAH* V, 344; Ehrenberg, *PA*, 166 (maintenance of 'no pay' principle, Aristotle, *A.P.* 33, 1; Thuc. VIII 97 1). Literary references suggest that Kleophon's rise and fall was linked to the *diobelia*, with which Archedemos (Xen. *Hell.* 1, 7, 2)

166   NOTES

and Kallikrates (*A.P.* 28, 3) were also associated; the latter, according to Aristotle abolished it, after having been the first to promise that he would add another obol to the two. Athenian tradition, Kurt von Fritz and Ernst Kapp, *Constitution of Athens* (1950), 172f. Help for the disabled, see *Note 165*

118 Like Bolkestein, 371–5, Berchem, *DBA*, 17, sees the *lex Sempronia* as the almost inevitable outcome of the *cura annonae* (concern for the food supply) 'qui, par une disposition universelle, a de tout temps incombè à l'État'. See also, H. Last, *CAH* IX, 57–60; E. Gabba, *Appiani Bellorum Civilium Liber I*, 337f; L. Piso, Cic. *Tusc.* III, 20, 48. A drain on treasury, Cic. *de off.* II, 21, 72; Oros. V, 12 (reflecting Livy); Plutarch, *C. Gracch.* 5; Appian, *B.C.* I, 21. Outline of the whole history of corn distributions at Rome, M. Rostovtzeff, *RE*, VIII, 172–82, *s.v. frumentum*. E. Badian, *Roman Imperialism* (1967), 34, 42f, 69, argues cogently that Cyrene and Cyprus were the sources of revenue for the corn laws of 73 BC and 58 BC, just as Asia had been for that of 123

119 Cic. *pro Sest.* 48, 103

120 Cassius Dio, XXXVIII, 13, 1 (Appian, *B.C.* I, 21, should perhaps be interpreted as meaning that Caius Gracchus' corn law was his only measure of consequence prior to his *re-election* to a second tribunate. The evidence on which Rostovtzeff held that Clodius merely brought back a law of Lepidus (consul 78 BC) introducing free corn is very uncertain. Saturninus, *auctor ad Herennium*, I, 12, 21 (note the language: 'Cum L. Saturninus legem . . . laturus esset . . . Saturninus ferre coepit . . . Caepio . . . impedimento est quo setius feratur'). M. Octavius, Cic. *Brut.* 62, 222; *de off.* II, 21, 72 (see H. Last, *CAH* IX, 95, 165f; T. R. S. Broughton, *MRR* I, 578 n. 3; A. E. Douglas, *AJPh* 1966, 304–6; also Douglas' note on the *Brutus* passage in his 1966 edition, 163f). Sulla and the following decade, Sallust, *Hist.* I, 55 11M; Gran. Licin. 43 B; *lex Terentia-Cassia* (73 BC); T. Rice-Holmes, *The Roman Republic*, i, 363f; R. J. Rowland, *A. Ant. Hung.* 1965, 81–3, estimates 180,000 beneficiaries by reference to Cic. *2 in Verr.* III, 163; *libertas* on coinage, *BMC, Imp.* I, 225, no. 138 (pl. 42, no. 1), a *sestertius* of Nero's reign. The legend on Hadrian's coinage, Note 130

121 Freeing of slaves, Appian, *BC* II, 120; Dion. Hal. IV, 24 (Berchem, 21, supposes that this may have caused Pompey to draw up an initial list of those entitled to a ration). Julius Caesar, Suet. *D.J.* 41, 3; Dio Cassius, XLIII 21, 4; Bolkestein, 357f

122 Mommsen, *Röm. Gesch.* (9th edition), III, 506; *lex Tabulae Heracleensis*, F. E. Adcock, *CAH* IX, 699; M. C. Frederiksen, *JRS* 1965, 188ff. Land law, Bolkestein, 364, 467–8, re. Suet. *D.J.* 20, etc. Domicile, Berchem, *DBA*, 22–3; Bolkestein, 377. 320,000, *Res Gestae divi Augusti*, 15

123 2 BC, Cassius Dio LV, 10, 1. *Congiaria*, Bolkestein, 337–9; Berchem, *DBA*, 119ff; P. M. Brunt and J. M. Moore, *Res Gestae Divi Augusti* (1967), 57–8. Philo, *leg. ad Gaium* 22. Van Berchem notes that from the first to the third

century each imperial *congiarium*, except for those of Domitian, is followed by issue(s) of commemorative coinage. Lower age limit, Suet. *D.A.* 41, Pliny, *paneg.* 26 (Berchem, *DBA*, 33–4). Manumission of slaves, Suet. *D.A.* 42

124 Exclusion of foreigners (doctors and teachers excepted), Suet. *D.A.* 42. 200,000 recipients, *Res Gestae*, 15; Cassius Dio LV, 10, 1. 150,000, Suet. *D.A.* 41; Cassius Dio LVII, 14, 2; Tacitus, *Ann.* I, 8. Citizenship the criterion, Schol., Persius V, 73 (*Romae autem erat consuetudo, ut omnes qui ex manumissione cives Romani fiebant in numero civium Romanorum frumentum publicum acciperent*); CIL VI, 10228, 10220, etc. (Berchem, *DBA*, 41ff). Large non-citizen population, Sen. *ad Helv.* 6, 2–3; Lucan, VII, 405; Juv. *Sat.* III, 62ff. Relation of this element to the *plebs sordida*, Tac. *Hist.* I, 4; *plebs infima*, Suet. *Otho*, 7; Z. Yavetz, *Athenaeum* 1965, 295ff. Estimates of the total population of Rome (and, therefore, of sections of it) are, however, hazardous, J. E. Packer, *JRS* 1967, 80ff. Little change till the Severi, Carcopino, *DLAR*, 290 n. 30

125 *Tesserae*, Berchem, *DBA*, 70ff. The epithet *nummariae* applied to them (*Res Gestae* 18; cf. Suet. *D.A.* 41) is taken by van Berchem (*DBA*, 86ff) to refer to their purchasing *function*, rather than to their physical shape or character; thus they are as represented on the coinage as oblong in shape and made of wood, and not identifiable with Rostovtzeff's *Bleitesserae* (*Klio* 1905, 3ff). Four-monthly scheme, Suet. *D.A.* 40. Cura annonae, *Res Gestae* 5, Suet. *D.A.* 37. Claudius, G. E. F. Chilver, *AJPh.* 1949, 7ff, minimises the changes, while Berchem, *DBA*, 73f, holds that there is no firm evidence for the eclipse of *praefecti frumenti dandi.* AD 6, Cassius Dio, LV, 26, 3 (Suet. *D.A.* 41); cf. Nero's action (Cassius Dio LXII, 18, 5; Tac. *Ann.* XV, 39) causing, on van Berchem's interpretation (*DBA*, 74–6), all the reserves to be put on the market in the interests of the *whole* population, so that the citizens temporarily ceased to receive their monthly free ration. Nerva, *BMC*, *Imp.* III, pl. 6, No. 1 and *xlviii;* G. Vitucci, *Arch. Class.* 1958, 310–4, *contra* Berchem, *DBA*, 77. Trajan, Pliny, *Paneg.* 28, 4, 26, 1–3 (M. Durry, *Panégyrique* (1938), rejects the view that the reference is to the *alimenta*). Severi, Berchem, *DBA*, 97ff, 178

126 Government scheme, R. Duncan-Jones, *PBSR* 1964, 123ff, citing earlier literature. Pliny, Sherwin-White, *LP*, 422. Representations on coinage, etc., M. Hammond, 'A Statue of Trajan represented on the *Anaglypha Traiani*', *Memoirs of the American Academy in Rome* XXI (1953), 127ff, where (as in his work, *The Antonine Monarchy* (1959), 462 n. 10) the very tenuous evidence for attributing the imperial scheme to Nerva is also noted (Duncan-Jones, PBSR 1964, 128)

127 R. Duncan-Jones, *PBSR* 1964, 128ff; A. Sirago, *L'Italia Agraria sotto Traiano* (1958), 288f. Non-repayable loans, Frank, *ESAR*, IV, 367; Laum, 172–3. Preliminary scheme, R. Duncan-Jones, *PBSR* 1964, 141–2; main-scheme, 129; *curiales*, 130ff

168 NOTES

128 Pliny, *ep.* X, 54, 55. Duncan-Jones, *PBSR* 1964, 128, notes the inadequacy of the emperor's estates

129 After Trajan, Duncan-Jones, *PBSR* 1964, 142ff. Hadrian's coinage, M. Hammond, *Memoirs of the American Academy in Rome* (1953), 172; see H. Mattingly, *BMC, Imp.* III, *clxiv*, for a possible pun on *liber, liberi* and *libertas;* also pl. 77, nos. 11, 12. Wholly beneficial?—A. Sirago, *L'Italia Agraria sotto Traiano*, 300

130 Bolkestein, 469ff; B. W. Henderson, *Five Roman Emperors (Vespasian— Trajan,* AD *69–117),* 212ff; cf. M. Hammond, *Memoirs of the American Academy in Rome* (1953), 172

131 Laum, 252; Pliny, *Paneg.* 26, 3–5, 28, 5; Livy, II, 9, 6 (exemption of *plebs* from *portoria* and *tributum*). See also, J. Gagé, *Les Classes Sociales dans L' Empire Romain* (1964), 126

132 B. W. Henderson, *Five Roman Emperors,* 220. Recruits in Italy, J. F. Gilliam, *AJPh* 1961, 247 n. 46. *Providentia* and *aeternitas,* M. P. Charlesworth, *Harvard Theological Review* 1936, 107–32, and *The Virtues of a Roman Emperor, Propaganda and the Creation of Belief* (1937), 15ff. Q. Metellus, note, in Gellius' version of his speech (I, 6), '*saluti perpetuae potius quam brevi voluptati consulendum est*'. Augustan legislation, H. Last, *CAH* X, 425ff; Pliny, *ep.* VII, 32, 1 (cf. Sirago, *L'Italia Agraria sotto Traiano,* 304)

133 Population decline argued, A. E. R. Boak, *Manpower shortage and the Fall of the Roman Empire in the West* (1955); criticized, M. I. Finley, *JRS* 1958 146ff (see also, P. M. Brunt, 167ff, in same volume). England, Owen, *EP,* 3, 14–5, 38, 53; Sirago, *L'Italia Agraria sotto Traiano,* 280f; J. Carcopino, *DLAR,* 77. Duncan-Jones, *PBSR* 1964, 130ff, argues, however, that the round-figure total of 300 was deliberately fixed by the government rather than dependent merely on the willingness of individuals to accept loans; see his suggestion (*Historia,* 1964, 199–200) that under Pliny's scheme at Comum more boys than girls benefited, 100 as against 75, calculated on the assumption that Pliny followed the emperor in allowing a larger sum for boys than for girls. Aurelius Victor, *epit. Caes.* 12, '*puellas puerosque natos parentibus egestosis*', but this is also the source of the doubtful statement that Nerva initiated the government scheme. Duncan-Jones, *PBSR* 1964, 130, refers to 'children of the poor', while in Lewis and Reinhold, *Roman Civilization,* II (1955), 354, Dessau 2927 (D. 36), '*pleb(is) urban(ae)*' is translated as though specifying children 'of the lower class'. Childlessness, Owen, *EP,* 397, 475, refers to this as a factor in English philanthropy

134 Oil, *BCH* 1882, 209; L. Robert, *BCH* 1935, 448; *Études Anatoliennes* (1937), 314. For use at home: it is perhaps doubtful whether Menas' provisions for 'use at home' at Sestos (D. 55) included oil; the type of oil referred to in inscriptions is not always easy to determine, *e.g.* Pliny *ep.* X, 23 (see Sherwin-White, *LP,* 594)

CHAPTER VIII

135 Jordan, *PE*, 279, calculates that almost one-third of Elizabethan benefactions went to education. The *ephebeia* of his own day is described by Aristotle, *A.P.* 42; its origin has been much disputed, but there is growing acceptance of the view that it existed in some form prior to the Lycurgan reforms of 336/5. C. Pélékidis, *Histoire de l' éphébie attique des origines à 31 av. J.C.* (1962), takes the extreme view that it goes back at least to the early fifth century and represents the outcome of a typical institution of the archaic Greek state. O. W. Reinmuth, *Transactions of the American Philological Association* 1952, 34–50 (also, *Gnomon* 1966, 793ff) is more cautious, but regards 336/5 as the date, not of the creation of the *ephebeia*, but of the enlargement of its programme; similarly, F. W. Mitchell, *Hesperia* 1964, 344–5, n. 34, *contra* M. P. Nillson, *Die hellenistiche Schule* (1955), 20. 40 talents subsidy, W. S. Ferguson, *Hellenistic Athens*, 10. Thetes included, C. A. Forbes, *Greek Physical Education* (1929) 128 n. 1

136 Sparta, W. Jaeger, transl. G. Highet, *Paideia*, III (1947), 171: 'the postulate that education should be the concern of the state is Sparta's real contribution to the history of culture'. Deficiencies of Spartan education, II, 325; also, H. Marrou, transl. G. Lamb, *History of Education in Antiquity* (1956), 150. Development of *ephebeia*, Pélékidis, *Histoire*, 117; he puts the intellectual side rather later than Reinmuth, in the early decades of the third century BC, but the absence of any inscriptions earlier than this is not decisive. The Sullan period, O. W. Reinmuth, *Hesperia* 1965, 255ff, *re. IG* II, (2nd edition), 1040, 1025

137 F. W. Mitchell, *Hesperia* 1964, 346, suggests that the withdrawal of subsidy was linked with the limitation of franchise. Single year, and voluntary course: some assign this change to a date before the end of the fourth century (doubted by Pélékidis, *Histoire*, 170–2, whose view appears somewhat misrepresented by Reinmuth, *Gnomon* 1966, 796f), but it will not in any case have been more than two or three decades later. Drop in numbers, Pélékidis, *Histoire*, 165ff, estimates drop from around 600–700 in the fourth century to 20–40 during the century beginning 267/6 (C. A. Forbes, *Greek Physical Education*, 152; J. Delorme, *Gymnasium* (1960), 469–72; Marrou, *HEA*, 107–8). Private generosity, E. Ziebarth, *Aus dem griechischen Schulwesen* (1913), 51ff (not all instances connected with *ephebeia*); Delorme, 316ff, Marrou, 187ff. Zosimos, *Inschr. von Priene*, 112, ll. 73ff. Preference for gifts of oil, Delorme, 467; Marrou, 389 n. 30

138 Library contributions, Pélékidis, *Histoire*, 263f; Delorme, *Gymnasium*, 331f; Marrou, *HEA*, 188. Religious duties, Pélékidis, *Histoire*, 211–56; O. W. Reinmuth, *Gnomon* 1966, 799; Ziebarth, *GS*, 148ff. *Neoi* at Mytilene, *SEG* III, 710 (*IG* XII, Suppl., No. 116). Cibyra, Ziebarth, *GS*, 53; Nillson, *Die hellenistiche Schule*, 38 n. 2. Decrees in honour of ephebes, Reinmuth,

Hesperia 1965, 262f. Delorme, *Gymnasium*, 472 speaks of military exercises as becoming '*un souvenir archéologique*'

139 Foreigners, O. W. Reinmuth, *The Foreigners in the Athenian Ephebeia* (1929); Marrou, *HEA*, 107, 384 n. 7. Membership of the *ephebeia* was a condition imposed at Athens on foreigners wishing to buy citizenship, but Reinmuth, *Gnomon* 1966, 798, questions whether extant ephebic lists can be used to show that Augustus' ban on the latter had any effect on entry into the former. Generosity of *kosmetes*, etc., Jones, *GC*, 223; Forbes, *Greek Physical Education*, 162f (distinguishing the gymnasiarch of *ephebes* from city gymnasiarch)

140 Early education, Marrou, *HEA*, 112–4. Literacy, F. D. Harvey, *REG* 1966, 585ff, discusses 'Literacy in the Athenian Democracy' (town and country, 619–20; women, 621–3; Plato and Aristotle oppose the trend). Mycalessus, Thuc. VII, 29, 5. *Paidonomoi*, *RE* XVIII, 2, 2387–9 (O. Schulthess)

141 Generalization, Marrou, *HEA*, 142ff, qualified in Nillson, *Die hellenistiche Schule*, 60; Jones, *GC*, 285, 352 n. 24; Forbes, *Greek Physical Education*, 82; Demosthenes, *de cor*. 257. Low fees, C. A. Forbes, *Teachers Pay in Ancient Greece* (1942), 29, 33

142 Miletus and Teos inscriptions, Ziebarth, *GS*, 10ff, 46ff. Marrou, *HEA*, 113, notes that almost half of Eudemos' fund is to be expended on sacrifices. Cult in gymnasia, Delorme, *Gymnasium*, 341f; Ziebarth, *GS*, 49f. England, Tudor-Stuart period (an an indirect attack on poverty), Jordan *PE*, 281ff; later, Owen, *EP*, 23ff (Charity Schools), 146ff (Ragged schools)

143 A possible instance of the donor's intention being overridden in the acceptance decree, see Note 12

144 Advertisement value of these donations, Rostovtzeff, *SEHHW*, 236; but internationally, too, such benefactions tended to be for higher education. For example, the lavish gift of 75 talents by Hieron and Gelon for the Rhodian gymnasium, *c*. 225 BC (Polybius V, 88), Rostovtzeff, *SEHHW*, 641ff

145 Charondas, Diodorus XII, 12, 4 (Bolkestein, 272f; Marrou, *HEA*, 388 n. 24; Harvey, *REG* 1966, 589 n. 10; Ziebarth, *GS*, 26)

146 Lack of public education, Plato, *Laws* 804 D, etc; Aristotle, *Pol*. 1337A (cf. *E.N.* 1180 (A26). Narrow citizenship, Plato, *Laws* 741 E, 846 D; Aristotle, *Pol*. 1278A. Upgrading?—Plato, *Rep*. 423

147 Plutarch, *Them*. 10 (Ziebarth, *GS*, 32–3). Solon, Aeschines, I, 19; Plato, *Crito* 50 D (rejected by Harvey, *REG* 1966, 589 n. 10, *contra* F. A. G. Beck, *Greek Education*, 92); A. R. W. Harrison, *The Law of Athens* (1968), 78 n. 3, takes the *Crito* passage as too free an interpretation of a law of Solon, Plut. *Sol*. 22, whereby a father who did not teach his son a craft was not entitled under the law to maintenance by the son later. Derkylos, Ziebarth, *GS*, 34; Marrou, *HEA*, 382 n. 3; F. W. Mitchell, *Hesperia* 1964, 337ff (followed in text). Some have used ps-Xen. *A.P.* 2, 10, to indicate the public provision of education (physical, at any rate) for boys at Athens; but see Forbes, *Greek Physical Education*, 82ff

148 Epikrates, Delorme, *Gymnasium*, 319, assumes he taught in the gymnasium. M. Guarducci, *Memorie, Accademia Nazionale dei Lincei, (classe di scienze morali)*, 6, II IX (1929), 629ff, supposes that others than the *ephebes* enjoyed such lectures

149 Schools of philosophy, Marrou, *HEA*, 47, 67, 70, 369 n. 3; see also, Laum, 243, C. A. Forbes, *Teachers Pay in Ancient Greece*, 24ff, who observes that Epicurus does not appear to have opposed fees where the latter were a token of gratitude, and that members of his school paid an annual contribution of 120 *drachmae*; later history, Cic. *ad fam.* XIII, 1, 3; Aristotle, *E.N.* 1164 B2ff

150 Polybius, *ap.* Cic. *de Rep.* IV, 3. Generalization, Marrou, *HEA*, 266–8, cf. 296. Pliny, see Sherwin-White, *LP*, 288, for references suggesting that such schools were common in larger *municipia*, for grammar if not for rhetoric. Municipal pride, expressed, for instance, under the Roman Empire in a bitter struggle between towns for honorary titles, Magie, *RRAM*, 635–8, 654; T. Frank, *ESAR* IV, 809; In England, Jordan, *PE*, 154; Owen, *EP*, 395 (or reflect on the dimensions of the 'wool churches' in neighbouring towns of East Anglia)

151 *Collegia iuvenum*, Marrou, *IIEA*, 299–301, 439 n. 1; Maria Jacyznowska, *Collegia Iuvenum* (1964), résumé in French, 84ff, argues that the *iuvenes* were parallel to the *neoi* rather than the *ephebes*, and closer to the professional or religious *collegia* connected with early cults at Lanuvium, Tusculum and elsewhere; she notes the access granted to slaves and freedmen, 86f, from the first century AD, but a high proportion were *seviri Augustales*

152 Vespasian, *AE* 1936, 128 (Magie, *RRAM* 572 and 1430–1, n. 15; Lewis and Reinhold, *RC* II, 295). Libraries, an account, with the Greek background (*librariae* in association with gymnasia), is given by C. Calmer, *Acta Instituti Romani Regni Sueciae X* 1944, 154ff. Comum, R. Duncan-Jones, *PBSR* 1965, 185. Ephesus, Dessau, 8971 (C. Calmer, 170f; Magie, *RRAM*, 584)

153 Nillson, *Die hellenistiche Schule*, 73; cf. G. M. Trevelyan, *English Social History* (1944), 363, Owen, *EP*, 247

154 Plato, *Rep.* 401; his advocacy of a strict censorship of poetry and drama is the outcome of his belief in the power of this 'unconscious education'. Pericles, Thuc. II, 41, 1: 'our city is a liberal education to Greece'. The provision of music and drama: at Athens, A. W. Pickard-Cambridge, *The Dramatic Festivals of Athens* (1953), 55ff (the opening sections of Lysias, 21, give a picture of how much might be spent by the wealthy on these occasions): elsewhere, Jones, *GC*, 280, 356 n. 46; Dio of Prusa wanted his city to be 'more open to the air, with wider spaces, with shade in summer, sun and shelter in winter . . . lofty buildings, etc.' (*Or.* XLVII, 15; H. von Arnim, *Dio von Prusa* (1898), 340ff)

CHAPTER IX

155 Hippocrates, *Parangeliai* IV, VI. For the date and character of the *Maxims*, see W. H. S. Jones, Loeb edition of *Hippocrates*, I, 308–11. Empiric School, L. Cohn-Haft, *The public Physicians of Ancient Greece* (1956), 39 n. 33

156 Asklepios, Cohn-Haft, *PPAG*, 27–30; E. J. and L. Edelstein, *Asclepios* (1945) II, 175: 'it was one of his claims to fame and admiration that he took care of the poor, and he had done so from the very beginning of his career', also *testimonia* from *Asclepios* I; Aristophanes, *Plutus*, 726ff; Julian, *Ep.* 78, 419 B (*T.* 421 and 320, Edelstein). Christian hostility, August. *c. Dei* III, 17; Justin, *Apol.* 54, 10; Lactantius, *Div. Instit.* IV, 27, 12 (*T.* 363, 332, 333, Edelstein). Kabiersch, *BPJ*, 74, rightly finds no evidence in Julian, *Misop.* 363 B, of the provision for poor in *pagan* temples, *contra* Bolkestein, 477. Hostels, Edelstein, 176; *T.* 719, 499; cf. Jordan, *PE*, 257–9, 55ff, and Owen, *EP*, 37f, both of whom cite R. M. Clay, *The Mediaeval Hospitals of England* (1909), *xvii–xviii*

157 A. G. Woodhead, *Cambridge Historical Journal* 1952, 235ff; cf. Bolkestein, 274ff

158 Aristophanes, *Acharnians*, 1030 with Scholiast (cf. *Suda*, s.v. δημοσιένων, reading ἰατροὶ καὶ... rather than ἰατροὶ ὡς δημόσιοι); Cohn-Haft, *PPAG*, 59. On the date of the Aristophanic *scholia*, Cohn-Haft, *PPAG*, 33. J. Bousquet, *BCH* 1966, 666, quotes a new instance of a doctor classed as a δαμοσιεργὸς in a second-century BC convention between Myania and Hypnia

159 Diodorus XII, 13, 4, rejected as evidence by Cohn-Haft, *PPAG*, 10 n. 29, and doubted by Woodhead, *CHJ* 1952, 238

160 Cohn-Haft, *PPAG*, 35 and n. 11

161 Phanodemus, Dittenberger, 495, of 343/2 BC; or cf., more generally, decrees in honour of presiding members of the Council, *SEG* XXI, 366, 369, 372, 376, 377, etc.

162 Foreign status, Cohn-Haft, *PPAG*, 52f, cf. 55 (a matter of availability). Men of culture, Plato, *Laws* 720 A–E refers to slaves as doctors, but not apparently as independent practitioners, nor as attending to free men normally (Cohn-Haft, *PPAG*, 14, 23ff)

163 Cos, Cohn-Haft, *PPAG*, 61–5 questions Herzog's view of doctors assigned by a 'board of health' to service in local demes of Cos and overseas posses-sions; D. 63 relates almost certainly to a Coan doctor working at Cos. Athens, Cohn-Haft, *PPAG*, 49, 56ff. Plato, *Gorgias* 455 A (see edition of E. R. Dodds (1959) with note), 456 B6, 514 DE, passages which do not prove *regular* elections of public doctors at Athens. Public endorsement: it is doubtful whether Cohn-Haft's translation of the *Acharnians* passage, 'I am not *qualified* to act the physician' would have the same degree of point, comically, as the usual version, 'But I am under no contractual obligations

to serve you as a doctor'. *Demokedes*, whose name means 'he who cares for the people', earned two talents, a huge sum, at Samos (Herod, III, 131). Cohn-Haft, *PPAG*, 20, cites other wealthy doctors. From the Roman Empire period we have a decree of Domitian in which he fulminates against doctors who took money for training slaves rather than free men (Lewis and Reinhold, *RC* II, 295)

164 Gifts, R. Pohl, *De Graecorum Medicis Publicis* (Berlin, 1905), 71f; similarly Jones, *GC* 219 (cf. Cohn-Haft, *PPAG*, 39 n. 31)

165 Provision for the disabled, Bolkestein, 273f. Solon, Plutarch, *Sol.* 31, 3 (which refers only to one specific case); schol., Aeschines, I, 103, Hesych. *s.v. adunatoi*; Aristotle, *A.P.* 49, 4; Lysias, 24, 22. J. J. Buchanan, *Theorika* (1962), I, accepts attribution to Solon, which was rejected by F. Jacoby, *FGH*, IIIB Suppl. I, 562–4, commenting on Philochoros, F. 197, who also doubted the limitation to the war-injured. A. Bocckh, transl. G. Lewis, *The Public Economy of Athens* (1842), 242, was, bearing in mind the limited evidence, too categorical in his assertion that such a scheme 'belonged exclusively to Athens, as charity was rarely met with among the Greeks'.

166 Plato, *Rep.* 406ff, in all except details the translation of A. D. Lindsay

167 *Iatrikon*, O. Nanetti, *Aegyptus* (1944), 119ff, who leaves obscure the connection, if any, with this tax of Diodorus' statement (I, 82) that 'in the course of military expeditions or service away from home in the *chora*, all receive treatment without paying any fee privately; for the doctors receive their keep ἐκ τοῦ κοινοῦ.' Are we to translate these words as 'from the community'? This does not square with our documents. As 'from the state'? Why then were only soldiers or travellers exempted from fees? See also C. Préaux, *Économie royale des Lagides* (1939), 132; Wilcken and Reinach, *Dictionnaire Daremberg-Saglio* III, 2, 1694

168 *Demosioi iatroi*, Cohn-Haft, *PPAG*, 68ff; O. Nanetti, *Aegyptus* (1941), 301ff; E. Boswinkel, *Eos* 1956, 181ff, relates title to situation arising from Antoninus' decree (*Digest*, XXVII 1 6 2–4, 10), and emphasizes the secondary importance of the doctor in some documents. Compare the elaborate picture drawn by Rostovtzeff, *SEHHW*, 1092f, offset by the conclusion that 'as regards the *laoi* I am afraid that it was left to the gods and the priests to help them to die in peace'

169 The first doctor ever to practise in Rome was the Peloponnesian Archagathos, who arrived in 219 BC, established a *taberna* at public expense, and was granted citizenship (Pliny, *N.H.* 29, 6). See, in general, H. Gummerus, *Der Ärztestand im römischen Reiche nach den Inschriften* (1932), 5ff. Medicine taken up late by Romans, Pliny, *N.H.* XXIX, 17. Edict of Vespasian, a copy at Pergamum, *AE*. 1936, 128; Magie, *RRAM*, 572, 1430f n. 15; K. H. Below, *Der Ärzt im römischen Recht* (1953), 23. Hadrian, *Digest*, XXVII, 1, 6, 8 (exemption from gymnasiarchy, billeting of troops, corn and oil purchasing magistracies); Gummerus, 9; Below, 24. Antoninus Pius, Below, 34, follows Pohl, *De Graecorum medicis publicis*, 23ff, 43, in

suggesting that it was after Antoninus' edict that the privileged doctors took the name of *archiatroi*, a title once held by court doctors of hellenized kings in Asia Minor and attested for the physician of the Emperor Claudius (Dittenberger, 804). See also, M. Wellmann, *RE* II, 1, 464–6; Magie, *RRAM*, 634, 1494f, n. 13. Free treatment for poor?—Below, 37f; Frank, *ESAR*, IV, 807 (who notes that *demosioi iatroi* had spread to the West, via the Greek colony of Massilia, by Augustus' reign: Strabo, IV, 1, 5, 181; Frank, *ESAR*, III, 417). Libanius, *ep. ad Celsum*, 635. Valentinian, *Cod. Th.* XIII, 3, 8, 368

170 *Valetudinaria*, K. Schneider, *RE* VIIIA, 1, 262–4; Sen. *de ben.* I, 1, 16; *de ira*, I, 16, 4. Slaves and freedmen, Cic. *ad fam.* XVI, includes a whole series of letters in which the health of his freedman, Tiro, is his main concern; cf. Pliny, *ep.* VIII, 24, 5; V, 19, 1–4; VIII, 16, 1–2

171 Cohn-Haft, *PPAG*, 40 n. 37, quotes from *Gospel of Wealth* (1933), 16. On the essential function of the city gymnasiarch Marrou, *HEA*, 114f; Ziebarth, *GS*, 65ff; Nillson, *Die hellenistiche Schule*, 56f; L. Robert, *Hellenica* VI, 127ff. Cf. use of the term *gymnasium* in inscriptions from Roman North Africa to mean distributions of oil (S. Lancel, *Libyca*, VI (1958), 143–52); D. 73. Attalus, *REG* 1906, 246 (Ziebarth, *GS*, 61). Veranius Philagrus, *IGRP*, 915 (Ziebarth, *GS*, 53)

172 Oil reservoirs, Delorme, *Gymnasium*, 304. Dioskurides, *Inschr. von Priene*, 123, ll. 5ff. Zosimos, *ibid.*, 112, ll. 56ff, 98–100. Dorylaeum, *OGIS*, 479 (a share in oil distribution, Nillson, 60); [Aristotle], *Oecon.* 1344 A23. Slaves at school, Marrou, *HEA*, 381 n. 1

173 Baths at gymnasia, C. A. Forbes, *Greek Physical Education*, 92, 238. Vaccius Leo, *IGRP*, 1302, *ll.* 38ff (Ziebarth, *GS* 76). M. Agrippa, Cassius Dio, XXXXIX, 43. Novaria, *CIL*, V, 6522. Timgad, P. Grimal, *Les villes romaines* (1954), 88. Italy has attested more *priced* gifts of baths than Africa, R. Duncan-Jones, *PBSR* 1965, 195. See also, A. Lussana, *Epigraphica* 1956, 87f. Rome, Carcopino, *DLAR*, 254. Victorian England, Owen, *EP*, 175. 'High living', Dittenberger, 716, *ll.* 106–7. *Destercoratio*, *AE* 1961, 97 (*Emerita* 1960, 146–9). M. Agrippa, Pliny, *N.H.* XXXVI, 104–8

174 Verona, Dessau, 557. 'Frivolous gifts', the judgment of Duncan-Jones on those attested for Italy, *PBSR* 1965, 233

DOCUMENTS

The following translations from original sources are arranged in three groups: the first (D. 1–46) offers evidence of charity or generosity mainly through the provision of cash or commodities; the second (D. 47–60) through the provision of educational facilities; and the third (D. 61–81) through the provision of medical or health facilities. Within each group the order of presentation is chronological (as far as can be determined), except where it would seem advantageous to juxtapose documents for comparison.

Besides references to the standard *corpora* of inscriptions, there are included references to recent publications and smaller collections of recent date where these are likely to be more readily accessible to the reader. Translations of fourteen of the Latin inscriptions will be found in Lewis and Reinhold, *RC*, II: all have been referred to with profit and, in the case of D. 35, 44, 74, closely followed. The translation of D. 22 derives from Frank, *ESAR*, II, 252; and that of D. 45 from an article by W. H. Buckler in *JHS* 1937. The French translations in Pouilloux, *Choix*, have also proved most helpful.

D. 1 Mid-fourth century BC; Tarentum (Italy) and other cities; Aristotle, *Pol.* 1320 B10

The example of the citizens of Tarentum may also be commended for imitation: the well-to-do share the use of their property with the poor and thereby secure the goodwill of the masses. [cf. *Pol.* 1263 A35]: Even now there are some states in which . . . each citizen has his own property, but when it comes to the use of this property, each makes a part of it available to his friends, and each devotes still another part to the common enjoyment of all his fellow-citizens.

D. 2 330–325 BC; Athens; Dittenberger, 304

[*l.* 6]: Demosthenes, son of Demosthenes of the deme Lamptrai, made the following proposal: since Herakleides of [Cyprian] Salamis continues in his service of the Athenian people with his heart set upon honour [*philotimeisthai*] and in doing all that he can that is good, and since previously he contributed at a time of corn shortage 3,000 *medimnoi* of corn at five *drachmae* a *medimnos*, being the first of the merchants who entered port, and again when a subscription-fund [*epidosis*] was established he contributed 3,000 *drachmae* to the corn-purchase fund, and for the rest, continues in his good will and energetic service towards the people: therefore, let it be resolved by the people . . . that he be made *proxenos* and benefactor [*euergetes*] of Athens, himself and his descendants, and that he have the right to own land and property according to the law, and that they serve militarily and pay property-tax along with the Athenians.

D. 3 Mid-third century BC; Samos (eastern Aegean); *MDAI* (*A*) 1919, 25 (*SEG* I, 366; Pouilloux, *Choix*, No. 3)

[*ll.* 23–5] : He was elected controller of the gymnasium by the people owing to the default of the person who was to serve, and maintained a high standard of discipline among the ephebes and *neoi*, acting with a sense of fairness and equity. [*l.* 36] : And when the state was troubled by a corn-shortage and the citizens, owing to the pressing nature of the need, appointed three corn-supply commissions, in all of these he displayed unfailing energy and enthusiasm [*philotimia*]; indeed, in the case of the first he advanced all the money for the deposit in accordance with the vote of the people, for the second he promised an amount equal to that of those who contributed the most, while for the third he not only contributed all the moneys for the deposit from his own private resources, but when the corn had been brought into the city and the commissioners for corn had borrowed money for this, he came before the assembly and promised that, since there were no funds available for reimbursement, he himself would repay the loan on behalf of the city and also the interest and all the remaining expenses; and this he did with all speed, repaying the lender without either making a contract with the city as regards these moneys or demanding that he be offered guarantors; rather, he made the common interest his main concern and the continuance of an ample food-supply for the people. As to the rest, he continues to display goodwill and enthusiasm for the people, both collectively and individually, by giving the best advice and arbitrating between disputants and assisting many of those in financial difficulty with contributions from his private resources. Therefore, so that we may show that we honour good men, and thus encourage in many of the citizens a like mind and purpose, it is resolved by the people to commend Boulagoras, son of Alexis, for his generosity [*arete*] and goodwill towards the citizens and to crown him with a golden crown on the occasion of the performance of tragedies at the Dionysia, and that the President of the games see to the proclamation and that the examiners [*exetastai*] have this decree inscribed on a stone monument which is to be erected in the temple of Hera; and the expense is to be met by the treasurer of sacred funds from the money at his disposal deriving from fines.

D. 4 *c.* 230 BC; Olbia (Black Sea); Dittenberger, 495

[*l.* 59] : And again in the priesthood of Pleistarchos, when there was a grave shortage of corn and when corn was being sold at 1⅔ *medimnoi* to the *aureus* and it was obvious that it would rise still further in price, and when, in as much as the price per *medimnos* became 1⅔ *aurei* at that moment, the people was in dire distress and thought it necessary to buy corn through state action and that the well-to-do should provide loans for that purpose, on the meeting together of the assembly he was the first to promise 1000 *aurei* for the purchase of corn which he brought and handed over on the spot; of this 300 *aurei* were to be without interest for a year, and while he made his gift wholly in gold, he took back copper in the case of 400; and he was the first to promise 2,500 *medimnoi* of wheat, of which he gave 500 at $4\frac{1}{8}$ *medimnoi* to the *aureus* and the remaining 2,000 at $2\frac{7}{12}$ *medimnoi* to the *aureus*; and, while the rest who promised in this emergency took their payment immediately from the funds provided, he met the cost himself for a year without exacting interest, and so through the ready service of Protogenes a very large amount of money and not a little corn was provided for the people . . . [*l.* 119]: Therefore the people in assembly, in great distress, brought before the eyes of all the dangers and perils which threatened, calling upon all men of means to come to the rescue and not to allow the fatherland, which had been kept secure over many years, to become subject to the enemy; and when no one offered himself either wholly or in part to meet the popular call, he himself freely promised to furnish the walls and to meet their whole cost.

D. 5 Second century BC; Aigiale, Amorgos (Aegean); *IG*, XII, 7515 (Laum, No. 50)

In the month of Apatourion, Architeles, son of Parmenion, Kratesilochos, son of Hegias, and Leonteus, son of Hegias, were chosen by the people according to the resolution to bring in a law for arranging the loaning out of the money which Kritolaos, son of Alkimedon, bestowed, and for the public feast and athletic contest, and to carry through all the other provisions; and they have introduced a law for the enrolment of Aleximachos, son of Kritolaos, as a hero, in accordance with the vote of the people and with the purpose of Kritolaos' gift of 2,000 *drachmae*, in the following terms: [*l.* 8]: The money is to be lent out in the month of Apatourion by the *archon* and the presiding committee of the Council and the officers in charge of rents and Kritolaos, son of Alkimedon. It is to be lent out at 10 per cent and the borrowers are to give as security landed estates to the value of not less than 2,000 *drachmae*, and the loan is not to exceed 200 *drachmae*. [*l.* 19]: And the principal is to be secured to the borrowers on the basis of the securities on which each borrowed the money, in the same way as with the tribal dues, in perpetuity; and the lenders are not to exact payment of it, and the borrowers are not permitted to pay down the money borrowed, but they are to continue with the loan on the securities on which they borrow in perpetuity. [*l.* 39]: And in order that the public feast may be carried out . . . two commissioners are to be chosen from the whole people of Aigiale, not less than thirty years of age, and those so chosen are at once to receive the money falling due and to buy a bullock of not less than two years and to sacrifice it. [*l.* 46]: And let the presiding committee and the gymnasiarch and the ephebes attend in procession upon the bullock from the town hall, and let all the younger men follow in procession. [*l.* 55]: And let them provide the dinner for all the citizens who are resident at Aigiale and the alien residents [*paroikoi*] and the foreigners and those of the Romans and their wives[?] who are present. [*l.* 58]: And let them supply sweet honey mixed with milk and provide the whole service for the dinner, making available wood and water and oil. And let the feast be a compulsory feast in the gymnasium, and let the commissioners set beside those in the dining-room a dinner, regardless of expense, and flowers, and let them set before them all the rest of what is sacrificed; but the hides let them sell straightway and expend the proceeds on the spot; and let the officers in charge give to each of the ephebes pork to the weight of a *mina*, and all that is set before them may be carried away from the dining room. [*l.* 70]: Let them issue rations of corn, having bought corn-wheat with the money, giving it on the first day to the citizens who are resident and the *paroikoi* and strangers staying with us, to each a man a *choinix* and to each child half a *choinix*. [*l.* 79]: And on the second day let them carry through the athletic festival, with the gymnasiarch employing for the prizes the whole of the ram and the half of the food provided, and the other half is to be for the presiding committee and the commissioners, and let them establish all the prizes for boys and men according to the gymnasiarch's law. [*l.* 82]: But let them not set up prizes for the *pankration*, but let Aleximachos son of Kritolaos be hailed as victor.

D. 6 2nd century BC (?); Samos (eastern Aegean); Dittenberger, 976 (Pouilloux, *Choix*, No. 34)

. . . among the most wealthy; and let them make the nomination in the month of Kronion in the second of the assemblies; and let the presiding-committee gather the assembly in the theatre and instruct the members to sit in their tribal sub-divisions [*chiliastues*], having marked off and defined their limits; and let anyone who refuses and does not sit in his own tribal sub-division [*chiliastys*] be fined a *stater* in the currency of the city; and if he declares that he has been wrongfully fined, let him enter a special plea and let the decision be made in the city court within twenty days. And let the presentation and election be carried out by the members of the tribal sub-divisions themselves. And in this assembly let the tribal-subdivisions examine the deposits and the guarantors, and whatever deposits they approve and whomsoever they approve as guarantors, let the presiding committee register them on the public records; and in like manner let them enter those who have been designated as *meledonoi* on the public records; and when the election is about to take place let the city herald utter a prayer that it may be for the best interest of those who by their vote elect the men whom they think will best manage the moneys, and let those declared elected exact the interest from the borrowers and make a written transfer to the elected members of the corn commission; and let these buy corn, that deriving from the 5 per cent dues provided by the district of Anaia, giving to the goddess a price not less than that which the people laid down ... five [*drachmae*] and two *obols*; and the money still remaining, if the people decides not to buy corn, let them keep themselves until others are elected to the office of the corn commissioners and then let them make a written transfer to the latter; but if they do decide to buy corn, let them make an immediate supplementary transfer to the already appointed corn-purchaser [*sitones*] and let him buy the corn from the territory of Anaia in whatever way he thinks will be most profitable for the people, unless it appear more advantageous to the people to buy corn from elsewhere; otherwise let the procedure be as the people decides. And let the presiding committee bring forward this matter each year, those who hold office in the month of Artemision, having given public notice of it in advance; and let the people designate in each year in the first of the assemblies for the election of magistrates, after the elective magistracies have been determined, two men, one from each tribe, to be in charge of the corn supply, being possessed of property to the value of not less than three talents each, and let these on receiving the interest from the *meledonoi* pay the price of the corn and whatever other expense arises, and let them measure out the corn. And let the people designate in the same assembly a corn-purchaser, his property being not less than two talents, and let the money from the interest be lent out, if anyone wishes to make a prior proposal, giving adequate securities and providing guarantors, and to provide the corn at a more advantageous rate; but those appointed to the management of the corn supply admit the securities at their own risk. And let them measure out all the corn that has been bought to the citizens in residence individually by their tribal sub-divisions, measuring out to each two measures a month free. And let them begin the distribution in the month of Pelusion and let them distribute in each successive month as long as the supply lasts; and let them not issue an allowance to one person on behalf of another unless someone is ill; and let them make the distribution from the first day to the tenth day of the month, but up to the thirtieth of the month in the case of those travelling. And each month let them give a statement in writing of those who have received a measure to the examiners [*exetastai*], by tribal sub-division, adding thereto the names of the recipients. And the members of the tribal sub-divisions shall have the right to appoint the same man as *meledonos* up to five years running. And if one of the borrowers does not pay back the money, whether in whole or in part, the tribal sub-division is to sell the security and, if there is a surplus, to return it to him who supplied it, but if there is a deficit, let it be recovered from the guarantor; and let the tribal sub-division give the interest accruing to those elected to control the corn supply; and if it fails to pay, let the members not receive the share in the distribution which is due to them until they honour their debt; and if any of the *meledonoi*, having received the money which he ought to lend, does not lend it, but keeps it himself wrongfully, let him be liable to a fine of 10,000 *drachmae*; and likewise, if he does not pay the interest to those elected to control the corn supply, let him be liable to the same fine and let the examiners register his property as forfeit to the tribal sub-division up to the amount which it was appropriate for him to repay, and with a view to a penalty, let them register him as deprived of his rights and let him remain so until he pays down the money; and let the members of the tribal sub-division also not receive the corn which is due, that is, those who designated the *meledonos* who has not paid his debt; but if the members of the tribal sub-division are ready to pay down the money, whether all or some of them acting jointly, which the *meledonos* has not repaid to the city, they shall have the right to do so, and whenever they have made payment let them receive the corn from the time of that payment. And let no one have the right to use this money for anything else, nor the revenue deriving from it, except for the provision of free corn; and if any presiding committee member brings forward a proposal or a public speaker proposes or a presiding officer puts to the vote a proposal that it should be used or converted to some other purpose, let each pay a fine of 10,000 *drachmae*, and likewise, also, if a treasurer or a *meledonos* or a member of the commission in control of the corn supply or a corn-purchaser give it or advance it for any other purpose and not for the free distribution of corn.

D. 7 *c.* 150 BC; Iasos (Asia Minor); *JHS* 1918, 100

[These men of their own will] desiring [further to advance] the democracy [made a contribution] of silver [from their own resources for the corn-supply, so that] the people might [ever live] happily, assured of a plentiful supply of corn, there being established the principle of equal rations [*sitometria*] for all the citizens [from the public fund in accordance with the law].

D. 8 Early or mid-second century BC; Samothrace (northern Aegean); *Samothrace*, II, i (1960), No. 5

And the price of the [surplus?] corn is to be paid to the corn supply officers [*sitothetai*] within the time laid down. And in order that money may be invariably available for the purchase of corn, the annual presiding committee of each Council, on the 21st of Maimakterion, is to arrange all [—] after payments made in advance to the sacred funds, [—] buying corn from whomsoever it may be necessary to buy. And the *sitothetai*, if there should be any lack of funds, are to announce it to the people, and the *argurologoi* are to give to the *sitothetai* immediately whatever they decide from the general revenue, whenever it has been collected . . .

D. 9 Before 100 BC; Istropolis (Bucharest); Dittenberger, 708 (F. G. Maier, *Griechische Mauerbauinschriften* (1959), No. 80)

[*l.* 3]: Since Aristagoras, son of Apatourios, being born of a good father and of ancestors who were all benefactors and priests of all the gods, wishing himself also to follow in their footsteps, on his return to his fatherland after the critical period through which the city had been passing, when the city was unwalled and the citizens were again in danger, together with their wives and children, showed the greatest energy and sincerity of purpose, on his appointment as officer for the repair of the city walls, in his attention to the work, and did not fail either in physical effort in anything which related to the building; and when the fatherland had been fortified and the citizens were coming back in groups from barbarian territory to the city, with some of the barbarians who were in control of the land he dealt shrewdly, while for certain of the citizens he advanced ransom-money, showing himself in every encounter with those who were thus being saved generous in his dealings, and in effecting very many settlements with citizens and foreigners in no case did he act in a mercenary spirit; moreover, as he advanced in years and grew in his reverence for the gods, as became him, first of all he honoured the gods, assuming the crown of Zeus and exercising his office as priest commendably, and he was praised by all the citizens, and then, coming forward of his own volition, he also took upon himself the official crown established by the city for Apollo; he honoured the city and the gods with festal gatherings to which all were invited and by sacred processions and by donations [epidoseis] to the tribes, wishing to make this clear, that there is gratitude alike from gods and from men who receive benefits for those who conduct themselves in the life of the city with reverence and with noble purpose; again, three years later, when the people, on account of the joint action of the barbarians who were in control of the land, were seeking a priest of Apollo, the Healer, men's private resources being under severe pressure, he made offer of himself [epididonai] and coming forward before the assembly he assumed the same crown, so obtaining double gratitude for himself both from the gods and from those he benefited. [l. 39]: And on his election as market controller [agoranomos] for a year he carried out his office as became a man of worth and honour, selling corn and wine at less than market price and bringing down the price of the remaining purchaseable goods to the greatest advantage of the citizens, and on receiving a panegyric in respect of this he rebuilt and set up an office for the agoranomos at his own expense; for this the people, welcoming his worthy and honourable action, appointed him agoranomos for a further two years, during which he gained equal distinction.

D. 10 *c.* 60 BC; Pegae (Greek mainland); *IG*, VII, 190 (*JOAI* 1907, 17ff; Laum, No. 22)

[*l.* 18]: And since often, on account of the straitened circumstances of the city, the ceremonial war-dance could not be held, he promised of his own volition 1,225 Alexandrian *drachmae*, so that from the interest on this capital the dance might be introduced each year.

[*l.* 22]: And in addition to all this, when we were wanting to give honour to Soteles and to set up his statue, appearing in the council and observing that the public funds were under pressure, he undertook to meet the expense of the statue and of its erection out of his own pocket, desiring thoroughly to please the citizens. And in order that the city might incur no expense on his account, when he set up the statue he sacrificed to all the gods and gave a dinner to all the citizens and residents [*paroikoi*] and to the Romans residing with us and to the slaves of all these and their sons and the slaves' children. In order then that others also may emulate such deeds for the advantage of the city, it was resolved . . . to commend Soteles, son of Kallinikos, for his goodwill and generous spirit, which he has shown unfailingly from his earliest youth, and to set up his statue wherever he wishes, in the most prominent place in the market, and to inscribe it thus: 'The people of Pegae [honours] Soteles, son of Kallinikos [its benefactor] for his goodwill and reverent spirit towards the gods, so that [all may know that the men of Pegai know how to honour those showing a generous spirit towards them]. And let the herald of the council summon him to a place of precedence, and his descendants . . .

D. 11 End of first century BC; Rhodes; Strabo, XIV, 2, 5, (652)

The Rhodians are concerned for the people in general; although their rule is not democratic, yet they want to look to the interests of the lower classes ['the poor']. Thus the people are supplied with provisions and the well-to-do support those who are not well-off, and there are certain public services [provided by the wealthy] concerned with the provision of rations; in this way, whilst the lower classes are provided for, the city does not lack what it needs, especially for naval expeditions.

D. 12 *c.* AD 42; Akraephia, Boeotia (Greek mainland); *SEG*, XV, 330 (*BCH* 1935, 438ff)

[*ll.* 9–14]: The generosity of Demetrios and Empedon when no money was available for the recently revived festival of Apollo and the Emperor.] [*l.* 48]: Empedon, the son of Empedon, and Demetrios, the son of Leonidas, and Pamphilos, the son of Soterichos, undertook on demand the office of *polemarch*, and, observing the straits to which the city was reduced, they accepted in addition, of their own free will, the office of *agoranomos* and that for the supply of oil; and to the traders and butchers and bakers who were accustomed to be irregular in their service of the city they supplied out of their own resources, as a gift, corn for the bakers and for the rest money as an interest-free loan for a year, through which we enjoy unfailing cheap supplies; and they provided oil with outstanding generosity, giving oil, boiled and very rich with perfume, and also making available white oil for unrestricted use; on account of all this [it is proposed] that there be voted by the archons and councillors and the people, that they be given places in the gymnasium and in whatever other place of prominence they desire and that statues be set up in gilt armour, with an inscription engraved: 'The city of Akraephia to Empedon . . . for their generosity and benefactions to her'; and that there be engraved on a pillar both the decrees and the inscription and that it be placed in the gymnasium in whatsoever place they wish.

D. 13 End of first century AD; Mantinea, Antigonea (Greek mainland); *IG*, V, 2, 268 (*BCH*, XX, 126, Laum, No. 5)

[*l*. 6]: Resolution of the Antigoneans: since Euphrosynus, son of Titus, our citizen, inheriting the goodwill displayed by his fathers towards the fatherland, so far from detracting anything from his family's worth, has enhanced it, always and every day contriving to provide some advantage for the city, being a man who, although possessed from birth of excellent moral qualities, has surpassed these in developing a character excelling his natural disposition, a man lavish in his gifts . . . He directed by statute that the income from the land should be used for the support of the corn purchase fund, providing for the unfailing supply of food in perpetuity.

[*l*. 32] [the decree goes on to praise Euphrosynus' wife, Epigone]: For they were linked together in a union of body and mind in their lives and they shared a common and undivided concern in always seeking to go beyond the other in devoting themselves to the performance of good deeds; thus, they rebuilt the temples which had been in utter ruins and they added dining-rooms to those existing and they provided the [religious] societies with treasuries, extending their piety not only to the gods but to the places themselves. Epigone, indeed, a woman of saintly dignity and devoted to her husband, imitated his example herself by taking up the priesthood ordained for every goddess, worshipping the gods reverently at sacrificial expense, in providing all men alike with a festive banquet.

D. 14 Early first century AD; Oenoanda (Lycia and Pamphylia); *IGRP* III, 493

He [C. Licinius Marcius Thoantianus Fronto] was town clerk, serving his native town with his heart set on honour [*philotimōs*], and he was a Roman and a citizen of Oenoanda who served as clerk of the Lycian confederacy, gymnasiarch and officer in charge of the corn ration providing corn at [?] *denarii*, and he held the office of priest of the *Augusti* with his most distinguished wife, Licinia Flavilla, with all reverence and magnanimity, and he was in charge of the corn ration a second time, distributing [*epididonai*] to the citizens both from the public supply and also from his own supply in a most difficult time; and he contributed to a public subscription for a distribution of money, ten *denarii* to each citizen, so that all who dwell in the city share this benevolence, and in every office he showed his concern for honour [*philotimeisthai*].

D. 15 First century AD; Epidaurus (Greek mainland); *IG*, IV², 65

In marketing corn on numerous occasions, whenever there was need, he harmed his private livelihood for the sake of the good of all; and he provided certain buildings for the city, and some of the public places he repaired, spending on these things lavishly and beyond what was normal, and in the magistracies he acted in a fair and just way towards all, and so too in his public obligations he met expenses with magnificent generosity; and in the rest of the needs which the city experienced he maintained the trust which the city placed in him, and in doing all this he harmed still further his private livelihood.

D. 16 Second half of first century AD; Atina (southern Italy); Dessau, 977 (Lewis and Reinhold, *RC*, II, 348f)

To Titus Helvius Basila, son of Titus, aedile, praetor, proconsul, legate of Caesar Augustus, who bequeathed to the people of Atina 400,000 sesterces, so that from the interest therefrom there might be supplied corn for their children until they came of age and that afterwards 1,000 sesterces per head should be given. Procula, his daughter set up [this monument].

D. 17 Late first century AD; Comum (northern Italy); Pliny, *ep*. VII, 18 (Bruns, 146)

Greetings from Pliny to his friend Carinus. You raise the question as to how the money which you have offered to our townsmen for a feast is to be safeguarded after your death. Suppose you pay over the money to the state—there is the fear that it will be mis-directed; suppose you hand over land—then once it has become public it will be neglected. For my own part I find nothing more expedient than what I myself have done. For, instead of the 500,000 sesterces which I had promised for the maintenance of free-born boys and girls, I made over to the administrator of public lands a piece of land from my estate which was worth considerably more, and then I took it back again burdened with a ground rent by which I was to pay 30,000 sesterces annually. In this way the amount due to the state is secure and the financial return is not subject to variation, while the land itself, because of the very fact that its yield greatly exceeds the rent, will always find an owner to work it.

D. 18 AD 101; near Beneventum (Italy); Dessau, 6509 (Bruns, 145b; Smallwood, 435; Lewis and Reinhold, *RC*, II, 346)

In the consulship of the Emperor Caesar Nerva Trajan Augustus Germanicus for the fourth time and Quintus Articuleius Paetus, those whose names are written below offered as security properties in accordance with the instruction of the best and greatest emperor, so that as a result of the contract the Ligures Baebiani may receive interest monthly as written below, and in accordance with his kindly purpose their boys and girls may receive maintenance allowances. [The terms of 66 mortgages follow, for example]: By Crispia Restituta, the Pomponian farms in the territory belong to Beneventum, the Aequan district in the Ligurian area, adjoining Nasidius Vitalis, valued at 50,000 sesterces, for [a loan of] 3,250 sesterces. Half-yearly interest, 88 sesterces.

D. 19 *c.* AD 102 and 114; Veleia (northern Italy); Dessau, 6675 (Bruns, 145a; Smallwood, 436; Lewis and Reinhold, *RC*, II, 345)

Mortgages on properties to the amount of 1,044,000 sesterces, so that in accordance with the kindly purpose of the best and greatest Emperor, Caesar Nerva Trajan Augustus Germanicus Dacicus, boys and girls may receive maintenance allowances as follows: legitimate boys, 245 in number at 16 sesterces each [per month], making a total of 47,040 sesterces; legitimate girls, 34 in number at 12 sesterces [per month], making a total of 4,896 sesterces; illegitimate boy, 1, 144 sesterces [per year]; illegitimate girl, 1, 120 sesterces [per year]. Total, 52,200 sesterces, which equals 5 per cent interest on the afore-mentioned principal. [The terms of 46 mortgages follow, for example, No. 1]: Gaius Volumnius Memor and Volumnia Alce through Volumnius Diadu-menus, their freedman, registered the Quintiac Aurelian farm and Muletas hill with the woods which is in the Veleian district, in the Ambitrebian area, bounded by M. Mommeius Persicus, Satrius Severus and public property, worth 108,000 sesterces; they are to receive 8,692 sesterces and to offer the aforementioned farm as security. [Then follows an earlier group of mortgages, dated before AD 102]: Likewise the mortgages taken on properties by Cornelius Gallicanus to the amount of 72,000 sesterces, so that in accordance with the kindly purpose of the best and greatest *princeps*, the Emperor Caesar Nerva Trajan Augustus Germanicus, boys and girls may receive support as follows: legitimate boys, 18 in number, at 16 sesterces [per month], a total of 3,456 sesterces; legitimate girl, 12 sesterces [per month]; total of the two sums, 3,600 sesterces, which equals 5 per cent interest on the aforementioned amount.

D. 20 AD 169–80; Sicca (North Africa); Dessau, 6818 (*CIL*, VIII, 1, 641, Bruns, 150; Lewis and Reinhold, *RC* II, 352–3)

To my fellow townsmen of Cirta, to my beloved Siccenses, I [P. Licinius Papirianus] wish to give 1,300,000 sesterces. I entrust this sum to you, dearest townsmen, that from the interest of five per cent there may be maintained each year 300 boys and 300 girls, the boys from the age of three to fifteen, each boy receiving 2½ *denarii* per month, the girls from the age of three to thirteen, each girl receiving 2 *denarii*. Townsmen and residents likewise should be chosen, provided that the residents shall be dwelling within the buildings which bound our colony, and these, if it shall seem good to you, it will be best for the *duoviri* of each year to choose; but care should be taken that an immediate replacement is found for any child reaching adult age or dying, so that the full number may always be maintained.

D. 21 Second century AD; Tarracina, Latium (Italy); Dessau, 6278 (*CIL*, X, 6328, Lewis and Reinhold, *RC*, II, 352)

Caelia Macrina, daughter of Gaius, left 300,000 sesterces in her will for the construction of this monument and . . . thousand for its decoration and upkeep. She also left in memory of her son, Macer, to the people of Tarracina 1,000,000 sesterces, so that the interest therefrom might be given to one hundred boys [and one hundred girls] on account of maintenance allowances, to each boy of the colony 5 *denarii* per month, and to each girl four *denarii* per month, for the boys to the age of 16, for the girls to the age of 14, so that, by means of constant replacement, 100 boys and 100 girls are always in receipt of it.

D. 22 Mid-second century AD; Antinoopolis (Egypt); *Aegyptus* 1933, 518 (*Greek Papyri in the British Museum*, Inv. No. 1905; Frank, *ESAR*, II, 252)

To [—] nomarch of Antinoopolis, from Lysimachos, also called Didymus, son of Heraclides, of the Matidian tribe and Callitecnian deme, living in his own house in the first quarter, seventh block. Petronius Mamertinus, former prefect, made known to us the benefits granted to us by the deified Hadrian, the founder of our city, by which he directed that the children of Antinoites who are returned by us, their parents, within thirty days of their birth, should be maintained from the proceeds of funds granted for this purpose and from other revenues. I therefore return the son born to me, Heraclides, also called Valerius, twenty days old, by my wife Ninnarous, daughter of Orsenouphis, Antinoite, the fee for whose birth certificate I paid through the most excellent senate, furnishing three guarantors of the marriage and parentage . . .

D. 23 Not earlier than AD 50; Aigiale, Amorgos (Aegean); *IG*, XII, 389

Since Kritolaos and Parmenion, the sons of Alkimedon, on becoming *choregoi*, provided all that was needed for the staging of the plays and carried through their office with an enthusiasm which called for honour [*philodoxōs*], being unfailing in their devotion and ambitious spirit of service [*philotimia*], and in addition supplied a ration of corn for the people and for all those dwelling in Aigiale and for the foreigners lodging in the city, and, sacrificing oxen to Apollo and Hera, they provided meat and a feast for the people on two days, providing all that was beneficial for the sacred gathering, with no thought for expense and in a spirit of ambitious service [*philotimia*]; so that our city may be seen to honour men of ambitious spirit [*philotimoi*] and honest worth, etc. [*l*. 30: Honours are awarded for *arete*, *eunoia* and *philotimia* towards the city, and for *eusebeia* (reverence) towards the gods].

D. 24 After AD 180; Corfinium (central Italy); *Epigraphica* 1958, 15–17

[Q. Avelius Priscus] for a public office gave five gladiatorial shows, and for the public office of *quattuorvir* gave dramatic shows, and for the office of aedile gave games in honour of the goddess Vetidina, and to help the corn supply he donated 50,000 sesterces to the state of Corfinium, and for the Avelian bath for women 30,000 sesterces and many feasts and distributions of money to the whole body of citizens from his own funds, and frequently he gave financial assistance to meet heavy obligations of the state. The people of Corfinium [dedicated] publicly [this monument] to mark his outstanding goodwill towards the city: Avelius Priscus accepted the honour but himself bore the cost.

D. 25 AD 145; Ephesus (Asia Minor); Dittenberger, 850; Lewis and Reinhold, *RC*, II, 349

[Letter of Antoninus Pius to the Ephesians]: The generous service [*philotimia*] which Vedius Antoninus is providing for you in his eagerness for honour [*philotimeisthai*] I have learnt from his letters rather than from yours; for since he wants to obtain help for the embellishment of the public works which he has promised you, he has revealed the great amount of building he is adding to the city, but you have not given it a proper welcome. I have agreed to his requests and welcomed the fact that he has not chosen the usual way of those engaged in political life, who for the sake of immediate prestige lavish their expenditure on shows and distributions and prizes for the games, but prefers a way by which he hopes to make the city more imposing in the future.

D. 26 Late second century AD; Camerinum (central Italy); Dessau, 6640

This man's father often met the burden of the corn supply when corn was dear and frequently he gave a feast. The people of Camerinum [dedicated this] in view of the very many and great benefits conferred on themselves by his father and himself. He accepted the honour, but he gave back the amount which they had collected. At the dedication he gave a feast.

D. 27 After AD 180; Ager Sorrinensium Novensium (central Italy); Dessau, 6595

To Marcus Aurelius Marcellus, son of Elainus, priest with right of jurisdiction of the Sorrinenses Novenses, *quaestor* of the public funds, patron of the associations of smiths and quiltmakers. To this man, first of all, the distinguished council, from the gifts which they had received, voted that a statue should be set up on account of his services. For the dedication of this statue he gave to the councillors bread and wine and forty sesterces, and moreover on account of the honour conferred upon him he gave 5,000 sesterces to the people for the corn supply in perpetuity.

D. 28 AD 136; Lanuvium, Latium (Italy); Dessau, 7212 (Bruns, 175; Lewis and Reinhold, *RC*, II, 273-5)

[Clauses from the charter of a funeral society. Preface]: At Lanuvium in the temple of Antinous, in which Lucius Caesennius Rufus, patron of the municipality had instructed that a meeting be called, through the agency of L. Pompeius ... *quinquennalis*, of the worshippers of Diana and Antinous, he promised that he would out of his generosity give to them the interest on 16,000 sesterces, namely 400 sesterces, on the birthday of Diana, August 13th, and 400 sesterces on the birthday of Antinous, November 27th . . . [Laws of the society]:

It is unanimously resolved that whoever wishes to become a member of this society shall give as a personal entrance fee 100 sesterces and an *amphora* of good wine, also he shall pay a monthly subscription of 5 *asses*. It is likewise resolved that whoever fails to pay his subscription for six months in succession, and the common lot of mankind befalls him, his funeral shall not be covered, even if he has provided for payment in his will. It is likewise resolved that whoever departs this life as a paid-up member of this body, shall duly receive from the treasury 300 sesterces, from which sum there shall be deducted a funeral fee of 50 sesterces, which shall be distributed at the pyre; the funeral procession shall go on foot . . . It is likewise resolved that if any slave belonging to this association is given his freedom, he shall be under obligation to give an *amphora* of good wine . . . List of dinners: March 8th, the birthday of Caesennius . . . father [of Caesennius Rufus, the patron]; November 27th, the birthday of Antinous; August 13th, the birthday of Diana and of the society; August 20th, the birthday of Caesennius Silvanus, brother [of Caesennius Rufus]; 4th [or 6th] of [—] the birthday of Cornelia Procula, his mother; December 14th, birthday of Caesennius Rufus, patron of the municipality . . . Likewise it is resolved that whoever is appointed *quinquennalis* in this society, the same should be exempt from presenting pottery miniatures during the period of his office; and in every distribution a double share shall be given to him; likewise to the secretary and to the summoner of meetings, being exempt from presenting pottery minia-tures, there shall be given a share and a half in every distribution. Likewise it is resolved that whoever holds the office of *quinquennalis* honestly, to him by way of honour there shall be given a share and a half in everything, so that others also may hope for the same by the proper performance of their duty . . . Like-wise it is resolved that the *quinquennalis* shall sacrifice on the holidays of his period of office with incense and wine, and shall perform the rest of his duties, clothed in white, and on the birthdays of Diana and Antinous he shall provide oil for the society in the public baths, before their banquet.

D. 29 AD 100–150 (?); Iuvavum (Salzburg); *JOAI*, XLIII (1956–8), 52ff

To Marcus Haterius Summus, son of Lucius, town-councillor of the munici-pality of Iuvavum, *duovir* with power of jurisdiction, the people [dedicated this] to an excellent citizen for his relief of the corn supply.

D. 30 First half of second century AD; Nacolia, Phrygia (Asia Minor); Dessau, 7196 (*TAM*, V, 95f; Laum, No. 121, Lewis and Reinhold, *RC*, II, 340)

Chapter of the will of Publius Aelius Onesimus, imperial freedmen: To my dearly loved fatherland of Nacolia, although I owe it very much, yet in keeping with the limited size of my estate I desire to be given 200,000 sesterces on the following condition, that according to the ruling of Cornelius ... and Cornelius [Hes]ycius, the money be lent out and that from the interest accruing during the next three years they may make a contribution to the corn fund, so that whatever amount of corn is possible may be obtained each year. And at the end of this three-year period I wish the interest on all the money to be divided out to my fellow citizens each year, following upon a registration of them on the most blessed birthday of our lord Trajanus Hadrianus. However, I wish half of the interest to be allotted for individual gifts [*sportulae*], in such a way that half of it is given out on the holiday called ...

D. 31 AD 138–61; Petelia (southern Italy); Dessau, 6468 (Duncan-Jones, *Historia* 1964, 199f)

To Manius Megonius Leo, son of Manius, grandson of Manius and great grandson of Manius, aedile, *quattuorvir* under the Cornelian law, *quaestor* of the public funds, patron of the township, *quattuovir, quinquennalis*; the town-councillors, *Augustales* and people gave this monument from money subscribed on account of his services. Chapter from his will: To the state of my fellow townsmen, if a pedestrian statue has been set up in the upper forum, with a stone foundation and a marble pedestal, on the model of that which the *Augustales* set up near to that erected to me by the townsmen, I wish to be given the 100,000 sesterces above mentioned, so that from the interest of six per cent on this money, every year on my birthday, which is March 23rd, there may be a distribution to the decurions at a feast, of 300 *denarii*, allowing for deduction from this sum for the service, the rest to be divided among those who shall be present at that time. Also to the *Augustales* on the same condition I wish 150 *denarii* to be given, and to the townsfolk of Petelia of either sex, in accordance with local custom, one *denarius* in every year, and also at the feast of the *Parentalia* fifty *denarii* and in addition the cost of the sacrificial victim, in accordance with the terms of the public contract. From you, best of townsfolk, I earnestly seek, in the name of the most sacred Emperor Antoninus Augustus Pius and his children, that you hold in perpetuity to my purpose and dispositions, and that you inscribe this whole chapter of my will on the pedestal of my pedestrian statue, which I besought you above to set up for me, that it may be the better known also to our descendants or, again, that it may act as a reminder to those who may be munificent towards their native city.

D. 32 After AD 100; Pisaurum (central Italy); *CIL*, XI, 6377

To Titius Valentinus, son of Gaius, of the Camilian tribe, *quaestor, duovir*, who by his will gave to the colonists of the colony of Iulia Felix at Pisaurum one million sesterces, so that each year from the interest on 400,000 a feast should be given to the people on the birthday of Titus Maximus, his son, and that from the interest on 600,000 gladiatorial games should be given every fifth year. Erected by the people of the city.

D. 33 Late first or second century AD (?); Stratonicea (Asia Minor); (*BCH* 1891, 184f, No. 29; cf. *BCH* 1927, 57ff)

[Voluntary priests for two years]: Theophilus son of Theophilus of Hierakome and priestess Tryphera . . . opening the sacred refectory of the god to every class and age and to the out-of-town visitors with the most ready goodwill and lavish generosity, entertained also the body of elders in the city with food to be carried away.

D. 34 Date uncertain; Spoletium (central Italy); *CIL*, XI, 4789

This man, military tribune of the legions XV *Apollinaris* and V *Macedonia* bequeathed by will to his fellow townsmen 1,500,000 sesterces, so that from the income deriving from this sum each year on the sixth of November, his birthday, there might be given to his fellow townsmen a feast and pastry and mead.

D. 35 After AD 100; Spoletium (central Italy); Dessau, 6638 (*CIL*, X, 4815; Lewis and Reinhold, *RC*, II, 356)

Gaius Torasius Severus, son of Gaius of the Horatian tribe, *quattuorvir* with power of jurisdiction, *augur*, built this [probably public baths] in his own name and in the name of his son, Publius Meclonius Proculus Torasianus, pontiff, on his own land and at his own expense. He likewise gave to the community to celebrate the birthday of his son 250,000 sesterces, out of the income from which on August 30th, annually, the decurions are to hold a public banquet and the townspeople who are present are to receive eight sesterces apiece. Likewise he gave to the board of six priests of Augustus and the priests of the *Lares* of Augustus and to the officers of the city-wards 120,000 sesterces, so that out of the income from this sum they might have a public repast on the same day. Because of his services to the municipality the council of decurions adopted him as patron of the municipality.

D. 36 Early second century AD; Comum (northern Italy); Dessau, 2927 (*CIL*, V, 5262; Lewis and Reinhold, *RC*, II, 353f)

Gaius Plinius Caecilius Secundus, son of Lucius of the Oufentine tribe, consul, augur *legatus propraetore* in the province of Pontus and Bithynia, sent to that province with the rank of praetor in accordance with a decree of the senate by the Emperor Caesar Nerva Trajan Augustus Germanicus Dacicus . . . He left [?] sesterces in his will for the construction of baths, with an additional 300,000 [plus?] sesterces for decoration and in addition 200,000 sesterces for upkeep; and for the support of his freedmen, a hundred persons, he likewise bequeathed to the municipality 1,866,666 sesterces, the income from which he desired to be spent afterwards on an annual banquet for the people. In his lifetime he also gave 500,000 sesterces for the support of the boys and girls of the populace of town [*plebs urbana*], and also a library and 100,000 sesterces for the upkeep of the library.

D. 37 First or second century AD; Tenos (Aegean); *IG*, XII, 3 1119 (Laum, No. 60)

The council and people [honours] Satyros, son of Philinos, who has filled every office and liturgy and has on four occasions held the *architheoria* [leadership of a sacred embassy] and bestowed upon the city baths and: (1) 5,000 *denarii*, so that from the interest therefrom the baths may be heated; (2) for the gods in Eriston 5,000 *denarii*, so that from the interest on the festival of the *Bouthusia* each year there may be given a *denarius* per head to those free Tenians who shall join in the feast in the temple; (3) in addition, for the same gods, 10,000 *denarii*, so that from the interest therefrom each year there may be apportioned in the temple, on the day of garlands and on the eighteenth day, to every free Tenian a certain sum, the amount to be according to the number of those who gather together; (4) and again 6,000 *denarii*, so that from the interest therefrom each year there may be apportioned to Andrian men and women, on the day fixed for the ceremony at his grave, the sum appropriate to the number of those who gather together; (5) and again 18,500 *denarii*, so that from the interest therefrom the amount of the poll-tax may be given on behalf of the free men and women and children.

D. 38 First or second century AD; *Ebusus*, Ibiza (western Mediterranean); Dessau 6960 (*CIL*, II, 3664)

This man bequeathed to the state of Ebusus [ninety] thousand sesterces, with the intention that from this sum each year the tribute to the Romans might be paid and that the citizens should not be compelled to pay tribute at a difficult time. The remaining [six] thousand are to be lent out and from the interest games are to be held each year, together with provision of five illuminated vessels on his birthday.

D. 39 Late second century; Termessus, Pisidia (Asia Minor); *TAM*, III, 4

In the month of Soterios, the thirteenth day in the regular assembly, it was resolved by the people, on the proposal of the presiding committee; since Atalanta, daughter of Preterabis, daughter of Pillakoas, daughter of Kinnunis, a widow, adorned both with nobility and with a sense of what is right, and who reveals to the full the quality of a woman emulating by her exertions the accomplishments of her forefathers in their ambitious services [*philotimeisthai*] towards the city, both in expenditure of no mean kind and in advancing moneys and in public subscriptions and gifts and priesthoods, has promised in time of great corn shortage to provide an ample supply for the commons, and in fulfil-ment of her generous promise [*philotimia*] she provides corn unstintingly from the month Idalianos of the present year . . . [bronze and golden crowns are voted in her honour, a statue in a prominent place, close to the Attalus arcade].

D. 40 After AD 180; Corfinium (central Italy); Dessau, 6530

[To a man who had held most of the local offices of Corfinium, including those of *sacerdos* and *pontifex*]: On account of the outstanding forebearance and high moral sense [*verecundia*] of this man, the distinguished council with agreement of the people voted that the bronze plaques of patrons should be conferred upon him and his sons. P. Mammius Aufidius Priscinus, having received the honour, straightaway held a glad celebration for the distinguished members of the council and their wives and children, and also for the people in a public feast, amid much jubilation. And for these services the council and people of Corfinium voted that a statue be set up to him, so that the love which he displayed to his fellow-citizens, both individually and collectively, should be requited, and for his children, boys belonging to the rank of knights, at public expense. For their inauguration he offered to the councillors and the whole people 50,000 sesterces, which are to be called the Mammian fund, from the interest on which they may receive a distribution on his birthday, 7th February. Now if on the day fixed this condition shall not be adhered to, then the distribution of that day shall belong to the town of Sulmo. Also he gave to the town-councillors attending the feasts and to their children 30 sesterces, to the board of six *Augustales* at the meal 20 sesterces, and to the whole people, to each attending the feast, 8 sesterces.

D. 41 Second century AD; Sillyon, Pisidia (Asia Minor); *IGRP*, III, 801 (*BCH* 1889, 486ff)

The council and the people honoured the priestess of all the gods and hierophant for life and one of the ten chief citizens, Menodora, daughter of Megacles, *demiourgos* and gymnasiarch for the provision of oil, who gave on behalf of Megacles, her son, 300,000 silver *denarii* for the maintenance of children and further gave both in her own gymnasiarchy and in the office of her son, as *demiourgos*, and in the gymnasiarchy of her daughter, to each councillor 85 *denarii*, to each member of the body of elders 80 *denarii*, to each member of the assembly 77 *denarii* and to the wives of each of these 3 *denarii*, and to each citizen 9 *denarii*, and to the freedmen freed *per vindictam* and to the [other] freedmen and non-citizens [*paroikoi*] 3 *denarii* per head.

D. 42 *c.* AD 120–48; Mons Fereter (central Italy); *CIL*, XI, 6481

[In addition to various buildings including baths] he left 200,000 sesterces for a distribution for a funeral feast; 100,000 for a foundation providing for a division of a sufficient amount of pastry and mead and bequests for those not named in his will; for the decurions 400 sesterces; for the board of six and *Augustales* 300 sesterces; for the common people 200 sesterces. The city folk on the thirty-third day after his decease, mindful of his benefits, from money contributed, amounting to 43,000 sesterces, set up [this monument] in the consulship of Bellicius Torquatus and Salvius Julianus.

D. 43 After 120 AD; Ager Sorrinensium Novensium (central Italy); *CIL*, XI, 3013

[For a man who had held local magistracies and the military rank of *praefectus fabrum, eques equo publico*]: When for his outstanding unselfish conduct the town-councillors, with the support of the *Augustales* and common people, offered to him statues to be paid for by subscription, he remitted the expense of the collection and himself instructed them to be erected, and for their dedication his heirs, in accordance with his bequests, gave to the town-councillors 16 sesterces, to the *Augustales* 12 sesterces, to the common people resident within the city wall 8 sesterces and to the children of all of these half the amount.

D. 44 AD 200; Oxyrhynchus (Egypt); B. P. Grenfell and A. S. Hunt, *Oxyrhynchus Papyri* No. 705 (Laum, No. 216; Lewis and Reinhold, *RC*, II, 447f)

[*ll.* 54]: The Emperor Caesar Lucius Septimius Severus Pius Pertinax Augustus Arabicus Adiabenicus Parthicus Maximus and the Emperor Caesar Marcus Aurelius Antoninus Pius Augustus, to Aurelius Horion, greeting. We commend you also for this endowment which you see fit to bestow upon the villages of the Oxyrhynchite district by presenting the resources for acquisition of property. The established rule shall be observed in this case also, so that your grant shall be expended as you desired and not be diverted to any other purpose. The request is as follows: 'To the most gracious emperors, Severus and Antoninus, the saviours and benefactors of all mankind, Aurelius Horion, former *strategus* and former chief judge of the most illustrious city of Alexandria, greeting. Certain villages of the Oxyrhynchite district, most benevolent of emperors, in which I and my sons possess lands, have been utterly exhausted by the burdens of the annual liturgies of the *fiscus* [imperial treasury] and of policing their districts, and there is danger that they will be ruined as far as the *fiscus* is concerned and that your land will be left uncultivated. Accordingly, in an endeavour to be both philanthropic and useful, I desire in the interest of their recovery to make each village some small endowment for the purchase of land, the revenue from which shall be earmarked for the maintenance and expenses of those who perform the annual liturgies for the . . . [the rest is lost].

D. 45 AD 237; Orcistus, Phrygia (Asia Minor); *JHS* 1937, 6f (*MAMA*, V, 202)

[A. Deed of Gift]: In the year of the consulship of Marius Perpetuus and Mummius Cornelianus, the sixth before the Kalends of June at Orcistus, I, Varius Aurelius Marcus, son of Theobulus, townsman of Orcistus, deposit

N

among the records as a mark of my gratitude the deed of gift hereinafter written: *dosis eucharistike* [gift of kindly favour]. Deeming it fitting as well as just to requite the native town that bred and loves me, I consider her by right entitled to a greater return, yet having regard to my own resources I give and bestow upon my native town, Orcistus, in money of account, 2,500 Attic *drachmae*, so that through this fund on Happiness-day in every year my fellow-townsmen may all share in a festival. They must conform to the express rule, which I desire shall above all be guarded and preserved, that for the future this money shall in every way perpetually remain undiminished and undiverted to other uses. One thousand *drachmae* are to be set apart, to be named 'Corn-purchase Fund' and to be lent out at interest forthwith; and from the revenue there shall be distributed annually to each of our fellow-townsmen one pound of bread or however much the town clerk shall serve out from purchases made as prescribed. In like manner the other one thousand five hundred *drachmae* are also to be set apart and lent out at interest, and out of the revenue there shall be held on Happiness-day in our town-gymnasium a feast for all the people [seven lines illegible] No sort of alteration in or diversion of this fund shall be allowed, for I desire that anyone altering it or diverting it to some other endowment shall pay [eight lines illegible].

[B. Decree]: For good luck. At a general assembly of the whole people, the elders also present on the front benches, on a motion put by the town-clerk, Aurelius Bassion, son of Alexander, it was resolved by the People of the Orcistenes: Whereas Aurelius Marcus, son of Theobulus, is a man by family tradition munificent [*philotimōs*] to the people and a benefactor to each and all, who on no occasion ever fails with public spirit nobly and amply to relieve the needs pressing upon his native town, where moreover he discharges with due diligence the highest offices and public duties, and hence, often, prior to this, at our assemblies and public meetings, acknowledgement has been made to him corresponding to the kindnesses that he has done; and now with unstinting generosity more than requiting the people for their praises of him, he has further given for public distributions and festivities a corn-purchase fund, so that through the munificence [*philotimia*] of this great gift the festival of Happiness-day will year by year make a braver show; therefore the people, mindful of these and of his other acts of kindness, have by general and popular vote decreed the erection in his honour, on the most conspicuous spot, of a statue with suitable inscription, so that his children and descendants may jointly and severally enjoy this honour in perpetuity by contemplating the gratitude of his native town enduring and worthily expressed . . .

D. 46 *c.* AD 250; Guelma (Libya); *Libyca*, VI, 1958, 143ff

To Q. Flavius Lappianus, son of C. Flavius Lappianus, of the tribe Papiria, *flamen* in perpetuity of the municipality of Calama, the distinguished knight, for his exceptional and unparalleled generosity and munificence towards the citizens, by which, among the rest, he took on his own shoulders every burden of responsibility, in this going beyond the generous gifts of his forefathers, the people of Thabarbus offered a statue costing 6661 sesterces; this offer was gladly and gratefully accepted by Lappianus but he returned all the money, being content with the honour alone; and providing a feast and gymnasium, with still further generosity, he dedicated it, together with the citizens.

D. 47 Mid-third century BC; *Teos* (Asia Minor coast); Dittenberger, 578 (Laum, No. 90; H. W. Pleket, *Epigraphica*, I (1964), No. 34)

[The extant part of the inscription begins]: and let the *paidonomos* [Controller of Youth] be appointed after the choice of the gymnasiarch, being not less than forty years old. And in order that all the free-born boys may be educated as Polythrous, son of Onesimus, in his concern for the people promised to them, thereby establishing a fair memorial of his own longing for glory [*philodoxia*], giving [*epididonai*] to that end 34,000 *drachmae*, there are to be chosen each year at election time, after the election of the clerks, three elementary teachers, to teach both boys and girls [details of graduated salaries follow] . . . and let there be appointed also two wrestling masters [details of salaries follow] . . . and let there be appointed a flute-player, one who plucks the strings or plays with the *plektron* [again, salary details] . . . an arms drill master and a master of archery and javelin-throwing are to be hired by the *paidonomos* and the gymnasiarch, referring the matter to the people.
[*l.* 16]. And he [the music teacher] shall teach those boys whom it is appropriate to select for the leading class and those who are a year younger than these both music and the playing of the lute, whether by plucking the strings or with the *plektron*, and he shall teach music to the ephebes and regarding the age of the boys the *paidonomos* shall decide. [*l.* 24]: Let these [the arms-drill master and the master of archery] teach the ephebes and the boys who are registered to be taught music. [*l.* 28]: And the *paidonomos* and the gymnasiarch are to see to it that the boys and ephebes are properly exercised in their studies as each is instructed according to the laws; and if the elementary masters dispute among themselves about the number of the boys, the *paidonomos* is to decide and they are to accept his ruling; and the examinations which are to take place are to be held by the elementary masters in the gymnasium and by the music teacher in the council-house. [*l.* 35ff: Provisions against misdirection of the fund and penalties (half of any fine going to a successful accuser); *l.* 60ff: Oath to be sworn by magistrates.]

D. 48 200/199 BC; Miletus (Asia Minor) Dittenberger, 577

[The resolution of the people, following upon the proposal of the committee of councillors]: since Eudemos, the son of Thallion, choosing to benefit the people and to leave a memorial for ever of his love of glory [*philodoxia*] has promised to give for the education of the free children ten talents of silver on behalf of himself and of his brothers, Menandros and Dion, the Milesians have resolved that Eudemos be commended for his concern for these high purposes and that it receive the careful attention of the council and the people. And in order that the arrangements relating to this endowment shall be carried through as is proper, Eudemos should pay the above-mentioned sum to the treasurers for routine expenses within the time stated in his promise, and the treasurers are to hand it over forthwith to the managers of the state bank, and these are to establish a state bank account for 'Eudemos' endowment-fund for the education of free children', and enter into the account the money donated and keep watch over it, and hand it over to the bankers who shall succeed them, until the people has decided regarding the income deriving from it. [*ll.* 17–25: Detailed arrangements relating to the 300 *staters* annual income and sanctions protecting it.] And those who wish to be gymnastic masters or to give elementary teaching are to register with the Controllers of Youth [*paidonomoi*] appointed for the coming year, and the registration is to take place each year from the fifteenth to the twentieth of Artemision, and the *paidonomoi* are to exhibit their names in the hall of Antiochos, and on the twenty-eighth day of the same month, on the gathering of the assembly, to set up in the *orchestra* a tripod and incense-burner; and the priests, those of Hermes, President of the games, in the boy's *palaestra*, and of the Muses, and the Sacred Herald and the *paidonomoi*-elect, who are about to enter upon office, and Eudemos, during his life, and afterwards the eldest of Eudemos' descendants, are to offer incense to Hermes and the Muses and to Apollo, leader of the Muses. And the Sacred Herald is to utter a prayer for the members of the assembly, that whoever elects gymnastic masters and elementary teachers whom he thinks will best look after the children and does not allow himself to be swayed by any influence contrary to what is just, that this man may be blessed, but that he may fare ill if he does otherwise. And after this let the *paidonomoi* hand over to the clerk of the Council the name of those registered, and let him introduce them one by one. [*ll.* 43–64: Oaths of gymnastic masters and teachers, four of each to be chosen; provisions for pay.] And the money paid out for this purpose, in accordance with the financial disposition, is not to be diverted to any other object in any way, and if anybody speaks or puts a motion or puts to the vote or misapplies or allots less than the sum laid down, let him be liable to pay a penalty of 500 *staters* to the priests of Hermes and the Muses. And the surplus of the sum set aside for this purpose after the payment of the salaries, let the *paidonomoi* take, and let them send to Apollo of Didyma the finest ox possible, every fifth year on the occasion of the Festival of Didyma, and in the other years of the *Boegia;* and they themselves are to take part in the procession and the boys chosen by them and their appointed overseers and, during his lifetime, Eudemos and afterwards the eldest of Eudemos' descendants. And let the *paidonomoi* sacrifice the offering sent and assign a share to all the boys and to the others who it is written are to accompany the procession. And the children are to be free from lessons on the fifth day in each month and the *paidonomoi* are to register this among the festival days as is laid down in the Code of the *paidonomoi*. And in order that the decision of the people and the love of glory [*philodoxia*] of Eudemos in respect of these things may be manifest to all, the wall-commissioners and the architect are to see to it that this decree is written on two stone pillars [*stelai*], the one to be set up in the boys' wrestling school, the other in the temple of Apollo Delphinios, in the hall consecrated by Eudemos, son of Thallion. And in order that Eudemos may be worthily honoured in respect of his enthusiastic purpose in these matters, let the people take counsel at the appropriate time. The people resolved to inscribe the decree on a notice-board.

D. 49 162 BC; Rhodes; Polybius, XXXI, 25 (Laum, No. 40)

The Rhodians had received 280,000 *medimni* of corn from Eumenes [Eumenes II of Pergamum], so that its value might be invested and the interest devoted to the payment of the fees of tutors and teachers of the boys. One might accept this from friends in case of financial embarrassment as one might in private life rather than allow children to remain uneducated for lack of means . . .

D. 50 160–159 BC; Delphi (Greek mainland) Dittenberger, 672 (Laum, No. 28; Pouilloux, *Choix*, No. 13)

[*l*. 6]: In eager response to our requests he [Attalus II of Pergamum] sent to the city for the education of the children 18,000 Alexandrian silver *drachmae* and for honours and sacrifices 3,000 *drachmae* . . . In order that the gift may stand for all time and that the teachers' salaries and the outlay for the honours and sacrifices may be secured by the interest from loaning out the money [provisions against misdirection of the fund, for the lending out of the money and for the arrangements of the festival of the *Attaleia* follow].

D. 51 Early second century AD; Comum (north Italy); Pliny, *ep.* IV, 13 (Lewis and Reinhold *RC*, II, 354f)

Recently, when I was in my home-town, there came to greet me the young son of a fellow citizen. 'Are you at school?' I said to him, and he replied that he was. 'Where?' I asked. 'At Milan,' he replied. 'Why not here?' I asked; whereupon his father, who was with him and had in fact himself brought the boy, answered, 'Because we have no teachers here.' 'Why have you no teachers?' I asked. It would be much to the interest of those of you who are fathers . . . that your children should go to school here rather than anywhere else. For where could they find a place more pleasant to attend than in their own town? Or where could they be better disciplined than under the eyes of their parents or at less expense than at home? Very little trouble is involved in collecting subscriptions and hiring teachers and meeting their fees with the money which you now spend on accommodation, on travelling-expenses and on those things which are bought outside the city (that is, everything); and, indeed, I who have no children as yet, am ready on behalf of our city, as for a daughter or a parent, to give one third of whatever you decide to contribute. I would even promise to donate the whole sum, were it not for a fear that this free service [*munus*] might sooner or later be rendered ineffective through personal influence. This defect can be met by one remedy only; that is, if the parents alone are left with the right of giving employment, so that the same people exercise the duty of correct choice and the obligation to pay a subscription. For those who are irresponsible perhaps in handling other people's money will at any rate be careful about their own, and they will take trouble to see to it that no unworthy candidate receives money from me, if he is going to receive it from them as well. Come to a common mind about this, then, and combine together in response to the spirit of my offer; for I am anxious that the amount which I am obliged to contribute should be as large as possible.

D. 52 (—); Eleusis (Attica); Dittenberger, 956 (IG, II, 1187; *Hesperia* 1964, 337ff)

[Philip's proposal]: since Derkylos, the general, has his heart set on honour [*philotimeisthai*] with regard to the deme of Eleusis, both generally and especially with regard to the education of the boys in the deme, it is resolved by the Eleusinians to commend Derkylos, son of Autokles, of Hagnous, and crown him with a golden crown to the value of 500 *drachmae* and to announce in the theatre at the tragic contest at Eleusis that 'the people crowns Derkylos . . . for his noble qualities [*arete*] and love of honour [*philotimia*] with regard to the deme of Eleusis'. Let him be given freedom from public burdens and a seat of privilege among the people of Eleusis and let the magistrate of the deme, whoever is in office, assign to him a share from the sacrifices equally with the Eleusinians; and the resolution is to be inscribed on a stone pillar and placed beside the gateway of Demeter and Kore; and the fathers of the boys are to attend to the inscription together with the magistrate of the deme. [Perhaps 'boys' = ephebes: see article in *Hesperia* 1964.]

D. 53 *c.* 200 BC; Samos (Eastern Aegean); *MDAI* (A) 1919, 29 (*SEG* I, 368)

[*l.* 13]: Since Epikrates, son of Demetrios of Heraclea, a Peripatetic, has stayed a considerable time in our city and through his instruction has greatly benefited the young men, wishing to do us a kindness, both privately giving his time to those pursuing their studies such as he met with, and publicly being ungrudging towards the people, in that he admitted all those who wished to have a share in his instruction, and for those of the common people who were unable to pay his normal fee he gave his lectures at no charge; now therefore, so that we too may be seen [to honour] good and worthy men and such as are able to benefit those of the younger men who are eager for knowledge . . . [His reward includes Samian citizenship.]

D. 54 Second century BC; Pergamum (Asia Minor); *MDAI (A)* 1907, 278

[*l.* 10]: Straton, gymnasiarch of Pergamum, [continued] to secure the publicly maintained teachers by the appropriate rewards [*philanthropiai*] and in addition to these two he brought in [another two?], meeting the expense out of his own pocket, so that nothing of the instruction which was necessary should be lacking; and thus for himself there is secured everlasting praise from those whom he has benefited, and for them there is established to good effect the most valuable renewal of those things which are advantageous to life; and throughout the whole year he established an unlimited supply of oil at his own expense; and on his entry into office he sacrificed a steer given by himself, praying to all the gods for the safety of the people and for their unity of heart [*homonoia*] and he carried out a distribution of pure oil and a distribution of the flesh of the sacrifice.

D. 55 130–100 BC; Sestos (Dardanelles); *OGIS* 339, (*IBM*, IV, 2 1000)

[*l.* 7]: Menas wished by his own endeavour always to provide something of service to the people, and for himself and for his descendants to secure a glory which would never be forgotten, arising from the gratitude of the citizen body for his kindness and favour. [*ll.* 10ff: Embassies undertaken for the city.] [*l.* 31]: Having been chosen gymnasiarch he attended to the discipline of the ephebes and the *neoi* and secured that all else in the gymnasium was well conducted in an excellent manner in his passion for honour [*philotimōs*]; and he provided the bathroom and the attached building and dedicated also a statue of white stone and provided in addition all that was needful and necessary; and on the birthdays of the king in each month he offered a sacrifice for the people and established races for the ephebes and the young men, and he held javelin and archery contests and provided also oil for anointing because of his longing for glory [*philodoxia*]. [*l.* 61]: And he excelled himself in his expenditure and in the rest of his conduct reflecting his love of glory [*philodoxia*]; for, entering upon his office on the day of the new moon, he carried through sacrifices to Hermes and Heracles, the gods whose altars are established in the gymnasium, for the welfare of the people and the young men, and he instituted races and javelin and archery contests, and on the following day, having sacrificed for favourable omens, he called to partake in the sacrificial rites not only those who partake in the activities of the gymnasium but all others as well, granting a share in the sacrificial rites also to foreigners; and in each month he carried through the appropriate sacrifices on behalf of the young men, acting with good and generous spirit in his provision for the gods who preside over the gymnasium and instituting archery contests and javelin-throwing and holding races, giving to the young men a share in the sacrificial rites carried out by him and through his love of glory [*philodoxia*] encouraging the young men to engage in hard exercise, as a result of which the younger men, being involved in a contest directed towards manliness, receive excellent training of character; and he gave to those who are active in the gymnasium for use at home a share in the sacred offerings associated with the contests of the gymnasium, extending his kindly act [*philanthropia*] also to non-citizens who take part in the gymnastic activities, and he conducted himself in the same kindly spirit also towards all those who gave lectures, wishing in the case of these too to secure for his fatherland glory through men of education . . . [*l.* 92ff: Menas is awarded a public encomium and is to be crowned annually with a golden crown at festivals; a bronze statue in the gymnasium is voted—which he undertakes to pay for himself—together one of the chief seats at all games, both for himself and for his descendants.]

D. 56 Towards 100 BC; Eretria, Euboea (western Aegean); Dittenberger, 714 (*AJA* 1896, 173ff)

The standing committee of the council proposed; in as much as Elpinikos, son Nikomachos, having been elected gymnasiarch by the people, conducted himself with honour in all the rest of the matters relating to his office, and, on the gathering together of a considerable number of boys and young men and of the rest who came under his direction as a result of his devoted service [*philotimia*], took thought for their discipline, remaining in attendance at the gymnasium throughout the year, and provided from his own funds a teacher of rhetoric and an arms drill master who gave instruction in the gymnasium to the boys and the young men and to anybody else who wished to receive benefit from such training; and in as much as he gave attention to the oil supply, that it might be of the purest quality, meeting the expense of this out of his own funds; and since he also carried through arrangements for many long distance races and at each performed a sacrifice to Hermes; and the prize offered by the people for the winner in the race from the temple of Heracles he provided himself out of his own resources, repaying the money offered by the people: and he carried through the games in honour of Heracles, meeting the cost of the prizes from his own funds, making the whole lavish outlay [*philotimia*] because of his good will for the people; and at the sacred gathering of the *Artemisia* he met the expense of the unguents out of his own pocket; accepting this expense not only for the citizens but for the rest of those who attended the gathering and shared the common privileges, and, in undertaking the sacrifice to Hermes, he invited by public proclamation both the citizens and those Romans who were resident, and on the fourth day he banqueted those who shared the common privileges, and on the fifth others of the citizens and many of the strangers . . . [*l.* 38ff: Award of an olive crown and monuments in stone bearing inscription, to be placed in the most prominent place in the gymnasium.]

D. 57 Towards 100 BC; Eretria, Euboeoa (western Aegean); *IG* XII, 9 235 (*AJA* 1896, 188)

The standing committee of the Council proposed: since Mantidoros, son of Kallikrates, on being chosen gymnasiarch by the people, conducted himself in all the matters relating to his office honourably and in a way worthy both of himself and his forefathers and of the trust placed in him by the people; and, on the gathering together of a considerable number of boys and ephebes and of the rest who came under his direction as a result of his devoted service [*philotimia*], took thought for their discipline in the place during the whole period of his office, attending in the gymnasium throughout the year; and since he made available an adequate supply of oil and unguents of the purest quality and, wishing to benefit the young men, readily provided out of his own funds a Homeric scholar, Dionysios, son of Philotas, an Athenian, who gave a course in the gymnasium for the young men and the boys and for all the rest who were suitably disposed for education; and since he performed each month the sacrifice to Hermes and Heracles for the boys and the young men and all the rest [the inscription breaks off].

D. 58 Latter part of first century BC Chalcis, Euboea (western Aegean); *IG*, XII, 9,916

[Resolution of the Boeotian synod]: *l*. 5: In the gymnasiarchy of Aulus Salarius, son of Manius: L. Cusonius Agatho gave to the synod three thousand *denarii* and the following were chosen gymnasiarchs for a month [sixteen names follow]; and while Aulus Salarius, son of Manius, promised to act as gymnasiarch throughout the year and held the office at his own expense, each of these gave 120 *denarii* for the gymnasiarchy to the synod, on account of which they were registered as gymnasiarchs. And the following were so registered on completing their course as *ephebes* [names follow] and the following were enrolled on receiving inheritances, etc.

D. 59 270 BC; Athens; Diogenes Laertius, X, 16–18

[The will of Epicurus]: On the following conditions I give all my property to Amynomachos, son of Philokrates, of Bate, and to Timokrates, son of Demetrios, of Potamos, to each severally according to the registration of the gift in in the Metroon, namely that they make available the garden and its appurtenances to Hermarchos, son of Agemortos of Mytilene, and to his fellow-philosophers and to whomsoever Hermachos leaves it as his successors in philosophy, to live and pursue philosophy therein. And I entrust the school in the garden in perpetuity to those who are its members, so that they may preserve it, together with Amynomachos and Timokrates, to the best of their ability, and to their successors, so that they too may maintain the garden in the way which is most secure, just as it is maintained by those to whom the members of my philosophic school bequeath it. And the house in Melite let Amynomachos and Timokrates provide for Hermarchos and those who pursue philosophy with him as long as Hermarchos is alive. And from the income deriving from the gifts made over by me to Amynomachos and Timokrates, let them to the best of their ability, in consultation with Hermarchos, allot funds for the funeral

offerings to my father and mother and brothers, and for the customary celebration of my birthday on the tenth day of Gamelion each year, and also for the
monthly gathering of the members of my school on the twentieth in remembrance of me and Metrodoros. Let them also join in celebrating the day in
Poseideon in memory of my brothers and also the day in Metageitnion in
memory of Polyainos, as we also have done.

D. 60 *c.* 288 BC; Athens; Diogenes Laertius, V, 52, 3

[The will of Theophrastus]: The garden and the covered walk and all the
dwellings which adjoin the garden I give to those of my friends here written who
are willing to devote their time to the common pursuit of philosophy in them—in
as much as it is not possible for all men to dwell in them permanently—on
condition that no one is deprived of his place nor treats it as his own, but that
they hold it as a sanctuary open to all, acting as a family and in the spirit of
friendship, as is right and proper . . . and they are to bury me in whatever spot
in the garden seems most appropriate, without undue attention either to the
burial itself or to the memorial.

D. 61 Mid-fourth century; Athens; Aristotle *A.P.* 49, 4

There is a law which lays down that those who possess less than three *minae* [300
drachmae] and who are physically maimed so as to be incapable of work are to be
examined by the council and to be given two obols a day for maintenance at
public expense.

D. 62 304–3 BC; Athens; Dittenberger, 335

And he [*sc.* Pheidias of Rhodes] continues to do that which is to the advantage
of the Athenian people and to treat those of the Athenians who seek his help
with praiseworthy devotion [*philotimōs*] and now he has offered himself
[*epididonai*] as a public doctor freely, displaying the goodwill which he holds
towards the city. [Cohn-Haft, *PPAG*, 59, offers as an alternative translation:
'now he has offered himself as providing free of charge an authorised medical
practice'.]

D. 63 Third century BC; Cos (eastern Aegean); Dittenberger, 943

[Praximenes proposed]: Since Xenotimos, son of Timoxenos, in previous
times took care of the citizens according to his medical skill, showing himself
eager to save the sick and now, in face of the onset of many virulent diseases and
the illness of the public doctors in the city resulting from the ill effects of their
attendance upon their patients, he of his own volition has been unfailing in his
provision of help for those in need, taking it upon himself to provide a remedy
for every illness, and allowing to no one undue favour but saving men's lives by
his ready service of all equally: it is resolved by the people to commend

Xenotimos, son of Timoxenos, and to crown him with a golden crown, etc.

D.64 218 BC; Gortyn (Crete); *I. Cret.* IV, 168 (Pouilloux, *Choix*, No. 15)

The *kosmoi* of Gortyn and the city send greetings to the council and people of Cos. Since Hermias, son of Emmenidas, having been elected by you and sent to us as a doctor, has made his stay among us worthy both of you who sent him and of himself, and also of ourselves who gave you the responsibility of the choice of the doctor; and since he has been irreproachable in all his dealings with us and has completed his stay of five years, looking after the citizens and the rest of those dwelling at Gortyn, and has by the enthusiastic and earnest application of his skill and his other care saved many from great dangers, never failing in his energy; and since, when many allies were with us at the time when we were at war, he displayed the same care for them and saved them from great dangers, wishing to show his gratitude to our city, and now he has come to the assembly and has asked of us his return to his own home, we have agreed and have sent to accompany him Soarchos and Kydas of our own citizens, wishing to express our gratitude to him; and since it has seemed good to us to commend Hermias for his merits and goodwill towards the city and also to commend the Coans in that they sent to us a good doctor and a worthy man; in order that all may know that we understand how to show our gratitude, it was resolved by us to give citizenship to him and his descendants . . .

D. 65 201–197 BC; Samos (Eastern Aegean); *MDAI* (*A*) 1957, 233, No. 64 (Pouilloux, *Choix*, No. 24)

[*l.* 3]: . . . [that Diodoros, son of Dioskurides], who has served as a public doctor [over many years among us] and has provided his service in accordance with his skill irreproachably, and who, in the rebuilding of the city and in the siege of the high points, when many were wounded, provided his services, be praised and honoured in the way that seems good to the council and people. And the council has framed a draft-resolution to introduce the matter at the time of the electoral assemblies: since Diodoros, son of Dioskurides, having received among us the office of public doctor, firstly, over many years in the previous period, restored to health by his careful and experienced treatment many of the citizens and of the others in the city who had fallen into a grave condition and was responsible for their recovery, as has often been borne witness to by many in the assembly at the time of the making of contracts; and, again, since on the occasion of the earthquakes among us, when many were laid low by grievous blows of every kind owing to the unexpected nature of the disaster, and when his care was needed with all speed, he came to the aid, giving his attention to all equally; and since, when the judges who had been sent for were arrived among us and some had fallen ill, on instruction from the people that he should look after them, too, he displayed his uncomplaining readiness to help all alike, and at the time of the return of the city into the Ptolemaic Empire, when many were injured in the sieges of the heights in the daily engagements, he disregarded personal distress and expense in his concern for the public good and for those who were repeatedly in need of his help, from his own resources [here the inscription breaks off].

D. 66 Early 2nd century BC; Tenos and islands (Aegean); Dittenberger, 620

May it be with heaven's blessing: in the archonship of Agathion, in the month Bouphonion, the fifteenth day, it was resolved by the council and people, on the motion of the presiding committee: in as much as Apollonius, son of Hierokles of Miletus, being a doctor, previously gave many demonstrations and by his skill and, in general, his spirit of goodwill showed himself worthy of the generous rewards [*philanthropa*] voted to him by the people; and in as much as, in going abroad and entering public service [*demosieuon*] in other islands, he displayed an equal devotion and enthusiasm, in terms of his skill and spirit of goodwill towards all he met with; and in as much as he came to the city when many fell ill and appeared before the assembly and, first, he promised that he would serve [literally, take upon himself a 'liturgy' for] the people freely during the six month period of office; and in as much as he did this with his heart set upon honour [*philotimōs*] and with all enthusiasm and saved many from serious illnesses and . . . now, taking up public service at a time when a new epidemic has broken out and threatens dangers to all the islanders, he has not thought fit to abandon the people, but continues in his public service conscientiously and makes himself available to all without excuse and remains faithful to his original choice: therefore, in order that it may be manifest that our people honours men who have shown their worth, etc., [honours previously voted are confirmed; he is awarded an encomium to encourage further service, also an olive wreath for *arete* and *eunoia*; the decree is to be inscribed on a stone which is to be placed in the temple of Poseidon and Amphitrite. A separate decree of the islanders follows].

D. 67 not before 200 BC; Brycous, Carpathos (eastern Aegean); *IG*, XII, 1032

Since Menokritos, son of Metrodoros, the Samian, has acted as public doctor for over twenty years and has continued in his energetic service in his love of honour [*philotimōs*] and through his skill, experience and general conduct has shown himself beyond all reproach, and when epidemic conditions developed and many, not of the people only but also of the residents, fell into the most critical danger, he displayed all energy and tireless service and thus was responsible for saving their lives and since, previously, serving as a paid doctor, while staying in Rhodes he saved many of the townsfolk when these were in a critical condition, accepting no fee, and continued to display a proper sense of devotion in his attendance upon each of the non-citizen class in the suburbs of the city; now, therefore, so that the people of Brycous may appear grateful and ready to honour doctors of real worth, etc.

D. 68 *c.* 86 BC; Gytheion (Greek mainland); *IG*, V, 1145 (*IBM*, II, 143)

[*l.* 9]: Since Damiadas . . . a Spartan doctor, on letters being sent to him, as had been voted . . . came to practise in our city, showing himself second to none in his skill, as befitted his reputation, and the best of [public] doctors, so laying claim to the highest regard of the magistrates and of our city, and since he became a [public] doctor among us and, having practised as such, was opportunely called upon by the people, and during a stay of two years among us provided the due treatment, skillfully serving those in need, showing unlimited energy and devotion [*philotimia*] in serving fairly all alike, whether poor or rich, slaves or free or foreigners . . . [*l.* 24]: He maintained a blameless reputation in all respects, providing proper attendance, which was open to all, as befits a man of culture and moral sense. And in the magistracy of Biadas and the month Laphrios, seeing the city in severe difficulties in respect of the property taxes, he promised to serve as a doctor in our city freely, going beyond all limits in the nobility of his spirit towards us [by his propriety of conduct] and in everything offering the greatest proof of his goodwill and devoted care for our city; for this reason the people made him *proxenos* and *euergetes* of our city and granted him enjoyment of the right to own land and a dwelling-place and all the other signs of favour [*philanthropa*] and honour.

D. 69 *c.* 100 BC; Eretria, Euboeoa (western Aegean); *IG*, XII, 9, 236

The committee of the council proposed: in as much as Theopompos, son of Archedemos, maintaining the good relations with the people inherited from his ancestors, and seeking further to increase his right-dealing with gods and men, having zealously pursued the life of virtue and honour from his earliest youth, wishes to establish clearly his devotion towards that which redounds to the advantage of the common interest and his eager desire to serve the people; and in as much as he shows himself faithful towards the whole people in his service and has conducted himself irreproachably in the offices which he has held, displaying his generosity; and in as much as, in his wish to leave an imperishable memorial for all time of his noble spirit and goodwill for the people, he has bestowed out of his own resources for the people, for the purpose of oil for anointing, forty-thousand *drachmae*, so that the aforementioned sum, being lent out on adequate securities, may provide revenue annually for the purchase of oil for the gymnasium, the distribution of which shall be carried out by the officers who are placed in charge of these matters, and that the people may be relieved from this expense . . . [*ll.* 33ff: Award of a gold crown and two bronze statues with honorary inscription; the decree itself to be inscribed on two stone monuments; public proclamation of these honours at festivals of Dionysos and of Artemis; inscriptions also to be added to the statues of sons and daughter set up by Theopompos.]

D. 70 First century AD; Comum (northern Italy); Dessau, 6728 (*CIL*, V, 5279)

L. Caecilius Cilo, son of Lucius, . . . who in his will bequeathed to the townsfolk of Comum 40,000 sesterces, the interest on which each year was to provide oil during the *Neptunalia* on the *campus* and in the baths and all bathing establishments which belong to the people of Comum.

D. 71 AD 161–169; Gytheion (Greek mainland); *IG* V, 1, 1208 (A. Wilhelm, *Griechische Inschriften rechtlichen Inhalts* (1951), 90ff; Laum No. 9)

I have left the aforementioned money so that those who are holding magistracies from year to year, when they also relax the rest of the public burdens, may loan it out, from the year of the generalship of Aristopolis, according to the resolutions of the councillors of the city and of the people . . . [*l.* 12]: And this money is to be lent out and those who borrow the money are to give adequate security in land, so that from the interest oil may be supplied for ever to the citizens of Gytheion and the non-citizens, and the magistrates and councillors are to display all energy and good faith each year, so that my beneficent act [*philanthropia*] may remain eternally for the gymnasium and for the city. [*l.* 31]: Let the fourth part of the 8,000 *denarii* belong to the accuser, if he prove the default of the magistrates, and the [remaining] 6,000 *denarii* are to belong to the city of the Spartans. And if the Spartans, too, neglect my gift, let the 6,000 *denarii* be dedicated to the divine Augusta; it is open to anyone who wishes, to prove the neglect of the Spartans and [make over] the money to the Emperor's house . . . I wish also the slaves to share in the gift [*philanthropia*] of oil for six days each year, three days during the festival of the *Augusti* and three of the goddess; and no archon or gymnasiarch is to hinder them using the oil . . . And I wish my gift and favour bestowed upon the gymnasium on the stated conditions to be published on three marble pillars; of these, one should be set up . . . in the market before my house, and one should be erected in the *Caesareum*, set close by the gates of the temple, and one in the gymnasium, so that both to the citizens of Gytheion, and to the non-citizens, my philanthropic and kindly act may be clear and well-known to all. [*l.* 48]: And I entrust to the city and the council also my house-slaves and freedmen, all of them, both male and female; and I beseech you, by all the gods and by the Fortune of the *Augusti*, even when I live, that, whenever I suffer the common lot of men, you may take the utmost thought, both individually and collectively, for the carrying out of my wish and for the house-slaves whom I honour and have honoured. [*l.* 51]: My idea is to achieve immortality in making such a just and kindly disposal [of my property] and, in entrusting it to the city, I shall surely not fail in my aim.

D. 72 AD 214; Theveste (North Africa); *IL Alg.* 3040

By his will C. Cornelius Egrilianus, prefect of the legion XIV gemina, in which . . . besides other things he gave 250,000 sesterces to the state, so that on certain days oil [*gymnasia*] should be provided for the people in the baths.

D. 73 Second century AD (?); Gor (North Africa); *CIL*, VIII, 12422

To Marius Marinus, son of Felix, *flamen*, *pater patriae*, because of his outstanding liberality towards his fatherland and his fellow citizens, who in his will gave to the state of Gor 12,000 sesterces, from the interest on which on his birthday, the Ides of September, each year the town councillors should receive presents [*sportulae*], and oil [*gymnasium*] should be given to all the citizens. After the town council had voted to him a statue on account of his liberality, Maria Victoria, his daughter and heir, content with the distinction and the site, set up the statue at her own expense and together with Ophelius, the first *sufetes* [?], *flamen* and *pater patriae*, her husband, gave a feast to the council.

D. 74 Second century AD; Barcino (Barcelona, Spain); Dessau 6957 (Lewis and Reinhold, *RC*, II, 348f)

Lucius Caecilius Optatus, son of Lucius, of the Papirian tribe, centurion of Legion VII Gemina Felix and centurion of Legion XV Apollinaris, honourably discharged by the Emperors Marcus Aurelius Antoninus [Augustus] and [Lucius] Aurelius Verus Augustus, included by the town of Barcino among those exempted from public obligations, attained the offices of *aedile*, *duovir* three times, *flamen* of Rome and the deified Emperors. He left a legacy to the municipality of Barcino as follows: I give, bequeath and desire to have given 7,500 *denarii*, with six per cent interest whereby I desire a boxing contest to be held each year on June 10th at a cost of up to 250 *denarii*, and on the same day 200 *denarii* worth of oil to be supplied to the public in the public baths. I desire these bequests to be carried out on condition that my freedmen and also the freedmen of my freedmen and freedwomen, who attain the honour of the board of six (*Augustales*) be excused from all the obligations of the office. But if any of them is assigned such burdens, then I order the said 7,500 *denarii* to be transferred to the municipality of Tarraco, with the same programme of shows as aforementioned to be held at Tarraco.

D. 75 Late first century BC; Praeneste, Latium (central Italy); *CIL*, XIV, 2979 (Laum, No. 17B)

C. Aurunceius Cotta, son of Gaius, gave to the colonists, the dwellers in the town, the foreigners, and the visitors and to their slaves free bathing at his own expense in perpetuity.

D. 76 First century AD; Bononia (Bologna, northern Italy); Dessau, 5674 (*CIL*, XI, 720)

[At baths originally built by Augustus and restored under Caligula] Titus Aviasius Servandus provided by legacy that from the income deriving from this sum men and young people of either sex should bathe free of charge for ever.

D. 77 Second century AD; Altinum (northern Italy); *Not. Scav.* 1928, 283

This man gave to the state of Altinum, 1,600,000 sesterces so that the Sergian and Putinian baths might be repaired from the expenditure of 800,000 and be enjoyed by the townsfolk, another 400,000, that from the income therefrom the baths might be heated, and 200,000 in perpetuity for their upkeep, and also 200,000, so that from the interest thereon, on his own birthday, the 7th [or 9th] of [?], and on the same day of that month, the birthday of Petronia Magna, his mother, and on the 16th of December, the birthday of L. Fabius Amminianus his father, the decurions, *Augustales* and board of six [*seviri*] might receive presents.

D. 78 Late second century AD; Murgis (Baetica, southern Spain); *CIL* II, 5489

L. Aemilius Daphnus, *sevir*, gave to his fellow citizens, the Murgitani, these baths, meeting all the expense; and on the day of their dedication he gave a *denarius* apiece to the citizens and residents by way of a feast; as long as he lived he promised that on the same day he would give to the same a *denarius* apiece and 150 *denarii* for the upkeep of the baths, as long as he lived.

D. 79 Not before second century AD; Comana, Pisidia (Asia Minor); *Anatolian Studies*, X, 1960, 51/2, No. 100 (*SEG* XIX, 830)

He has filled all the offices appropriate to his rank and all the liturgies with great distinction, and in addition he has given 30,000 silver *denarii* as capital for a perpetual distribution for his fatherland and again 4,000 *denarii* for the repair and revetting of the baths at Cretopolis . . .

D. 80 Mid-second century AD; Athens; Philostratus, *Lives of the Sophists*, II, 548 (Lewis and Reinhold, II, 350f)

There was also a great spirit of generosity in this Atticus [Tiberius Claudius Atticus, father of Herodes Atticus]. When for instance Herodes was in control of the free cities of Asia, seeing Troy poorly supplied with baths and the inhabitants drawing muddy water from wells and digging cisterns to catch rain water, he sent word to the emperor asking him not to allow an ancient city and a city close to the sea to perish for lack of water, but to give them three million *drachmae* for a water supply, seeing that he had already given even to villages many times that amount. The emperor approved of the suggestion, as being in accordance with his way of thinking, and he placed Herodes himself in charge of the project. But when the expenditure had reached seven million *drachmae* and the officials in charge of Asia kept writing that it was shocking to spend the tax from five hundred cities on a source of water for a single city, the emperor reproved Atticus regarding this; whereupon Atticus replied in the language of the most lavish of benefactors: 'Do not, my Emperor, be annoyed about trifles; for the amount spent over and above the three million sesterces I myself am giving to my son and my son is giving it to the city.' Again, his will, in which he left to the Athenian people a *mina* [one hundred *drachmae*] for each citizen annually, proclaims the magnanimity of the man, to which he gave expression in other ways also, in sacrificing one hundred oxen to the goddess on a single day on many occasions and in providing a sacrificial feast for the whole people of Athens in their tribes and families; again, whenever the Dionysia came round and the statue of Dionysus was brought down to the Academia, he would provide drink in the Ceramicus both for citizens and strangers as they lay on beds of ivy leaves.

D. 81 Second century AD; Aspendos, Pamphylia (Asia Minor); *IGRP*, III, 804 (*BCH* 1886, 160)

Tiberius Claudius Erymneus, of the tribe Quirina, one of the ten chief men, gymnasiarch providing oil available on demand, son of Tiberius Claudius Italicus, one of the ten chief men, high-priest, *demiourgos*, gymnasiarch and president of the great five-yearly games, the *Caesarea*, who gave for the supply of water eight million sesterces and undertook three embassies to the emperors freely.

o

INDEX

Ethiopia, 64
Eubiotos of Athens, 93
Eudemos of Miletus, 55, 121, 128
Eumenes II of Pergamum, 122
Eubulus, 98f
Euphrosynus of Mantinea, 95
Euripides, 120
Evans-Pritchard, E. E., 29

Fabatus, 113
Faustina, 110
Felix, L. Aemilius, of Theveste, 59
Finley, M. I., 28f
Francotte, H., 96
Frank, T., 13, 68
Fraser, P. M., 96

Galatia, 97
Gallicanus, 109
Gellius, Aulus, 86
Gelon of Syracuse, n. 144
Glaukos, 28
Gomme, A. W., 69f, 74
Gortyn, 133, 136f
Gracchus, C., 101f
Gracchus, T., 16, 67f
Gregory of Nyssa, 60
Gytheion, 50, 133, 142

Hadrian (Emperor), 21, 110, 140
Henderson, B. W., 112
Hera, 51
Heracleides of Salamis, D. 2
Hermarchus of Mytilene, 127
Hermias of Cos, 133
Herondas, 123
Hieron of Syracuse, n. 144
Highet, Gilbert, 48, 62, 64
Hippocrates, 131, 133
Hobhouse, Arthur, 24

Homer, 28, 63, 65, 78f, 118
Horace, 62, 63

Iambulus, n. 88
Iasos, 96
Ibiza (Ebusus), 92
Irus, 63, 78
Isaeus, 40
Isocrates, 35, 41, 74
Israel, 11, 77, 85
Italy, 91ff, 103, 107, 110, 112

Jacoby, F., 138
Jews, at Alexandria, 84
Jordan, W. K., 12, 40, 44, n. 62
Josephus, 84
Julian (Emperor), 132
Juvenal, 48, 62, 64, 87, 94

Kolophon, 51
Kritolaos of Amorgos, 58, 130, D. 5, D. 123

Lappianus, Q. Flavius, 50
Laum, B., 18, 22, 23, 111
Laurium, 98
Leo Manius of Petelia, 50, n. 105, D. 31
Leo, L. Vaccius, 143
Lepidus, Aemilius, n. 120
Libanius, 98, 140
Livy, 112
London, 40, 144
Lucania, 53
Lucretius, 37, 87
Lycurgus, 116
Lysias, 29

Macer, C. Licinius, 103, 110
Macnaghten, Lord, 12, 14, 89, 116

Hellenistic age—*cont.*
123, 134, 139
Hellenistic comedy, 88
Hellenistic kings, 42, 56
homonoia, 38ff, D. 54
honorary decrees, formula for, 50; for public doctors, 135; for ephebes, 118f, 135
honos: see honour
honour, in club and state, 36f, 49; graded, 38, 50f; and 'immortality', 55ff; for descendants, 55; titles, 60; qualification in distributions, 91; through trivial acts, n. 44
hospes, 35
hospitals, 132, 141
humanitas, 84, 86ff, 103; and law, 87; and *paideia*, 86f; and Greek distribution theories, n. 114

iatrikon, 139
iatros dēmosieuōn, 133ff; free medical attention(?), 132ff, 137, 169; forgo salary, 135; commonly non-citizen, 136; salary equals retainer(?), 136; at Cos and Athens, 136; men of culture, 136, 137; fiscal immunity, 140; immunity limited, 140
ideal state, 65f, 81
immortality, through giving, 55ff; founding of *gymnasia*, 121; of philosophic schools, 127
infamia, 34, 41, 52
investment, small scope for, 35

jurymen's pay, 100

kosmetes, of ephebes, 119

labourers, landless, 63, 64
law-courts, pressure on wealthy, 40f, 48; 'pity' within, 80, 84
legal personality, in relation to charities, 17ff
lex, Terentia-Cassia (73 BC), n. 120; *Tabulae Heracleënsis*, 103; Cincia, n. 46; *Julia agraria*, 104
liberalitas, 32, 48
libertas, 103
library, of gymnasia, 118; municipal, 129
literacy, in Greek cities, 120
liturgy, 37, 39, 109, 119; gifts in aid of, 93; *antidosis*, n. 33
loans, interest free, 54, 85, D. 3, D. 4, D. 12, D. 39; non-repayable, 109f
Lyceum, Aristotle's, 127

magistracies: see offices
marriage-gifts, 28f
medical ethics, 131f
medicine, forensic, 139
mercenaries, 68f
middle-class, in classical cities, 71f
miners, 65
misericordia: see pity
municipal pride, 128
Muses, altar of, 126

neoi, 118, 128, 129
New Testament, 35, 71, 84
non-citizens, receive benefits, 90f; exclusion, 97; as merchants, 98; in *ephebeia*, 119; at oil-distributions, 142; at baths, 143; see D. 5, D. 10, D. 23, D. 33, D. 55, D. 56, D. 64, D. 65, D. 67, D. 68, D. 71, D. 75

offices (public), acceptance of as a gift, 52, D. 9; calling for expenditure, 89, 93, 105, D. 4; inducement to hold, 93

oil, uses of, 115, 118; reservoirs, 142; foundations for, 142; in baths, 143; for clubs, 52ff

Old Testament, 77

oliganthropia, 73, 113f

Olympian gods, 132

orphans, 73f

ostracism, 120

paideia, and *humanitas*, 86

paidonomoi, 120, 122f, D. 47, D. 48

paroikoi: see non-citizens

philanthropos, philanthropia, 35, 38, 42, 60, 80, 118, 122, 137; and *humanitas*, 87

philodoxia, 43, 77f

philos, philia, 33, 36, 37; see friendship

philotimia, 43, 77f, 125

pietas, 87, 92, 111, 112

pity, as a motive for charity, 12, 61, 77ff; in Greek tragedy, 78f, 81; altars of, 80; in law-courts, 80; and justice, 81, 85; and fear, 81; reference to on epitaphs, 84; in democratic cities, 85

poll-taxes, charities for, 92

'the poor', the term in classical usage, 62; in 'oriental' usage, 64; as colonists, 68; and family limitation, 69ff; in fifth-century Athens, 72; assimilation to slaves, 72, 75, 76; and the gods, 77f; not favoured in private distributions, 89; discriminated against, 91f; at sacrificial feasts,

90f; contend with slaves, 94, in public distributions, 95ff; in *diobelia*, 100; how advantaged, 98f; produce children, not tax, 112; and *alimenta*, 114; education, VIII; medical treatment, IX; benefit from gymnasia, baths, 141ff

Poor Law, Elizabethan, 67f

praefecti alimentorum, 111

praefecti frumenti dandi, 107

priesthoods, lavish expenditure, 52f, 89f

property, private, necessary for gifts, 42f; in colonies, 68

providentia, imperial, 113

proxenos, 51, 133

ptōchos: see beggars

puellae Faustinianae, 110

recruitment, legionary, 112ff

religion, Greek and Roman, 89f; 'oriental', 80f, 90f, 111; see Christianity

reverentia for fellow-men, 87

rites at grave, 56f

Roman character, meanness, 48; greed, 94; cruelty, 88, 129; *pietas*, 87, 92, 111, n. 97; see *humanitas*

sanatoria, 141

sanctions, protecting public funds, 21f, 95

sewage, 144

sick, state corn ration secured for the, 96

sitometria, 97f

sitonai, 53